BEST SPORTS STORIES
1955

E·P·DUTTON&CO.INC
1852 1954
CREATIVE·102 YEARS·PUBLISHING

Edited *by* IRVING T. MARSH and EDWARD EHRE

BEST
Sports Stories
1955 Edition

•

A Panorama of the 1954 Sports Year

AND A SPORTS RECORD BOOK, INCLUDING THE
REVIEW OF THE SPORTS YEAR, AND THE 1954
CHAMPIONS OF ALL SPORTS

*WITH THIRTY OF THE YEAR'S BEST
SPORTS PICTURES*

E. P. DUTTON & CO., INC.
NEW YORK   •   1955

PRINTED IN THE UNITED STATES OF AMERICA
BY THE WILLIAM BYRD PRESS
RICHMOND, VIRGINIA

Library of Congress Catalog Card Number: 45-35124

TO THE MEMORY OF

GRANTLAND RICE

FROM WHOM WE HAVE ALL LEARNED

TABLE OF CONTENTS

FOOTBALL

BOXING

GOLF

TENNIS

RACING

BASKETBALL

HUNTING AND FISHING

MARATHON

HOCKEY

TRACK AND FIELD

DOGS

GENERAL

IN MEMORIUM

FOR THE RECORD

ILLUSTRATIONS

PREFACE

This is the start of the second decade of the *Best Sports Stories* series, inaugurated so timidly back in 1945. During that eleven-year span, there have been included more than 500 stories by almost 300 writers, more than 300 pictures by almost 200 photographers. During that eleven-year span, also, the series has become more and more accepted, by writers and photographers of sports events as well as by the people who like to read about them, even in retrospect. For this the editors are exceedingly grateful.

As long as we're handing out words of gratitude, may we also express our appreciation to our judges, John Chamberlain, Bob Considine and Quentin Reynolds—sports fans all—who have served in this capacity for many years and who have helped in the growth of the series.

Anyway, getting down to this year's competition and the winners:

As in all previous years, the judges received the manuscript, whittled down from more than 600 entries, with all stories "blind". That is, there was no title or author indicated. Each story was "slugged" (newspaper terminology for identification mark) and the judges came up with the winners after the first round, unlike some previous years when there had to be a recount.

Of the winners of the three $250 prizes, only Jimmy Cannon is a repeater. He captured the news award back in 1947 with his story on the Louis-Conn fight. Matter of fact, for John Gilooly, winner of the News Coverage Award, and for Herman Hickman, the football coach turned author, winner of the Magazine Award, this is the first appearance in the series.

Here is the box score of the judges' voting:

News Coverage Division

Author and Story	Chamberlain	Considine	Reynolds	*Pts.
Gilooly's *Golf in Braille*	3	3	—	6
Cashen's *That Team Named Desire*	2	—	2	4
Hunter's *The Rhodes Story: Chapter I*	—	—	3	3
Young's *Dodgers on the Rocks*	—	2	—	2

11

Author and Story	Chamberlain	Considine	Reynolds	*Pts.
Rendel's *Canine King*	1	—	1	2
Nason's *Hurricane Rocky*	—	1	—	1

News Feature Division

Canon's *The Beautiful Racket*	—	1	3	4
Kuechle's *So You Want to Be a Quarterback*	3	—	—	3
Clarke's *The Monk and the Ball Game*	—	3	—	3
Eisenberg's *Dizzy Dean of the Links*	—	—	2	2
Roeder's *Baseball Pagliacci*	2	—	—	2
Maule's *Old Satch*	—	2	—	2
Martin's *Tears, Country Style*	—	—	1	1
Mitchell's *"Some of My Best Friends Are Ghosts"*	1	—	—	1

Magazine Division

Hickman's *Rasslin' Was My Act*	—	3	3	6
Graham's *My Friend Grantland Rice*	—	2	2	4
Linn's *"We Conquered," He Cried, and Fell Dead*	3	—	—	3
Herndon's *Baseball Wife*	2	—	—	2
Meany's *Baseball in Three Languages*	—	1	—	1
Murray's *"I Cover the Big Leagues"*	—	—	1	1
O'Neil's *Duel of the Four-Minute Men*	1	—	—	1

*Based on 3 points for a first-place vote, 2 for a second and 1 for the third.

Said John Chamberlain of his selections:

What I like about sports writing is that, to a far greater extent than other types of magazine or newspaper work, it seems to resist the dead hand of the "formula." Games may be conventionalized, but the human factors that come into play in them are seldom the same. Bring a writer with a "free" franchise together with a new situation, and it is not strange that a good literary product results. My choices:

Coverage

1. "Blind Golf" (Gillooly's *Golf in Braille*)
2. "Army-Navy" (Cashen's *That Team Named Desire*)
3. "Dogs" (Rendel's *Canine King*)

The story of "Blind Golf" competition would offer some singular values in any event, but when you have a blind golfer who is also afflicted with arthritis and "football" legs you have something that is, fortunately, extremely unusual. Most writers would have been tempted to overplay the agony. The author of this particular news story held himself under commendable restraint. The value— courage, humor—come through all the better for that.

The No. 2 story, about the Navy "team named desire" and its victory over Army, sticks to the line of action. But the "desire" comes through in every line. Not many coaches keep up with the highbrow theatre of Tennessee Williams, and the coach who can deal in epigrammatic literary allusions is a rarity. Eddie Erdelatz set a neat stage for a sports writer, and your author has caught the spirit of the play.

As for "dogs" and my No. 3 choice: I wouldn't have believed that a cocker spaniel could be so individualized in such a few words.

Features

1. "Quarterback" (Kuechle's *So You Want to Be a Quarterback.*)
2. "Clown" (Roeder's *Baseball Pagliacci*)
3. "Casey" (Mitchell's *Some of My Best Friends Are Ghosts*)

The idea of explaining how a pro quarterback wrestles with signals might seem obvious, but it took a first-rate reporter to make the "obvious" clear. I've heard of something called "close-in" reporting, which usually turns out to be an effort to substitute a tape recorder for the value-choices of a good writer. This particular story is real close-in reporting, for it explains certain minutiae that a tape recorder would miss completely.

The story of Slivers, the baseball clown, is a real contribution to history. I'd always thought that Schact and Altrock were the pioneers in this sort of thing.

The story of Casey's ghost, and of the ghost's ghost, is a wonderful parlay. Casey Stengel isn't so dumb, but why does he give this sort of stuff away? Artemus Ward used to collect for his own humor, and so did Will Rogers.

Magazines

1. "Marathon" (Linn's *"We Conquered" He Cried, and Fell Dead*)
2. "Wife" (Herndon's *Baseball Wife*)
3. "Bannister" (O'Neil's *Duel of the Four-Minute Men*)

Last year I liked a news coverage story about Doroteo Flores, the Indian marathoner from Guatemala. I thought I knew all about the marathon after reading that. How wrong can a man be? The magazine story about the Boston Marathon, its origins and annual destinations, gives a lot more.

The story of Monte Irvin's wife Dee, and of her reaction to the "costliest broken ankle in sports history" (but was it much more costly than Bobby Thomson's?), is a beautiful piece of sustained and restrained human interest.

For No. 3 in the magazines, there is Bannister and the account of the battle of the under-four minute milers. This is an artful blend of sports writing and investigation into medical science as it relates to exhaustion. Good human study, too, of two strange characters.

I've been judging these sports stories for a long time now. Every year there are some surprises. I wish I could say the same for the Washington reporting that I read.

This is Bob Considine's report:

Coverage

1. I think the "Blind Golf" story is one of the finest news stories I've ever read. It transcends the sport concerned, the score, and all else except the fine heart and spirit which the event asked of Frederick Kerr Schields, and of the writer.

2. The tipsy account of a Brooklyn loss (Young's *Dodgers on the Rocks*). How our sports pages cry for nimbler approaches to telling the old story of who, what, when, where, why, etc! This is a delightful mockery.

3. Marciano (Nason's *Hurricane Rocky*) is my third choice. Why? Because it tells more than the score of the Marciano-Charles fight, which score the reading public knew for many hours before this story could reach print.

Features

1. The story of the Cistercian monk (Clarke's *The Monk and the Ball Game*) is a remarkable feature, a kind of once-in-a-lifetime for a sports reporter. It took a great deal of tenderness and understanding to write this piece. And it took intelligence enough to let the facts speak for themselves . . . the touching, poignant, yet inspirational facts.

2. A lot was written about Satchel Paige during his decades in baseball, but I doubt if anyone quite caught Satch as well as the

writer of this splendid interview with the Great Man. (Maule's *Old Satch*) This writer has learned his trade well. He never interrupts when something important is being said—as here.

3. There's a savage splendor to the boxing story which starts, "Listen to the boosters' lies." (Cannon's *The Beautiful Racket*) This boy had a gut full and wrote what has passed through every honest boxing writer's mind since the time of the cestus. Wonderful indignation! Wonderful control of that indignation!

Magazines

I don't remember a better crop of magazine stories than the group presented for this contest. I'll have some sleepless nights for leaving out the one about Ed Furgol, Marciano, O'Malley, Mrs. Irvin, Wally Butts' daughter, the happy baseball writer, Private Eye Jack Larkin, and Bannister. But you want answers not apologies:

1. The wrestling piece (Hickman's *Rasslin' Was My Act*) gets my first nod for several reasons. Only an occasional blue moon provides such an article. With tens of thousands of people being added annually to the sucker list of those who believe in professional rassling—via TV—this was a needed declaration. It could have been an ill-tempered expose. Instead, it made some of the liveliest and most amusing reading of 1954.

2. An obituary would not normally rate high among the best magazine pieces on sports. But how often in sports history does a Grantland Rice die? The writer knew and loved and respected and studied his hero, and has done a fine job of keeping Rice alive for future generations of sportswriters. (Graham's *My Friend Grantland Rice*)

3. "Language" (Meany's *Baseball in Three Languages*). This study of the International League is exhaustive as play in that league must be exhausting. A brilliant job of creative research into the Tower of Babel.

From Quentin Reynolds:

Features

1. "Boxing" (Cannon's *The Beautiful Racket*)
2. "Patton" (Eisenberg's *Dizzy Dean of the Links*)
3. "Slaughter" (Martin's *Tears, Country Style*)

The story on boxing is a masterly indictment of a sport that seems to grow less attractive each year. It is a savage satire on boxing, as it is conducted today, and I think it wins first place hands down. It was written by a man filled with anger and with pity too—pity for the two dead boxers and for all boxers who inevitably begin to disintegrate as their skills lessen and the elastic leaves their legs.

Billy Joe Patton came from nowhere last year to become the favorite of the golf galleries. He makes an attractive subject, and it is handled skillfully in this feature. Just as good is the fine article on Enos Slaughter and of his hurt pride when he was traded by St. Louis to the Yankees.

Magazines

1. "Wrestling" (Hickman's *Rasslin' Was My Act*)
2. "Rice" (Graham's *My Friend Grantland Rice*)
3. "Reporter" (Murray's *I Cover the Big Leagues*)

The story on professional wrestling is not only hilariously funny but is the first story I've read by a wrestler that puts the absurd but popular pastime in its proper perspective. The writer is frank to say that all matches are rehearsed in advance, but he is quick to add that the wrestlers themselves look upon their profession as entertainment, not as sport.

Second place I think goes to the fine story about Grantland Rice. This is the Granny Rice we all knew; he is not glorified or sanctified—merely humanized, and by one who obviously knew him well. Third place goes to the amusing story of the relationship between baseball writer and player, and the occasional hazards which arise out of this relationship.

Coverage

1. "First Series Game" (Hunter's *The Rhodes Story: Chapter I*)
2. "Army-Navy" (Cashen's *That Team Named Desire*)
3. "Dogs" (Rendel's *Canine King*)

"The Indians came back to Manhattan today, back to a Manhattan they had once peddled for a keg of whiskey. And they sold out again, this time for a pint—a pint-sized home run. . . ."

That's how this brilliant story of the first 1954 World Series game began. This story is baseball writing at its best. I think it deserves first place.

Right behind it is the fine story of how underdog Navy whipped Army. In third place I put the story of how the buff-colored cocker spaniel Rise and Shine captivated the hearts of public and judges to win Best in Show at the Westminster Kennel Club event. It takes masterly writing to make a dog show exciting, but this story is exciting.

☆　☆　☆

As far as the prize photo competition was concerned, the editors found it exceedingly difficult to choose between Paul Vathis's *Bubble Gum Catcher* and Frank Lyerla's *Come Clean Boys*. Even though they are completely different in type, each had interest and tremendous action. So, they compromised. They split the $100 prize between the two photographers.

To all the prize winners, therefore, our sincere congratulations. To those who also ran, well . . . wait till next year.

IRVING T. MARSH
EDWARD EHRE

Best News Story

GOLF BY BRAILLE

By John Gillooly

From The Boston Record, July 18, 1954

Copyright, 1954, Hearst Corporation
Reprinted by permission of copyright owner

Worcester—

HERE NOW was something to see. None of the competitors did. For this was the U. S. Golf Championship for the Blind involving 23 sightless competitors, each of them an anatomical marvel adept at that neatest of tricks—keeping the head down while at the very same time keeping the chin up.

The first 18 of this 36-hole championship were staged yesterday at Wachusett Country Club in nearby West Boylston and the leader was Frederick Kerr Shields, Detroit businessman, whose story is incredible.

Shields shot a 104 to lead the perennial winner, Charlie Boswell of Birmingham, Ala. by four strokes with the deciding 18 holes coming up today.

Get this. Shields is 57 years old. Along with being totally blind, he has creeping arthritis; he wears what he calls a sacroiliac belt, or corset; he has "football" legs which barely carried him over the mountainish 6430-yard course.

His caddy lugged around a camp stool for him to sit on as his guide—a seeing-eye human—lined up his shots. On the 15th fairway it crashed under him giving him a bad tumble. He had requested the USBGA (U. S. Blind Golf Association) to give him permission to use an electric car—a caddy-cart—to motor him around the course. His request was refused. On Strike It Rich he would collect a fortune.

So Shields made it on tedious foot, fairly tottering over the final four holes as a gallery of 1500 eddied around him for his painstaking finish. Shields dropped his final putt at 7:10 p.m. He was among the earlier starters in the tournament which began at 8:30 a.m. He had only a brief time out for lunch.

Hundreds lingered around the decorous Wachusett clubhouse

for a look at Shields, the blind leading those with 20-20 vision and teaching a powerful lesson and making a lark of life's vicissitudes. "I'll cool off now with a double scotch, get a good night's sleep and walk the 18 more tomorrow," said Shields. "But I'll insist on playing alone. I want no partner. I'm too slow. I'll hurt a partner's game."

Born in Scotland, at Ruther Glen, a suburb of Glasgow, Shields came to the U. S. in 1912 bringing with him a links legacy. Around Paterson, N.J., he played considerable soccer and rugby—acquiring his "football legs" and naturally played a lot of golf. He was a 9-handicap golfer later when a member of the Oakland Country Club (Detroit) where the noted Al Watrous is pro.

Suddenly he went blind. "I had driven to Florida in 1948 and was having dinner with my wife and brother-in-law when the lights went out for good. It was creeping arthritis which made me blind," said Shields speaking freely, unemotionally about his personal disaster. "Started low in my spine, crept up to the head, through the skull and hit the optic nerve. It's rather rare. Only a few cases in the country that I know of."

Shields is as unafflicted by total hopeless blindness as all the others in the "golf in the dark" tournament, which is gay, jovial, a caprice. It's rich in humor. There's no room in their golf bags for pathos.

One of them made a rotten shot from a trap. He knew from the touch. His partner, next hit an equally sorry chip. He knew from the sound. "I'm blind, what's your excuse for that one," the trapped golfer joked.

Shields, nibbling his double scotch, was informed of the epigram over refreshments counter at the 19th hole: "Ve get too soon oldt, und too late schmardt." Shields was tickled as the words were read to him.

It hit him. For when stricken blind in 1948 he sold his clubs, abandoned his favorite sticks and his beloved sport. He became old too soon, overnight, when some cruel fate turned the switch on his lights. It was only five weeks ago that he heard about the U. S. Blind Open—or Shut, as one of the blind golfers joked.

The city of Detroit recreational department became interested in Shields' ambition to play again. It hired a coach, Andy Miller, a very competent golfer himself, to be his guide. "Give Andy the credit, he's wonderful," spoke Shields of his new "eyes" which he acquired only five weeks ago. Shields and Miller "played" but 45 holes together in preparation for this tournament.

Quite as extraordinary as the golfers are their guides, gentle, loyal, patient. They lead the golfers around the course by gripping a club together. They measure off the yardage, inform their golfer of where and how hard to hit, place the ball, line up the clubhead. Sometimes the golfer will "read" the green with a particular kind of braille—crouching or getting down on hands and knees to feel the carpet to the cup and test its contours.

Shields—father of two sons, Fred who is a salesman and Bob who is a captain in the Marines and recently returned from Korea and jet piloting—let guide Miller do all his thinking, as he termed it. Shields just did the swinging, not too long but mostly accurate. He had only 36 putts, two per green. He hovered close to par except on the 510-yard 17th when, to escape a water hazard, he pulled one into an unplayable lie and took a ten.

Otherwise he might have the title cinched with a longer lead over the annual champion, 38-year-old Charlie Boswell, a Jimmy Demaret of the links, lustrous in gingham shirt, pink cap, burnt-orange slacks and the latest in spikes. By contrast, Shields was adorned in golf garb he might have worn back in Ruther Glen, Glasgow. His spikes were of Ouimet vintage.

Boswell had three pars on the front nine for a 45 but then the slow pace—it took him almost eight hours to go around—unsettled his game. Boswell, major in the infantry and blinded by anti-tank shell fire in the Ruhr Valley—wound up with 108.

Boswell played football for Alabama. He was in the Rose Bowl game against California in 1938. He played against Sam Chapman and Bob Herwig in that game. "Herwig's the fellow married Kathleen Windsor, wrote 'Forever Amber,'" Boswell reminded. Boswell's guide was Sam Jaffe, Birmingham automobile dealer who took time off from his job to steer Boswell around Wachusett.

The Blind Bomber from Birmingham, as Boswell is affectionately known, has broken 100 often. He may need to break it again today to keep Shields and his arthritis and his football legs from achieving what would be one of the noblest, most inspiring sports victories of all time.

Fractured Ben Hogan recovered from a near-fatal auto crash to regain golf dominance; Ed Furgol with a withered arm won the U. S. Open; Babe Didrickson Zaharias conquered cancer to win the U. S. Womens Open. Superwoman. Here, just possibly, behind those green-tinted glasses and under that sweat-stained golf cap could be Superman, Frederick Kerr Shields, crippled, sightless.

Best News-Feature Story

THE BEAUTIFUL RACKET

By Jimmy Cannon

From The New York Post, December 13, 1954

LISTEN TO THE boosters' lies. The fight racket is a glorious adventure. It's a force for decency. It frees the impoverished from tenement and hovel. It transports them to great public halls where strangers gladly call their names. Wealth is their reward. Fame is their prize. They're the brave and the graceful and the honored. The hell they are.

They're frightened kids working at a filthy trade. It's not a game at all. It is only a game for a man sitting before his television set or leaning against a bar. It's merely a game for spectators who come whole into an arena and leave unbroken.

How can it be a game when men suffer to provide entertainment? Is there joy in public humiliation? There is no fun in concussions. Look at their clenched faces if you doubt me and read the transcript of old anguish.

The bums who get rum money for selling their blood to banks do it privately with only a nurse to watch them. You honor yourself when you give blood in the interests of the sick. Even those who have deformed this philanthropy into a sickening profession can regard the tortured act with pride. But pugs give their blood publicly and for money alone. Oh, it is a beautiful racket.

It's good and I enjoy it when it's right. I should be ashamed of liking it, but I'm not. I know fine men who work at it and aren't twisted by it. The big people like it, too, and tell crowds in the ballrooms of hotels how important boxing is in this country. What do they have to say to Ed Sanders, who died after a fight in Boston, and Ralph Weiser, who perished in a place called Klamath Falls, Ore.?

Please say a few words to Ed Sanders and Ralph Weiser. They're entitled to know about the glorious sport of boxing. It's possible they died without realizing the splendor of their calling.

22

They're entitled to know all about it. It's awful to keep secrets from such as these.

Don't save it for a boys' club or for a boxing writers' dinner or for a talk before a business men's lunch. Tell it to Ed Sanders and Ralph Weiser. They died in doubt.

It is not enough to explain how it shapes the body into a straight, hard leanness. Remember it all and hold none of it back. The brain is a queer organ. It is not improved by the fight racket. It softens and curdles. Punches aren't night school. They educate no one. The nose is not made handsomer by blows either.

The nose bends. The bone shatters. The flesh spreads. The breath comes in snorting pants. The eyes are not helped by the fight racket either. They blur and the lids fray. The flesh about them darkens and pinches them in lumpy wrinkles. The brows become ledges made by pain.

No dentist ever advised a patient to have teeth loosened by force. So you're not allowed to go into a fight without a mouthpiece to guard your teeth. Of course, you become toothless with a mouthpiece, but you usually lose them one at a time. Anyway, a fighter can afford false teeth. If he isn't talented enough to make enough money to buy them, what the hell good is he? The bum shouldn't have a license.

There is always talk of honor at the banquets, but seldom is the heart discussed or the liver or the kidneys. The butchers handle that kind of guff. The honored guest, Mr. Chairman, is concerned with the future of our youth. It saves them from criminal associations and gets them out of the alleys and into the gyms where they can meet the chivalry of the fight racket as exemplified by Frankie Carbo and Eddie Coco.

Why, Mr. Chairman, doesn't the respected speaker describe the hallucinations? It is like being a patron of a private movie. The way the world is, Mr. Chairman, perhaps they are better off, lodged in their visions. The world's no bargain, ladies and gentlemen. The insane lead sheltered existences. In no other trade can you become deranged faster and get paid while you're going crazy.

Think of those unfortunates who go whacky with love or whiskey or loneliness or drugs. They're amateur basket cases. They don't lay up a quarter, but the fighter is paid to lose his mind. The fight racket takes care of its own.

It's better than going to night school. The most innocent can be corrupted. The most naive may be made cynical. It teaches them control and obedience. You do what the manager tells you.

Isn't that the way the Army runs? And how many times was it said that a hitch of soldiering made a real man out of a silly boy? The fight manager lives by the direct order. That's the way the services operate and who knocks them? Dirty bums like sports writers knock the fight racket. Know why? They're lousy no good stool pigeons.

So tell them about death, speaker of the evening. Tell them about Ed Sanders and Ralph Weiser. Tell them about the last purse they fought for. Their end was death. Nobody blames anyone. The other guys could have been killed, too. That makes it all right. Isn't that a square proposition?

But no manager could have been killed by Ed Sanders or Ralph Weiser and no second and no judge and no referee and no sports writer or no promoter or no matchmaker or no press agent or no boxing commissioner. Only the fighters die.

Boxing belongs to Ed Sanders and Ralph Weiser now. They own it more than anyone ever did, including Jack Demsey, Benny Leonard, Joe Louis or Ray Robinson. No one will try to cut in with what they won in their last fights. They may keep that for themselves.

Best Magazine Story

RASSLIN' WAS MY ACT

By Herman Hickman

From The Saturday Evening Post, February 6, 1954

MY FIRST KNOWLEDGE of Dan Parker, the distinguished sports columnist of the New York Daily Mirror, was in 1932. I had just arrived in New York City to embark on a career as a professional wrestler, and his column in those days was "must reading" for the fraternity, just as Variety is for other branches of the entertainment field. He must have had a pipe line into our booking office, because his column kept picking the wrestling winners on the nose. He even got so brazen as to name the particular hold that would end a match, and the time of the fall.

It became a guessing game for the powers that be to try and cross him up on the results. Sometimes his information was so late that it was impossible to switch the outcome. The average wrestler didn't have to go by the office in Times Square to get the script for the evening's show. He could read it in Dan Parker's column. I can tell you that it was very demoralizing for a young and ambitious professional.

I remember one night when we fooled him. It was during the famous Jim Londos-Ray Steele series at Madison Square Garden, which, I understand, drew gates of around $70,000 for each match. Dan Parker came out with the prediction that Londos would win this particular match with his famous "airplane spin" in fifty minutes, and thus retain the heavyweight wrestling championship (Jack Curley Division). But did Dan miss it! Londos won, but not until fifty-seven minutes and thirty seconds, and then not with an airplane spin at all but with a series of flying tackles.

I'll say this for Dan. He was a gentleman. The next day his column came out all draped in black, and with the heading, AN APOLOGY TO THE PUBLIC. He said that he was deeply humiliated to have been off on the time of a professional wrestling match by as much as seven minutes and thirty seconds. As for his

25

not getting the winning hold right, there was just no excuse for that.

I felt pretty good about it all until I read his column a few days later. It was a question-and-answer affair. Question: What becomes of old broken-down wrestlers? Answer: They are still wrestling.

The wrestling bug bit me while I was a student at the University of Tennessee. Every Friday night I would go to the Lyric Theater in Knoxville and watch the matches. Soon the promoter, Sam Seigel, started giving me complimentary tickets. It wasn't long before he began taking me backstage to meet the wrestlers.

To a big-eyed East Tennessean, it was wonderful to hear their talk of faraway places—St. Louis, New Orleans, Memphis, Houston. They certainly were glamorous figures to me. I even began to like the "villains," who used such dirty tactics in the ring. I could not understand how these men, perfect gentlemen in their dressing rooms, could be such bullies when they wrestled. None of the wrestlers ever showed any nervousness about their coming matches, although I knew that they must be really on edge, the way I was before a football game.

I met them all during the next few years. The big names were all on the "gasoline circuit," as the Southern territory was called, because the cities were so far apart that the wrestlers had to jump into their cars after a match and head for the next engagement. They could not make connections by train, and airplane travel then was just a name. When I became established on the circuit myself, driving from one city to another after a hurried alcohol bath— usually there weren't any showers in the dressing rooms—and three or four silver-dollar-sized hamburgers, I would think about how I once dreamed of the excitement of new cities and new faces every night.

Here's a sample itinerary. Slip quietly out of Griffith Park in Washington, where the matches have been held outdoors. Grab something quick to eat at the nearest lunch wagon. Walk four blocks to an appointed rendezvous, where two of the boys are waiting in an automobile. Drive a couple more blocks and pick up your opponent. He was disqualified for choking you just an hour ago. Now he is busily engaged with ham sandwiches and a quart of milk as he flops alongside you on the back seat.

It is midnight Thursday, and our next match is in Knoxville, Tennessee, over 500 miles away, on Friday. We head out toward Charlottesville, then Waynesboro. We'll pick up old U. S. 11 between Staunton and Lexington. Then we will be on the beam heading due south.

We play three-handed poker for hours by the flickering overhead car light. The driver is ruled out, but we each take turns at the wheel. We play a spelling game, which I usually introduce. If a word of over three letters ends on an individual, it costs him a dime, and he has to start a new word. If we get a neophyte into the game with old hands who know the "lock" words, it can be an expensive spelling lesson.

We sing. We sleep a little. We stop at our regular all-night filling station after we hit Route 11, have soft drinks and more cold, slightly stale sandwiches, and are off again. We arrive in Knoxville at noon, separate before we get downtown, and go to our hotels. By driving all night we have saved a one-night hotel bill. We will spend this night in Knoxville; then drive all the following night en route to the next town.

The same "villain" who strangled me in Washington does the same thing to me in Knoxville, and is disqualified again. It is more serious here because this is my home territory. It takes three deputy sheriffs and two members of the fire department to get him safely to his dressing room.

After the matches, this is a night for rest and relaxation. I go by Weaver's Restaurant and order "the works." A crowd gathers to talk to me, and among them are some of the Tennessee football players. They look at me enviously as I talk of the places and people I've seen.

"How does it feel to be in the big time, Herman?" they ask.

"There's nothing like it, nothing like it," I tell them expansively, as I push the remains of a two-pound porterhouse away from me. It's the first real meal I have had in two days.

Saturday afternoon we meet again. I have my friend, French Harris, drive me ten miles out on the highway, because I'm well known around here and must not be seen fraternizing with my opponents. They pick me up, and we're off to New Orleans for a Monday night match. Then comes Birmingham on Tuesday, Atlanta on Wednesday, Nashville on Thursday, and back to Knoxville on Friday. Meanwhile I keep asking myself why I didn't get a job coaching some small-town-high-school football team or try to work my way through law school, as I had planned.

But in 1932 money was a scarce item, and there weren't many jobs floating around even if you did weigh 230 pounds, had made the All-American football team, and could recite a conglomerate collection of verse. So, when Rudy Dusek, the oldest and the mastermind of the Dusek brothers, undertook to sell me on the idea of becoming a professional wrestler, he did not find it difficult. He mentions something about the possibility of making $1000 a week and becoming champion of the world. He could have got me for less than half of that, and he did.

Up to then, I knew nothing about the inner workings of the wrestling game. I was worried about my lack of experience, but when I started asking about that, they passed it off with, "You're big and you're strong, and you're an All-American football player. We'll teach you everything you oughta know." That was all I knew until I arrived in New York City.

I was really scared when I got off the train at Pennsylvania Station. I decided to take a taxi to the Greystone Hotel at 91st and Broadway, where I was to meet Toots Mondt, who would take charge of my training. I pictured a big gymnasium with a lot of tough guys hanging around. I had read about how there were gangsters all up and down Broadway. This might be their hangout.

It was about eleven a.m. when I arrived at the Greystone. I asked at the desk for Mr. Mondt. They said that he was expecting me. I was getting more nervous all the time as I stepped off the elevator. I had read hundreds of pages about Joe (Toots) Mondt. He was Mr. Big in wrestling. I rang the bell to his apartment.

A big voice boomed, "Come in!" I walked falteringly into the living room, and I could see him through the open bedroom door. Was I disillusioned! There he was in a big oversize bed, having breakfast, and wearing pink silk pajamas. His pleasantly round face was bordered with a big smile, and his baby complexion matched his pajamas.

"How are you, kid?" was his greeting. "Rudy Dusek and Sam Seigel have told me a lot about you. You should be ready for your first match in a couple of weeks. We've got a room all fitted out with a wrestling mat on the next floor. That's your gym. I'll have two or three of the boys work out with you each day, and you'll be ready to go in no time."

He ordered a big breakfast sent up for me and asked, "How's your cash, son?" I told him that I had some money, but he pulled a fat roll of bills out of a pair of trousers hanging across a chair. He flipped off five $100 bills and said, "Well, you might need a little more to tide you over until you get going good. You can pay me back then."

I want to digress for just one moment here and say that I've been mixed up in many kinds of enterprises since my wrestling days and have met many kinds of people, but none can compare with the wrestlers for generosity, friendliness and real straight shooting. This term may sound a little incongruous when applied to participants in a "sport" that was fixed every night. But they never thought of it that way. They considered themselves performers attempting to please a crowd every night, just as a tumbling act might do on the vaudeville circuit. There have never been any gambling scandals in wrestling, because there has never been any betting mixed up in it. The athletic commissions in the different states consider the matches exhibitions, and in most places the referee gets in on the act with the wrestlers.

My training period progressed to the satisfaction of my mentors, Toots Mondt and Rudy Dusek. I worked out in the gymnasium room three or four hours each day. Men like Jim McMillen, who was an All-American guard during the Red Grange era at Illinois; Earl McCready, the Canadian who was intercollegiate heavyweight wrestling champion at Oklahoma A. & M.; Tiny Roebuck, the great Indian football star at Kaskell Institute, and Ernie Dusek, a younger brother of Rudy, would work with me every day, after they had wrestled the night before in Albany, Boston or Baltimore.

They taught me how to "work," which means putting on a performance, instead of "shooting," which means straight wrestling. They showed me how to take a fall without getting hurt, how to "go" with a wristlock without getting a dislocated shoulder, how to slam an opponent without injuring him. This latter is done by making his feet hit the mat first with a resounding thud, and not his head. They taught me to work "loose." Some of the best, like McMillen and the Duseks, could appear to be tearing a man's head off with a headlock, all their muscles straining, and yet their opponents could not even feel the pressure of their arms.

To get the proper dramatic effect, usually one wrestler in each match was "clean" and the other was a villain. Ordinarily you were typed in one role or the other, although some of the wrestlers would play the villain in one town and the hero in the next. I was presented as the clean-cut-college-boy type and because of my football background, the flying tackle was my key hold. Whenever I used that offense, it was usually curtains for my opponent.

Later I became noted for my "belly bounce." I would beat my opponent into submission by bouncing up and down on him—al-

ways remembering to break the bounce with my hands hitting the
mat first, so as not to start an epidemic of internal hemorrhages—
after I had weakened him with the flying tackles.

But I get ahead of my story. My debut was one to remember. I
opened in Syracuse at the cavalry armory. My opponent had been
selected with care. In fact, I had worked with him in my hotel gym
many times. I was to work with him in many places under many
names. Bill Nelson was quite a character. He must have had 3000
matches. He was semiretired from active duty, being engaged in
the office with the bookings. Toots and Rudy figured that I couldn't
go wrong with him.

I remember that Ed (Strangler) Lewis, one of the great "shooters" of all time and an equally outstanding "worker," was in the
main event that first night at Syracuse. I was in the second preliminary with Bill Nelson—Wild Bill in that town. I don't think
that Lewis or Hickman either was much of a draw in Syracuse.
The crowd was thin, and the odor of the horses was thick. Andy
Kerr, the Colgate football coach, who had coached me in the East-
West game, brought John Orsi, his great All-American end, and
some other members of the squad to see my debut. I was a little
embarrassed when they started inquiring about my strategy for the
match, and asked me if I weren't nervous. Sure, I was nervous—
even though I knew how it was coming out—but I had learned
my lessons well.

Wild Bill refused to shake hands with me in the center of the
ring before the match. The crowd booed. He complained about the
oil on my ears and hair. The crowd booed. He had an argument
with the referee about what constituted a fall in the state of New
York, and threatened to leave the ring. The crowd hated him
already.

The bell rang. I put out my hands to start wrestling, and he hit
me with a left to the jaw. I staggered. He hit me with a right to
the body which sounded like a pistol shot. I reeled. He started
kneeing me in the groin and pulling my hair at the same time. The
referee broke his illegal hold and warned him. He came right back
and knocked me down with another left hook to the jaw. He put a
"punishing" Japanese toe hold on me.

I suffered and suffered, but I would not give up, because I had
so much courage. I would not even try to crawl to refuge outside
the ropes, because I was a clean-cut college boy and would not re-
sort to anything in the least dishonorable.

Then it happened, and it wasn't in the script. For some reason, the referee broke the hold and had Wild Bill over in a corner of the ring, lecturing him about his dirty tactics. I didn't see them, because I was too busy suffering. I must have lain there on my stomach for a full minute with my feet bent over my back, not realizing that Bill was not still there. Then I happened to glance back over my shoulder and saw both of them.

I wanted to crawl under the ring and die, but instead I recovered my composure and started launching my flying tackles. He ran from me. He cried to the referee. He got outside the ring and asked for mercy. But I was riled up now, and nothing could stop me. The crowd was going wild.

The referee started counting him out. Wild Bill protestingly came back in the ring. I hit him with one tackle, then another. Each time he would sail into the air and hit the mat with a thud—the back of his heels. He couldn't get away from my terrific onslaught. He was a helpless mass in the middle of the ring, so I rushed over and pinned his shoulders to the canvas.

"Nice going, you old mountaineer hillbilly; you made it look good," Bill whispered to me. These were pleasant words from an old trouper to a neophyte during an out-of-town tryout. I had busted one line, but the master had forgiven me. I was ready for the big time.

The job of booking wrestlers in twenty or thirty cities all over the United States each night of the week is a complex operation. The Curley office in New York, which was really run in the early '30's by Toots Mondt, Jack Pfeffer and Ed White, Jim Londos' manager, was the center of all activities. From here went the instructions to the hinterlands as to the lineup and outcome of the week's matches.

All the wrestlers had code names. For instance, Jim Londos was Chris, Ray Steele was Glendale—his hometown—George Zaharias was Subway—his first trip to New York, he got mixed up and rode all day from one end of the line to the other, so the story goes. Jim McMillen was Football, Rudy Dusek was Mitch. I was Cannonball.

In those days the Postal Telegraph Company was still in existence, in addition to Western Union. The New York office would send out the instructions on one wire service and have them confirmed on the other. This is a sample message: "Cannonball moon Subway around thirty-five confirm." It meant that I was to lose— look up to the moon—to George Zaharias in about thirty-five minutes.

To be a good attraction for a promoter, you had to be either greatly liked or greatly hated. A mere scientific exhibition of clear wrestling skill won't draw at the gate. There must be a hero and a villain. The hero doesn't always win, but when he loses, the villain must always beat him by foul means.

I think that amateur wrestling, as conducted in high schools and colleges, is a wonderful sport. I have coached college wrestling and I enjoyed it. The contestants must be in top physical condition to go all out for nine minutes—the length of a regular college match. It would be physically impossible to wrestle like this for an hour or more, the way the professionals sometimes do.

But amateur wrestling has never been a big spectator sport and never will be, because it is impossible to inject the thrills and pathos in a shooting match that the professionals create in their exhibitions. I have seen many shooting matches by top professionals in the gymnasium, and they are just as dull and uninteresting to the average spectator as the college matches.

So wrestling, in order to draw crowds, must of necessity be "rasslin'." It always has been and always will be an exhibition. Taken in this light, I can see nothing harmful in it. As entertainment it is usually better than a lot of movies, and it should not have a bad influence on any member of the family, because virtue is always supreme.

I get quite a kick out of some of the old-time sports fans who say, "Wrestling today is just a hoax and a vaudeville act, but I remember back in the days of Hackenschmidt and Gotch and the Zbyszkos when it was really wrestling. Why, I've seen them stay in one hold for fifty minutes, and wrestle many a night for two hours, and none of this rough stuff either. They were scientific.'

They were scientific, all right, and maybe excellent shooters, although myths can flourish with the passage of time. I can tell you one thing, and that is that their so-called scientific wrestling matches were exhibitions, and not very exciting ones, either. I saw many of those early matches, which were for the most part put on by foreign wrestlers, and I later worked with some of them, such as Stanislaus and Wladek Zbyszko.

The style of that time was a carry-over from the old German beer gardens, where the longer the performers wrestled, the more beer they could sell the customers. Some of them told me that they would "wrestle" five or six hours during the course of the evening in the Graeco-Roman style, in which no holds are allowed below the waist, and when anyone is thrown to the mat, it constitutes a fall. They would lock in each other's arms and stay in one position for an hour or so. Then one would straighten up his arm slowly, flexing his muscles mightily, and the customers sitting around the tables would go wild and more beer would flow. Finally, when the wrestlers got thirsty, one would be thrown to the mat with a mighty thud, and they would rest for thirty minutes. And so on through the night.

The only public shooting match I ever saw took place in Madison Square Garden in 1933 between Strangler Lewis and Ray Steele. Ed Lewis was representing what was then the Paul Bowser branch of the industry, and Ray Steele was the standard-bearer for the Curley wheel. They were both excellent wrestlers. Lewis may have been the best of all time—on the basis of my personal observations in the gymnasium. Both were most popular with their fellow wrestlers.

This match was supposed to decide the "real" championship. I don't know yet how the powers that be ever let the match happen, but I do know that I have never seen such tension around the Times Square office as there was the week before the match. I was booked in the Broadway Arena in Brooklyn for the same night, along with seven other unfortunates. Ordinarily a wrestler never goes to a wrestling match, but this was different. We made our plans. We knew that in order to reach the Garden in time for the Lewis-Steele event, we would have to get four matches over with by nine-thirty. Never did the old Broadway Arena see such fast and short matches.

The match had already begun when we got to our seats. Lewis was fat, fifty and balding, with a big chest, big belly and small legs. He was built like the great Babe Ruth. Steele, approaching forty, had the body beautiful. He weighed around 220 pounds to the Strangler's 250.

From the very start it was no contest. Steele could do nothing with the Strangler. Lewis was a big cat, darting in, going behind, making Steele look like a boy on a man's mission. The fans yawned and started stamping their feet for action. The wrestlers, on the other hand, sat with their eyes glued on the ring. They watched every movement intensely. They were thrilled with the skill of Lewis. They were seeing the master give a pupil the lesson of his life.

Lewis and Steele were personal friends. I have no doubt that the Strangler could have pinned him at any time. Steele had courage, but realized that he was hopelessly outmatched. Some whispering probably occurred, and Steele started punching Lewis with his closed fists. So it ended with the referee disqualifying him after the match had gone about twenty minutes.

We saw Ed next morning at Grand Central Station on his way to another match in Buffalo.

"How was Ray?" we asked.

"Good little man, good little man," he replied, between puffs of his cigar.

My first match for the heavyweight championship of the world was held in the baseball park at Memphis in 1932. I had not been defeated in about fifty matches, so a bout with Jim Londos, the perennial champion, was a natural in my home state of Tennessee. I was drawing big crowds everywhere in the South, so the authorities did not want to see me beaten, even by the champion, except under extraordinary circumstances. I was told to go about fifty minutes, and then, after Londos had narrowly escaped defeat, to take a dive from the elevated ring platform out into the infield and be counted out.

There is a mistaken idea that wrestlers rehearse every move of their matches. Usually, the only orders you receive are as to who is to "moon." Only if there is to be an unusual finish is it discussed. A good match must be extemporaneous. The wrestlers must feel the reaction of the crowd. They must attain the moment of the highest excitement, and then have the finish come with dramatic suddenness.

Most wrestling fans know that the matches are pure exhibitions, but they forget everything they know when an exciting bout is in progress. I have seen more violent reactions from fans at a wrestling match than I ever saw or heard during a football game. Men and women alike wildly cheer and boo—the two reactions that the performers like to hear.

Jim Londos looked and acted the part of a champion. He trained hard, had no bad habits, and when he walked into the ring he carried himself like the king. I understand that he was an excellent shooter, and I know that he was a great showman and worker. He had the lightest touch in the ring of anyone I ever met.

His strategy against me was to keep away. He had decided to be the "villain," or at least the cautious type who was slightly afraid of me. The partisan crowd in Memphis was overjoyed when I broke his wristlock with pure brute strength. When he failed to get me above his head for his famous finishing hold, the airplane spin, he looked at me with amazement. Then, when I hit him with two flying tackles, he crawled outside the ropes for a rest as the crowd booed. Twice I had him pinned for a count of two—a count of three with both shoulder blades touching the mat constitutes a fall —but he managed to get away from me before I could finish him.

After forty minutes the crowd excitement had reached its crescendo. The moment had arrived. I hit him with a flying tackle and knocked him all the way into the ropes with such force that he bounced back, and I hit him again on the rebound. He went down, and as he staggered to his feet I let him have another shoulder block in his midsection. He sailed high into the air.

This was the end of a champion. The crowd could sense that just one more flying tackle and he would be done. I felt the elation of the crowd myself—once a ham, always a ham—as I prepared for the kill. I backed into the ropes to get more spring for my final assault. As I dove through the air, Londos fell flat to the mat. I sailed out of the ring, which was six feet above the ground, going between the second and third ropes.

I was aiming for some soft laps in the second row of the ringside seats, but either my aim was poor or the soft laps saw me coming, because I missed completely and landed flat on my back in the infield on a lighted cigar butt. I was to lie there unconscious while a count of twenty was being tolled over my inert form. I have been through some tough moments, but it took all my fortitude to withstand that burning cigar butt. I thought of Barrymore, of the theater, of "the show must go on," as the slow count of twenty was intoned.

When I heard the magic number of "twenty," I rolled over on my face just as someone dumped a whole bucket of ice water on me. Then three or four people dragged me off by the heels as they would a dead bull. I had failed at my first championship attempt, but had fought the good fight, and I still have a big scar to show for it where that cigar burned a hole in my back.

Many years have passed since my rasslin' days, and I look back on them with pleasant memories. I know that there have been few legitimate professional matches since Milo of Croton was six times champion of Greece, and Theseus laid down the wrestling rules in 900 B. C. I even have my doubts about whether that historic match between Ulysses and Ajax was a shoot. I do know that I met a lot of good guys who were the straightest shooters I've ever known, and that I got to see a lot of "faraway places." I still don't think you can get a better night's entertainment than you will by seeing your favorite "hero" tangle with a "villain." This plot has had the longest run in show business, so it must have something.

The World Series

THE RHODES STORY: CHAPTER 1
By Bob Hunter

From The Los Angeles Examiner, September 30, 1954

Copyright, 1954, Los Angeles Examiner
Reprinted by permission of copyright owner

New York—

THE INDIANS came back to Manhattan today, back to a Manhattan they once peddled for a keg of whiskey.

And they sold out again, this time for a pint—a pint-sized home run that, while just about the shortest on record, still was sufficient to boost the underdog Giants to a 5-2, tenth-inning triumph over the Indians in the opening struggle of this 51st World Series.

A record throng of 52,751, largest in Series history at the Polo Grounds, first sat in silent bewilderment and then broke into a bedlam of noise as it became apparent this innocent pop fly had ended what had been a desperate contest.

It was a pop fly that suddenly became the fourth pinch home run in World Series history that did it.

There was one out when Bob Lemon walked two men, and up came Dusty Rhodes, a remarkably effective bench warmer all season.

He hit the first pitch for a tall line drive, the ball soaring high and catching a friendly wind blowing towards the right field stands.

It looked all along, however, as though Dave Pope would have room to get under the ball, but it carried just to the very rim of the box seats, barely inside the foul line, less than 290 feet from home plate.

That's a bunt in some parks.

I thought the ball actually hit the wall on the fly, and thus would have been in play, but the umpires quickly raised their fists in a majestic circle, and the triumphant three-man parade started for home.

Perhaps you at your TV vantage spots had a better shot of it than we did here.

In fact, as I write this the 400 writers here are expressing some 400 different views on just what did happen.

Maybe you can tell me.

A popular version that soon became a minority was that the ball hit the overhang above the lower box seats.

This was quickly ruled out, however, simply because the ball lacked sufficient carry for such a contact as that.

Finally, it was agreed that a fan, sitting in the front row, reached out and deflected the ball.

That's when I saw it bang off the green concrete wall and flop tauntingly at Pope's feet.

The cameras undoubtedly were zeroed in on that spot in right field so you probably missed Lemon's immediate reaction to the dinky, but nevertheless, historic incident.

He flung his glove a monumental mile.

In fact, it was higher than the homer, and farther.

Lemon's act was certainly an appropriate expression of what all the frustrated Indians must have felt, although somewhat less picturesque.

They left 13 men on base, seven of them in the last three innings, as they muffed scoring chance after scoring chance.

You don't do that in a series like this, and then win it, especially when you're up against guys like the Giants, who'll grab everything on the premises that isn't nailed down.

Durocher's boys would take a hot stove.

They did today.

From the beginning—and you must have had the identical feeling there in front of your mirrored diamond—it was just a question of when the American League champions would start pouring on the coal.

But when the darn thing did wind up, what do you know, it was the Giants who were dancing a jig at home plate and immortalizing a guy for hitting a pop fly.

But, as I said before, Leo's outfit is that kind of a team.

Give 'em an inch and they'll steal the yardstick.

There were two men on and none down in the top of the eighth when the Giants put on one of their typical acts.

Vic Wertz, who already had three base hits, was next up and I would have had him bunting all the way.

But silent and sedate Al Lopez let Wertz decoy the Giants on one pitch, and had him bunt, which he failed to do, on the second strike.

So, the husky first baseman who was bailed out of a sentence with the Orioles earlier in the year, had to hit away, and he almost made Lopez a great manager and the Indians a one-up series leader right on the spot.

He plowed into Lefty Don Liddle's next serve and pumped it out almost 500 feet into dead center.

It would have made three of Rhodes' headline hoist.

But centerfield here is a bad place to hit a ball.

That's where Willie (Say Hey) Mays has his private pasture, and he doesn't like any loose horsehide shrapnel falling around him.

So Willie—and you must have had a beautiful picture of this beautiful catch—wheeled in that fluid fashion of his back to the wall and gaffed it.

At the start of the drive, it looked as though even Willie had no chance to get near it.

But did you see the way he actually outran the ball to save the game right there for the Giants and Reliefer Marv Grissom and all the fans in Manhattan?

It looked for sure, when first hit, the ball would sail straight on out of the park into the gray, forlorn and deserted structure back of centerfield, some three blocks away.

That bleak baseball bier is desolate Yankee Stadium.

Afterwards Willie explained his catch simply: "I had it all the way."

The Indians almost won it again in the ninth, and in the top of the 10th Lemon came within a couple of inches of being headlined as the hero.

With two on and two out he lined a blue dart, but it struck rigidly in Whitey Lockman's glove, just a couple of inches above the ground.

The Indians paid the penalty that time for having a runner on first, as well as third.

With the man on first, Lockman played closer to the bag, to hold him on, making it possible for him to take the hero's mantle away from Lemon.

Without a man on first Lemon would have had a hit and the Indians would have had a run.

I thought Durocher made a mistake selecting Sal (The Barber) Maglie instead of Johnny Antonelli, a 24-year-old kid who could start three times in the series, and relieve in a fourth game, if Leo handed him the ball.

Maglie has to have his four full days, Coach Frank Shellenback told me before the game.

That means he might never have been able to come back in the Series had Cleveland won today, and stayed on a hot break.

But Leo, as I said in yesterday's story, is a gambler.

He doesn't know what the word caution means.

To him, every boulevard stop is green.

So he played a long shot instead of the chalk, and right now has the heavily-favored Indians on the run and the odds-makers busy revaluating their big blackboards.

He comes back with Antonelli tomorrow against Early Wynn, a beautiful spot for the Giants to short change the Indians again.

And right this moment Leo, the gamblin' man, is smiling in the clubhouse, probably telling the boy to fetch him a new pair of dice.

He has no more use for the hot ones.

That would be too easy for Durocher.

THE RHODES STORY: CHAPTER 2

By Curley Grieve

From The San Francisco Examiner, October 1, 1954

New York—

JAMES "DUSTY" RHODES teed off again today with two key blows that sent Cleveland's Indians crashing to defeat and gave the New York Giants their second straight World Series victory, 3 to 1.

A dramatic homer by Rhodes terminated yesterday's thriller in the tenth.

He came on earlier today—in the fifth. And this time he delivered a single which scored Willie Mays with the first Giant run and was a vital factor in their second, which quickly followed.

And then this new pinch-hitting Colossus, who stepped into Monte Irvin's left field post, added the heroic touch with a home run blast in the seventh that barely missed knocking a news-reel cameraman off the roof of the stadium, two stories up.

There was something symbolic about the way the tensely fought duel ended, as Johnny Antonelli, on the ropes and reeling all afternoon, fought like a tigress protecting her young for that final out in the ninth.

Rugged Vic Wertz, who had singled in his first appearance today to make it five hits in six trips up, and who was robbed by Mays' incredible catch yesterday, had a chance to get the last laugh on his tormentors.

Two men were on base—Al Smith and Rudy Regalado. A homer would have meant three runs and probably victory.

What happened? After a painstaking duel of wits between pitcher and batter that seemed to last for an interminable time, Wertz flied out to Rhodes as if paying him final tribute.

Thus Antonelli, a throw-back to the Giant school of the Carl Hubbel era, beat a master craftsman in Early Wynn, who retired the first twelve men to face him and yielded only four hits.

The Tribe climbed on the Giant ace for eight but didn't have the right man to deliver in the right place—and so left thirteen men stranded on the sacks for the second straight day.

Leo Durocher, called by admirers the Little Shepherd of

Coogan's Bluff, seems to have reduced the game to a simple formula:

Get men on base and then push the button for Rhodes.

Dusty, who whacks the ball from the left side of the plate, now has thrilled more than 100,000 spectators with his fantastic exploits. Today's crowd totalled 49,099 and the fans were on the edge of their seats most of the afternoon as Antonelli edged out of one tight spot after another.

The Indians have only one solace. They are now going home to entertain the Giants in their expansive stadium, where the foul lines are 320 feet instead of 258 and 280.

The big California Bear, Mike Garcia, will attempt to remove the Rhodesblock tomorrow, if a far-fetched pun is permitted. Garcia, a fire-baller of the first rank, had a 19-8 seasonal record.

Durocher, who certainly has the Hollywood touch since he took up residence there, will use Ruben Gomez. Gomez has seventeen victories against nine defeats.

For a while this morning, it seemed that the game might be postponed. Rain had fallen during the night and dark clouds were threatening.

The humidity made the heat stifling at game time.

But later the sun came out and a cool breeze drifted in from left field to make conditions nearly perfect. Even so, the Indians probably always will believe they should have stood in bed.

They got off on the right foot.

Al Smith sent the first ball Antonelli hurled screaming to the top of the grandstand roof in left field, a mighty poke for a man who chokes his bat three inches up on the handle.

Following this, Wynn moved through the Giant lineup with a marksman's efficiency, shooting down one after the other.

The way he mixed up his knucklers, curves and fast balls, it looked as if one run was all the margin he needed. He had a no-hitter working for four innings—three men up and three down, a total of twelve over the stretch.

And then it happened—under circumstances remindful of that fateful tenth of yesterday. It also was launched by the issuance of a walk to Mays.

That one little opening—the first man up and on, and that man the fabulous Say Hey Kid—started the chanting throughout the jammed horseshoe stands.

The roar increased in intensity as Hank Thompson rifled a single to right that sent Willie The Wonder scampering to third, and it burst like a clap of thunder when number 26 was spotted trudging out from the dugout with lumber on his shoulder to bat for Monte Irvin.

This was a crisis for Wynn, and he knew it. He got one strike on the pinch-hitting genius, a long foul. Then the veteran right hander came in with a pitch that put Dusty on his back. It was a fast fall. If it had reached the head, it would have maimed or killed him.

Early made it plain he was fighting for his life and Rhodes better not take any toeholds.

With the call two strikes and one ball, Rhodes hit a high fly into shallow centerfield. Larry Doby, who was playing deep as a concession to Rhodes' power, ran and ran but couldn't reach it.

He picked it up on the hop and fired to third. But by that time Mays had scored, Thompson had slid safely into third and the alert Rhodes was racing for second. He made it ahead of the relay. Wes Westrum was purposely passed.

Wynn took a hitch in his belt and fanned Davy Williams. He got Antonelli to hit a slow grounder to second, but Bobby Avila and George Strickland couldn't pull off the double play, and Thompson rolled home with the winning run.

Two innings later, Rhodes avenged that near decapitation. He slammed Wynn's last ball to the distant roof, 150 feet up from the 294-foot marker. The cameraman made a stab at the putout, but the best he could do was deflect it back on the field.

That was the end for Cleveland. Manager Al Lopez made a weak stab with pinch-hitters in the eighth, and Don Mossi, powerfully built lefthander from Jefferson High of Daly City, whose parents are here watching the series, retired the Giants in order in the eighth.

The Indians are getting superb pitching, but the power that carried them to the American League pennant has not been evidenced at the right times.

Doby, the supposed big stick, has been a complete bust, and the reason can be seen almost every time he gets to the plate. Sal Maglie and Antonelli just waste a pitch to put the ball in his ear, as the saying goes.

Doby doesn't like it. He struck out three times today. Twice he was up in crucial situations.

Antonelli gave it to Wertz in the same way . . . but Wertz stayed in there with him.

Lopez threw Wally Westlake of Sacramento into right field for

Dave Philley and Wally delivered a single his first time up and walked the second. Westlake, brother of the Seals' Jimmy, bats right handed and is a pull hitter.

Strickland was the third out in the first and third innings and left five men stranded. Only in the eighth inning did the Indians go down in one-two-three order.

Antonelli walked six and fanned nine. Four times he used a change of pace pitch for the third strike. He showed a fast ball that was blazing in the later innings.

Even so, the Tribe had him set up for the knockout wallop and twice, in the first and seventh, Durocher marched to the mound for a conference.

Both sides played errorless ball, but the support the Giants gave their young southpaw ace was on the spectacular side. Shortstop Al Dark pulled him out of tight spots. Thompson at third made a sensational diving stop and fine throw while prostrate.

Under ordinary circumstances Westlake's blow in the first would have meant a run. It followed walks to Al Rosen and Wertz. Wally hit to center and Mays swept in and picked it up with his glove hand and threw in the same motion toward home. Lockman cut off the relay but the crippled Rosen had no chance to score and was wisely held up at third.

In the seventh when Rosen got into scoring position after a fielder's choice, Lopez sent Rudy Regalado, the USC product, to second as relief runner. Regalado finished out the game at third.

But no matter how critical one is of the Indians' failure with men on base, it cannot be denied that Antonelli didn't flinch in the jams.

Like Rhodes and Mays, he was there with the mostest when it counted.

That kind of spirit is going to be tough to conquer and Cleveland, trailing by two games in the best out of seven, has a rugged uphill climb.

Every Box and reserve seat, totalling 66,000, is sold out for the Indians' homecoming tomorrow. A throng of 75,000 to 80,000 is expected.

Also expected, I guess, is Dusty Rhodes.

He now has three straight hits, two of them homers. He also has two scalps, those of Lemon and Wynn.

If Garcia, the big California Bear, can't get the job done, the Indians better smoke their peace pipes and retire for the winter.

THE RHODES STORY: FLASHBACK

By Joe Reichler

From The Associated Press, October 3, 1954

Cleveland—

"THE GUY I can't hit I ain't seen yet."

It was long after the Giants had whipped Cleveland for the third straight time and Jim (Dusty) Rhodes, in his own quaint manner, was attempting to explain his phenomenal hitting in the World Series.

"I just love to hit," the superb pinch-hitter drawled in the quiet of the dugout after nearly all of his teammates had gone. "That's what baseball is all about—hitting. Isn't it?"

There are no false airs about Dusty. This stalwart son of Alabama, who now makes his home in Rock Hill, S. C., is a man of his convictions. He says what he thinks at all times and lets the chips fall where they may. For instance, he is mad as a hornet at Leo Durocher, his manager, for not letting him start a game in the Series and he doesn't hesitate in telling him so.

"Sure I'm mad," he said. "And Leo knows it, too. Why shouldn't I be? Show me one guy who doesn't want to play in a World Series. But he must be right the way he's doing it. It's paying off.

"Sure, Leo has confidence in me. But that's because I have confidence in myself."

To those who don't know him, Dusty sounds like he's bragging when he talks about his ability to hit. There is no false modesty in Dusty. He has tremendous confidence in his ability to hit any pitcher alive and the way his bat has been on fire in this Series, who is there to doubt him? Certainly not Cleveland's big three of Bob Lemon, Early Wynn and Mike Garcia.

Rhodes has been simply phenomenal. In his first four times against Cleveland pitching, rated as the best in the majors, Rhodes clubbed two homers and two singles to drive in seven runs. On three of those occasions, he delivered in the role of a pinch-hitter. Dusty has overshadowed even the fabulous Willie Mays.

Durocher yanked him off the bench yesterday to hit for Monte

44

Irvin in the third inning and he promptly smashed a scorching single on the first pitch to right to score two runners. The Giants went on from there to win 6-2.

"Leo said to grab a bat, so I grabbed one and swung at the first good pitch before he could change his mind," Rhodes explained. "What's the use of waiting around? I'm up there to hit, ain't I?"

Rhodes raised his eyebrows when asked whether he felt any pressure upon being called to hit in clutch situations in World Series play with so many millions of persons looking on.

"Are you kidding?" he asked sincerely. "What's there to be nervous about? These games with Cleveland are just exhibitions. The season's all over. We did all the straining beating out Brooklyn to get here. Now we're here. This is just fun.

"I can't understand why everybody's so excited about my hitting. I'm not. Sure I got a kick out of those homers but I got a bigger thrill three years ago out of watching my first World Series game on television than playing in it. The first television I ever saw was when Bobby Thomson hit that homer to beat Brooklyn for the 1951 pennant.

"I didn't particularly care about the Giants. I was a Chicago Cub fan. I was with Nashville and we had a working agreement with Chicago. I rooted for the Giants because I hated Brooklyn. I don't know why. I just don't like the name Brooklyn. Never did.

"Funny thing, the Giants paid good money to get me and the Cubs could have got me for nothing. But they passed me up. They said I was a 12 o'clock guy in a 9 o'clock town. But I'm glad they passed me up."

In fact, for a time it seemed the Giants didn't want Rhodes either. It was touch and go whether he'd be released before the 1954 season began.

"I felt I could win a regular job if given a chance for the odds were against me," the 27-year-old outfielder said. "When I arrived in camp for spring training, I knew the regular team already had been picked."

To what did he attribute his spectacular hitting during both the regular season when he swatted close to .350 and during the World Series when he equalled a World Series record with three pinch hits?

"I just don't worry," he said. "Bruce Haynes, the scout who discovered me, used to say: 'Worry is worse than a Colt 45. It kills you!' He was right.

"I always knew I could hit, but Leo didn't play me. I became a better hitter when I learned to relax. I go up to the plate loosy-goosy, dragging my bat behind me. You can have those guys who are tense and grip their bat like they're going to break it in half. They ain't worth a bit. Give me those guys who stroll up to the plate like they ain't got a care in the world. They're going to deliver. I remember when I was in Nashville, the manager used to eat my heart out because he said I was lazy. I only hit .398 down there. I only looked lazy. I would have hit over .400 but I got thrown out at first twice on line hits to right field."

Rhodes is married and has two children, both boys. Dusty, Jr. is six and Ronnie is four and a half. Dusty is in the first grade.

"I had tickets for the family for the first two games in New York," Rhodes said, "but Dusty, Jr., didn't want to leave school to see his old man play. I said 'Come on' and we went. Dusty got excited when I hit that pinch hit homer and as we drove into the park the next day, he said: 'Gee, Daddy, that homer was great. Will you hit another for me today? And please swing at the first pitch, just as you did yesterday.' You see, he was sure his old man was going to play. I wasn't so confident but when I got the chance, I didn't disappoint Junior. And I swung at the first pitch, too."

A strapping six-footer who weighs 180 pounds, Rhodes is surprisingly a light eater. In fact, the southpaw slugger insists he doesn't care for food.

"All I eat for breakfast is coffee and doughnuts," he said. "Usually I have a sandwich for dinner, sometimes nothing. Steak? Never eat it. I haven't had three meals a day since I started playing professional ball. I don't like to eat. Have no appetite. Only time I eat good is when I'm home and the missus forces me to sit down at the table. You see, if I don't eat, the children won't, so I have to eat."

Dusty's Rock Hill neighbors, all 25,000 of them, plan to give their favorite son a "Welcome Home" party when he returns after the World Series. They already have named him honorary mayor of Rock Hill for that day. Rhodes can't understand why all the fuss.

"I'm the same guy I was when I left," he said. "I've just been lucky. Leo could have called on anybody else on the bench and they would have done the same thing. They're all my friends in Rock Hill. I know every one—all 25,000 of them. They know they shouldn't do it. I'm no hero. I haven't done anything but hit a little old baseball."

ALL QUIET ON THE RESERVATION

By Red Smith

From The New York Herald Tribune, October 3, 1954

Cleveland—

As the teams changed positions in the third inning, the recorded bars of a once-popular song, "Side by Side," issued from the public address horns in Municipal Stadium: "We ain't got a barrel of money; maybe we're ragged and funny." A small shudder ran around the great concrete gaboon where 78,102 sufferers sat through the cloudless afternoon or paced restlessly beyond the wire fence which bounds centerfield.

The Indians were ragged, all right, and as funny as a dentist's drill.

At that early stage in the grim proceedings, Leo Durocher had defied both fate and all the gods of dramatic creation, yet the Giants were still grinding away remorselessly reducing the Indians to something unrecognizable and more than slightly untidy.

The practically peerless leader had been invited to honor the script that the Giants had followed winning the first three World Series games. Cleveland had again set the stage by walking Hank Thompson purposely to fill the bases with one out and Monte Irvin due next at the plate.

Awaiting his turn, Irvin kept looking over his shoulder toward the New York dugout. To his astonishment, no Dusty Rhodes came lounging up the steps with a big blunt implement. Bewildered, Monte went up and struck out.

For a man married to an actress, keeping Rhodes on the bench was an outrageous piece of disrespect for the theatrical verities. For such behavior, the Giants deserved to lose, but there was nobody in the joint to give them their comeuppance.

The Indians who succumbed four days straight couldn't beat a fat man down Euclid Ave. As defeat followed defeat, baseball historians groped back into memory for a comparable example of passive non-resistance. The Pirates who lost four straight in 1927, the Cubs who did the same in 1938 and the Reds who accom-

47

plished it the following year—all smashed by Yankee teams—may have been as helpless, it was conceded.

No loser ever showed a seamier side, though. The spectacle drew a net gate of $1,566,203.38, furnishing more boodle for the players than their predecessors ever collected. It is understood the Indians will accept their share. For participants it was the richest series; for competition, it was the poorest.

There were exciting games, however, and splendid plays. In their last stand, the Indians put up a bit better than token resistance, cutting into a New York lead of 7 to 0 and making gestures threatening enough to set Durocher to switching pitchers hastily.

Al Lopez even managed to infringe on the Durocher-Rhodes pinch-hitting copyright. With two on and two out in the fifth inning, he sent Heinie Majeski to bat for Ray Narleski, and Heinie whacked a home run.

Heinie thus became the fifth pinch-batter in World Series history to make a home run. His had added features, though, for there had been two Giant errors before he appeared, and Don Liddle should have been out of the inning. This made Majeski the first pinch-hitter to knock in three unearned runs.

As soon as Majeski's fly cleared the wire fence, Hoyt Wilhelm went to work in the Giants' bullpen. It was a curious spectacle, a relief man warming up hastily to replace a two-hit pitcher.

Liddle stayed in, however, and pitched well. Vic Wertz had doubled in the second, and Majeski's homer was the only other hit until Cleveland got three singles in the seventh, with Rudy Regalado carrying on the pinch-hitting tradition and batting in a run. Then Wilhelm arrived, got the inning finished, but stirred up a bit of fuss in the eighth.

Starting that inning, Bobby Avila swung at a third strike that was hopelessly out of the catcher's reach and got to first base easily. Larry Doby flied out, but Al Rosen singled, and here came Wertz, the only mean Indian of the Series. Durocher hollered to the left-handed Johnny Antonelli for help.

He got it. Antonelli threw unhittable stuff past Wertz. He paralyzed Wally Westlake, who gazed miserably at a third strike. A great quiet came to the reservation.

Afterwards, stragglers in the crowd gathered to watch while a large man in a tan sports jacket, evidently an unwise bettor, perched on the grandstand wall while another man lathered his head and shaved his hair in ingenious patterns. When the job was done, he still looked better than the Indians.

Other Baseball

BASEBALL IN THREE LANGUAGES

By Tom Meany

From Collier's, August 20, 1954

ALL A BALLPLAYER needs to get by in the International League these days is the ability to hit the curve ball and to go without sleep. It also helps if he has a smattering of Spanish, a soupcon of French, a fondness for plane rides and the digestive processes of an anaconda.

There's never been such a league. Originally, the International League claimed a right to its title by harboring three Canadian and five United States cities on its roster. This year there have been some changes. The circuit now has one Cuban entry (Havana), three Canadian teams (Montreal, Toronto and Ottawa) and four United States teams (Rochester, Buffalo, Syracuse and Richmond)—thus making it possible for International League umpires to be abused in three languages, a distinction they probably would be glad to forego.

Frank J. (Shag) Shaughnessy, president of the International League and father of the play-off system now in almost universal use in the minor leagues, had to adopt desperate measures to launch his league on this 71st season. Springfield, Massachusetts, fell by the wayside after attracting (if that's the word) only 85,281 cash customers for all of 1953, and Baltimore withdrew after it obtained the American League franchise of the St. Louis Browns. That left Shags with six clubs and a million headaches.

In a bold stroke, Shaughnessy added Havana and Richmond. Those clubs have helped keep the league afloat. Richmond, averaging 5,000 fans per game, claimed to be the first minor-league team in the United States to pass 100,000 paid admissions. Hardly had Richmond's president, Harry C. Seibold, made his claim when Roberto Maduro, Havana president, announced that *his* club was the first minor-league team in the Western Hemisphere to reach *150,000* paid admissions.

With Richmond and Havana added to a league whose southern-most franchise previously had been Baltimore, travel and schedul-ing have been major problems. The league resembles the legendary old vaudeville circuit of Baltimore, Philadelphia and El Paso—in which El Paso was used to break the jump between Baltimore and Philadelphia. Richmond is roughly 400 miles from its nearest neighbor, Buffalo; Havana is another 1,000 miles from Richmond.

Harry Simmons, secretary of the league, didn't have much time to draw up a schedule, since it was mid-January before the fran-chise shifts were approved. To save transportation costs, opposing clubs visit Richmond and Havana only twice, playing a total of 11 games in their two five-day stands. That kind of scheduling can cause complications. The Buffalo Bisons, which were rained out four times during their first visit to Richmond, had to play nine games in five days on their second trip there.

As excellent a job as Simmons did with the schedule, it couldn't have been carried through without air travel. The Wright Broth-ers' invention suddenly became as important to the International League as Abner Doubleday's. Just to give you an idea, around one o'clock of a morning in early May, half the league found itself sitting at the airport in Syracuse, waiting to go elsewhere. The Richmond Virginians and the Bisons, having completed a series in Buffalo, had shared a plane to Syracuse. When they arrived, they found the Syracuse Chiefs and the Cuban Sugar Kings wait-ing at the airport. The Virginians and the Chiefs then piled into one plane for a trip to Richmond and the Sugar Kings and Bisons boarded another to fly to Havana.

Not all of the ballplayers—or the sports writers, either—are keen about soaring into the wild blue yonder. President Shaugh-nessy was questioned at a press conference about the wisdom of putting two of his ball clubs into one plane.

"Suppose something should happen to that plane?" he was asked.

Shags pondered a moment. "In that case," he said, "I guess we'd have to go back to a six-club league."

Buffalo has had some unhappy experiences with plane delays. Once the Bisons left Buffalo at midnight and didn't get to Havana until two fifteen the next afternoon, more than five hours late. Then, returning from Havana after a night game, they reached Richmond four and a half hours behind schedule and boarded the bus which was to take them to the hotel for some much-needed rest (they had been up for more than 24 hours)—only to discover that the bus wouldn't start. They had to get out and push.

Naturally, the traveling is roughest on the long Cuba-to-Canada jumps. Here's a typical tale of woe, told by outfielder Ray Coleman, who started the season with Havana but later was traded, somewhat to his relief, out of the International League to the Texas League.

"We left Havana with the Rochester Red Wings and reached Miami an hour later," said Coleman. "Then we had to go through customs. Then we boarded another plane for New York, which we reached four hours later. There was another plane change, and then we flew to Rochester, where we dropped the Red Wings. Then we took off for Toronto, to open a series. But before we could get to the hotel for some shut-eye, we had to go through customs again.

"In that league, the boys don't worry so much about their batting averages. Most of them will feel that they've had a great year if they're still alive by the end of the season."

In 30 years of traveling with ball clubs, including a Dodger-Yankee exhibition series as far away as Caracas, Venezuela, I don't think I've ever had a rougher time than I did some weeks ago when I accompanied the Montreal Royals on a typical swing from Richmond to Havana to Montreal. I picked up the club on a Saturday night at the Richmond airport. The restaurant there was closed and the players had to divide forces and eat at two small roadside diners. Furthermore, there were no facilities for feeding the four Negro members of the team, and manager Max Macon had to pick up sandwiches and milk for them. The players had had their last big meal about nine hours before, and what they picked up at the counter joints had to last them until breakfast at the Hotel Nacional in Havana about ten hours later.

The plane left for Miami at 1:45 a.m. and took a little more than four hours to reach there. Then there was a delay of about three hours before the 58-minute trip to Havana. Again the airport restaurant was closed.

At last we reached Havana, and after Cuban customs was cleared, a bus took the ball club from Rancho Boyeros Airport to the hotel, a trip which somehow seemed more perilous than the plane flight.

It was 9:30 a.m. when the squad reached the registration desk at the hotel. Manager Macon informed the players that the bus

for Gran Stadium would leave at twelve-thirty—for a Sunday double-header. "They'll be calling us the Montreal Somnambulists," said Dixie Howell, the catcher.

Rocky Nelson, a first baseman turned back to the Royals by Cleveland, decided against going to bed. "Three hours' sleep would kill me," he declared. "I might never get up." Catcher Charley Thompson, who had been sent from Brooklyn to Montreal along with pitcher Joe Black, claimed that, counting cat naps on the plane, he'd had 20 minutes' sleep all told.

Nevertheless, Montreal managed to split the double-header, with Black pitching a fine game in the nightcap.

A few days later, in its getaway game, Montreal played Havana to a 10-inning scoreless tie. The game was called at 11:30 p.m. to allow the Royals to catch a plane, but for some reason the plane didn't leave until 1:15 a.m.

Next stop, Miami. After customs, another couple of hours passed before the plane took off for New York. Then, at New York's Idlewild Airport, there was a change of planes and another wait of an hour, followed by the flight to Montreal, the clearing of customs at Dorval Airport and the arrival, at about 2:00 p.m., at the hotel. A game scheduled for that night had thoughtfully been canceled. Macon grinned and said he'd generously decided not to hold a workout that afternoon.

"A workout!" muttered one of the players incredulously. "What does he think we've just had?"

Both Shaughnessy and Simmons are planning next year's schedule so as to leave an open date on either side of the hops to Cuba—an innovation which is expected to improve not only the players' health but also their nerves; a brush with Havana's baseball *fanaticos* is apt to be a frightening experience for those who haven't had time to steel themselves.

I had seen the Habaneros in action before, at exhibition games in the spring and in their own winter-league games, but this was my first experience with them since their team was elevated to Triple A status (the highest ranking in the minors, unless you take the "open" classification of the Pacific Coast League seriously).

In one game I watched, 21 fans were jailed for throwing cushions, and Havana manager Reggie Otero and coach Johnny Welaj were bounced by the umpires. The cushion-heaving started when umpire Joe Linsalata, a Brooklynite who backs up for nobody, called a drive by Havana's Clint Hartung foul after it cleared the left-field barrier. There were two on and Otero couldn't have been more indignant if his pocket had been picked. When order was finally restored and the disturbers of the peace hustled off to the calaboose, Hartung slammed the next pitch to dead center for a triple. Whereupon all the nonjailed fans promptly roared, "Foul!" at the top of their lungs and began whistling shrilly, the whistle being the Cuban equivalent of the Bronx cheer.

Hitherto, the French-speaking fans of Montreal have been said to have the lowest spectator boiling point in the league, but this year sports writers covering the Royals awarded the palm to the fans of Havana. "It's just no contest," says Lloyd McGowan, who has been following the Royals for the Montreal Star for some 25 years.

Butch Bouchard, the great hockey player of Les Canadiens, went along to Havana on the trip I made with the Royals, and he agreed. He was still talking about the Cuban fans weeks later. "I thought hockey fans were excitable," he said, "but I never saw anything like those fans in Havana."

"How do you think they'd react to a fast, physical-contact sport like ice hockey?" I asked.

"I hope they never see an ice hockey game," Butch said. "There'd be nobody left alive when the game ended—either in the stands or on the rink."

Lloyd McGowan was in the Gran Stadium press box one day recently when an announcement came over the loud-speaker, in Spanish. "What is it?" he asked uneasily. "A call for the militia?" "No," said a companion who had a loose knowledge of the language. "They're going to give presents to the kids who come to the park next Sunday. I couldn't make out what presents, though."

"Knives, probably," said McGowan.

The Havana fans are home-team rooters first, nationalists second. For example, Chico Fernandez, a Cuban playing for Montreal, gets hooted mercilessly at Gran Stadium.

When they can't tear down the visiting ballplayers, the Cuban fans may turn on their own darlings. During one of the games I saw, Sandy Amoros (then with Montreal, later recalled by Brooklyn) topped a ball down the first-base line. Emilio Cueche, the Havana pitcher (and a big-leaguer in the making, incidentally), fielded the ball and outraced the speedy Amoros to the bag. One fan, after making the expected unpleasant comment about Amoros, turned his wrath on Cueche, claiming that the pitcher was show-boating because he had run to first instead of throwing. A neigh-boring fan dissented by parting the critic's hair with a bottle.

Havana's fans bring gourds and drums to the games and keep up a steady thumping in tom-tom rhythm, creating an effect some-what similar to the off-stage drum in The Emperor Jones. Dixie Howell, who played winter ball in Havana on several occasions, calls it The Headhunters' Serenade.

"It's the closest you can get to playing baseball in a jungle," says Dixie.

In addition to musical noisemakers, the fans use mechanical noisemakers such as klaxons. From time to time, they also in-dulge in old-fashioned community sings. When the Sugar Kings have men in scoring position, one of the favorites is a number called, I am informed, Open the Door, Dearie. When the home team is trailing, or even when it has lost, a rallying song is You'd Better Sing, Don't Cry. A visiting pitcher belted to the showers is ushered off with a mass waving of handkerchiefs, plus a cheerful little ditty entitled (so I was told) Tut-ankh-Amen for You. The songs, of course, are in Spanish, but I'll bet the lyrics are dillies.

The language problem in the International League is especially difficult for newsmen and ballplayers who speak only English. Just when they're getting used to words like *jon ron* for home run and *lanzador* for pitcher in Havana, they bounce to Montreal where a homer is a *coup de circuit* and the pitcher is *le lanceur*. (Another language note: hot dogs, which are as much a part of baseball in Cuba and Canada as they are in the U. S., are *perros calientes* in Havana and *chiens chauds* in Montreal.)

While the ballplayers sometimes find enthusiasm of Havana's fans disconcerting, the games actually are well policed—on the field by the umpires and in the stands by President Batista's na-tional police. Open gambling always had been a feature of ball games in Havana, but owner Maduro promised Shaughnessy he would stamp the betting out. He did, simply by seeing to it that 400 gamblers were arrested at the opening game. If there is still any gambling at Gran Stadium it is discreet.

Maduro took a tremendous gamble in making baseball's oldest minor league truly international. To get into the league, Maduro offered to pay the travel expenses of every other team in the cir-cuit between Richmond (the nearest league city) and Havana. In other words, he foots the Richmond-to-Havana round-trip bill for each of the seven other teams (25 men to a team) twice a season.

The cost runs about $34,000 for the year, but Maduro points out that his radio and TV rights have boomed so since the club's advancement from the Florida International League (Class B) that he comes out way ahead financially. The games are broadcast daily and telecast three times a week for an annual return of $65,000.

Havana's Gran Stadium is definitely big league. It has an elevator to the press box; a private box for the President of Cuba, glass-enclosed and air-conditioned; a bar and restaurant; an excellent playing field, and a fine lighting system, far superior to that of most minor-league parks. It also has a Western Union representative in the press box, Miguel G. deSoria, who is a triple-threat linguist: he speaks Spanish, French and English.

The only aspect of Gran Stadium that isn't big league is the price of tickets. The scale goes from 30 cents in the bleachers to a dollar for box seats. Grandstand seats are 60 cents. For doubleheaders, the prices are upped to 40 cents, 80 cents and $1.40. The box seats were sold out before the season opened.

While Havana and Richmond are manfully holding up their end of the International League's treasury, some of the other clubs, notably Ottawa, have not been drawing well at all. And since Ottawa is owned by the Philadelphia Athletics, whose own vaults are not exactly bursting, there may be further franchise shifts by 1955. Mexico City and Caracas are prominently mentioned. The Venezuela capital is only seven hours and a half by air from New York.

"If Shaughnessy brings Caracas or Mexico City into the league," said one of the players thoughtfully, "the next step should be to move the league's headquarters from Montreal and rent space in the UN Building."

END FOR THE YANKEES

By Harold Rosenthal

From The New York Herald Tribune, September 13, 1954

Cleveland—

A CRUSHING double defeat, 4 to 1 and 3 to 2, today at the hands of the best Cleveland club in history swept the Yankee pennant hopes into the dustbin, but all developments like "magic numbers," hitting streaks, and personal won-lost pitching records must be subordinated to the fantastic crowd which flooded every cranny of the lakefront Municipal Stadium. It numbered an eye-popping 86,583, which is the largest ever to see a non-World Series game since the boys first tried it for size in Hoboken.

There were 1,976 press, radio and sundry complimentary customers in the crowd, which thereby robbed it of the distinction of being the largest paying baseball gathering in history. That honor is still reserved for that Sunday afternoon outpouring which saw the fifth game of the 1948 World Series. There were 86,288 customers that day. Passes for press and radio are not counted in the World Series figures and there are no other complimentaries.

The crowd had been assured by an unprecedented advance sale which had started a month ago, but it required pleasant weather to boost it to record proportions. The gates were opened at 9 a.m. for the sale of the few remaining bleacher seats and then the standees were admitted to both the reserved section and the fenced-off area in the outfield.

By game time the Stadium was a mass of humanity, half in sunshine, half in shade. The sun-flooded customers sat in their shirtsleeves, those in the shade looked longingly at those with topcoats.

Wherever the customers sat, however, they were united in a common sentiment—beat the Yankees, beat the five-time world champions, knock their ears off, make it eight and one-half games behind, and fix them good. They got their wish.

Those two masterful twenty-game winners who have played so important a role in Cleveland's unprecedented charge to the pennant, Bob Lemon and Early Wynn, gave this crowd precisely what

56

it had traveled hundreds of miles to see. Lemon won his twenty-second, Wynn his twenty-first.

Lemon pitched a six-hitter in the opener; Wynn came through with a three-hitter (two hits in the first inning) in the second. Early also fanned a dozen, which equals a performance achieved by Baltimore's Bob Turley the last time he faced the Yankees. This, however, was no game involving Baltimore and the Yankees. This was for the big kewpie doll.

Lemon was in a tight ball game for a half dozen innings until Whitey Ford came up with an aching shoulder and had to leave. Allie Reynolds, the mere mention of whose name used to strike terror into the Indians' hearts, took up the cudgels and absorbed the loss. Reynolds gave up two runs in one inning and another in the last he worked.

The second was close all the way in the runs-scored department, but actually it was a picture of Wynn toying with the onetime proud New Yorkers. He spotted them two runs on Yogi Berra's twentieth homer in the first frame and permitted them precisely one bunt single by Hank Bauer the rest of the way. It is a pity that a performance of this kind must of necessity be overshadowed by a mere sea of people, but they'll be talking about this turnout—and reciting the number 86,563—long after Wynn's name has grown fuzzy in the record book.

And what a crowd it was! It consumed mountains of hot dogs, a lake of beer, tons of pop corn. It sprawled along the runways, where the best views furnished a glimpse of the infield and nothing else. It choked the runways in left and right field, where the patrons were rewarded with nothing more than a view of two or three outfielders. They never knew who was up at the plate. They merely stood, listened, and sweated.

Sweating along with them were the Yankees, desperate in their knowledge that this was the end. Tommy Byrne, the retread reacquired ten days ago from Seattle in the Pacific Coast League, pitched well enough in the nightcap to win most games—a seven hitter, but they were denied even the dubious pleasure of a split.

The sweep was the first suffered by the Yankees since mid-1953 when the Senators inflicted a similar indignity. There was no talk of magic numbers in that July setback and the Yankees went on from there to a fifth straight American League pennant and a World Series victory over the Dodgers.

From here today they go nowhere. The so-called "magic number," any combination of Yankee defeats and Indian victories, is three. The Yankees could get the bad news while finishing up in Detroit Tuesday and Wednesday. Or the agony could be prolonged a couple of days and it could come as a week-end crusher while they are aimlessly going through the motions of a series in Philadelphia.

Actually they were just going through motions today against a Cleveland club with a chance to break the all-time mark for victories won in the American League. They have 104 right now with eleven games to go. The record is 110 by the 1927 Yankees. It's reasonable to assume that the Indians could win six of their remaining games.

This assumption is based on the fact that the Indians' big hitters are hitting. Bob Avila, the league's leading hitter, got a couple of singles in the opener and three in the nightcap. Al Rosen's two-run double off Reynolds sewed up matters in the opener. And then, of course, there is the awesome pitching array, as fearsome as some of those Yankee mound line-ups of the past. Only this time the decorative patches on sleeves are those of grinning Indians. They've plenty to grin about.

Mantle, on his way to another big strikeout year, fanned three times in each game and hit 100 whiffs on the nose . . . His personal high is 111, in 1952 . . . Wynn fanned the Yankee side in the ninth, Slaughter, Mantle and Berra . . . Berra, playing every day and catching both ends of double-headers, is worn to a nub . . . He also has a bad index finger on his catching hand . . . Avila has hit in twelve successive games . . . No Yankee club under Casey Stengel's stewardship has ever been this far behind . . . The Indians' management, adhering to its policy of no television on home games, which has helped its attendance considerably, turned down $75,000 to put this one on video . . . They also rejected a plea by the Mayor here, too.

The Indians finished the season 11 and 11 with the Yankees . . . No team in Stengel's regime has ever beaten the Yankees in a season series, and that mark is still pristine . . . Rosen has driven in 100 runs for the fifth straight year, the only current American League player who can lay claim to that distinction . . . Not too many players over in the other league can claim this, either . . . Lemon and Wynn join Willard Nixon, of the Red Sox, as four-time winners over the Yankees this year . . . Sale of standing space in the outfield transferred the bullpens to the sides of the playing field.

LEGACY OF THE A'S

By Don Donaghey

From The Philadelphia Evening Bulletin, October 13, 1954

THE ATHLETICS, as they seem destined to pass from control of the Mack family, and from Philadelphia after 54 years, leave to living fans and generations yet unborn a legacy of baseball history certain to keep fresh for another half century.

The story of the A's since they opened for business in the new American League in 1901 is the story of Connie Mack, and laterally, of the struggle of his sons to keep the show going.

A review of the club's span as Mack property—nine pennants won—five of eight World Series won—the fat and lean years—becomes inevitably a review of Connie's span as the club's boss.

When Ban Johnson decided his American League, an independent minor in 1900, was fit to go major, invade the east and give battle to the old established National, he picked Cornelius McGillicuddy to take charge in Philadelphia.

Connie, then 38, had been through for two years as a catcher. He had managed the Milwaukee club of the upstart league with moderate success for four years. His name had long since been cropped to fit box scores.

Ban's reasoning was that Mack, as an old Pittsburgh Pirate hand, was known in Philadelphia and that the fans would be receptive.

Calling a new Philadelphia club the Athletics was smart promotion. The very name endeared the team to the fans. Except for a brief spell in the '90s, there hadn't been a Philadelphia team so styled since before the Civil War.

Into the venture Connie put his 17 years experience as player and manager, and "not more" than $10,000. For that he got one-quarter of the original 500 shares. The rest went to Charles Somers, a wealthy Clevelander who bankrolled Johnson.

Before that first season ended, the late Benjamin F. Shibe, a sports goods manufacturer in Kensington, bought out Somers. "Uncle Ben" was long described as a co-founder of the A's.

In the look-around for a ball yard, Connie encountered political obstruction traceable to the distaste of the Phillies' owners for the invasion.

On the advice of "two newspaper fellows," he leased a clearing at 29th & Columbia and got a hurry-up job on wooden stands—mostly uncovered and holding about 9,500.

Those local journalists were Frank Hough, a sports editor, and Sam (Butch) Jones, night bureau chief of the Associated Press.

For the advice about the ball park selection and other services, each received from president Shibe a one-eighth share of the stock.

At mention of that reward to the newspaper fellows, it is appropriate to digress from the review of the A's as producers of hits, runs and errors—as pennant winners and pushovers—and recap the complexities of the business relations of the House of Mack and the Clan Shibe.

Never elsewhere in baseball have the details of ownership been the object of so much fan curiosity. Throughout the era ended the club has had a following of busybodies who craved the lowdown on the Mack-Shibe set-up.

The play-by-play, with some plays missing:

Somewhere in the first decade of operation the shares were increased from 500 to 1500 and the holdings of Ben Shibe, Connie, Hough and Jones increased proportionately.

By 1913 the shares had acquired so much worth that the newspaper fellows were ready to take a fat profit and get out.

With money lent him by Fen, Connie bought out the combined one-quarter interest of Hough and Jones and so became a 50-50 partner. Then he pledged the shares as collateral for the loan.

The loan was repaid from Connie's share of the take on the sale of stars of his scuttled 1914 pennant winner.

In the '20s he gave sons Roy and Earle a share of stock each to qualify them for places on the board of directors, leaving himself 748 shares.

When Ben died in 1922, his will divided his holdings evenly among the four children—Tom, John, and two daughters.

But the 50-50 Mack-Shibe control endured until John's death in 1937, soon after Tom's. Then the Macks acquired John's shares and were in the driver's seat.

In the '40s, Connie cut up his shares, keeping 302 for himself, and dividing the rest among Mrs. Mack, Roy, Earle and Connie, Jr.

In 1949 the alignment of the interests of Connie, Jr., and his mother with the Shibe heirs amounted to 872 shares, valued at $2,000 each. That was control for the "Shibe faction."

In the reorganization of 1950, Roy and Earle became the come-back boys of the year when they followed through on the short term option given them by Connie, Jr., and bought those 872 shares for $1,750,000. The money was raised by mortgaging the ball park to the Connecticut General Life Insurance Company.

Connie became the fourth A's president, and the only president-manager in the majors. Tom Shibe succeeded his father in 1922. John took office when Tom died in 1936, and after his health failed, gave way to Connie the next year.

Next to Connie, John had been the color guy in the club's high command. He ripped and snorted, ducked interviewers and cameras—once demanded that Lefty Grove be fired for damaging the leather hide of his pinochle throne in the Shibe tower.

But in his grumpy way, he was a hard off-the-field hitter. He was high in the councils of Pennsylvania Democrats and a one-man pressure group in the battle which gave Sunday baseball to the State in 1934.

The A's Sunday test violation with the White Sox in 1926 was his idea. Later he flirted seriously with a proposal to take the A's to Camden for Sunday games, in a park to be built on Admiral Wilson Boulevard—"ten minutes from City Hall."

Back to the beginning of the "American Baseball Club of Phila-delphia":

The A's premiered at Columbia Park before 15,000 with seven errors and a 5-1 licking by Washington. But the White Elephants —nickname through the discourtesy of John McGraw—were on their way to fourth place.

To insure a reasonably good showing that first season, Connie had taken the precaution to raid the Phillies for able hands, includ-ing the famed Nap Lajoie.

In the first month of the 1902 season, the Pennsylvania Supreme Court okayed the Phils' injunction and the A's lost Lajoie and four other good ones. They didn't let that stop them. With rein-forcement by Rube Waddell and Danny Murphy, they won their first pennant. There was no World Series.

In 1905—Chief Bender was now one of them—they were in again, and almost wished they were out when the Giants beat them in the Series, four shutouts to one. The Chief was Mack's winner.

Shibe Park, in all its single decked glory, opened on April 12, 1909. The A's beat the Red Sox, 6-1, Eddie Plank pitching, before 30,162 (no passes). There was no left field bleacher. The spill-over crowd was roped off and the cops swore by their badges and keys that another 30,000 played the game by ear from the outside.

When the opening day patron first in line laid down a $5 bill for three grandstand tickets, he got the heave-ho. So early in the day, the Shibe Park counting house didn't have change for a five.

Connie and Ben were uneasy about their venture. They suspected they had gone too far out on the municipal limb in choosing a far flung site like 21st & Lehigh. The lot cost $150,000 and the completed plant was described as a million dollar job.

For that first opening the park had a grandstand and two uncovered bleachers to the right and left—seats for 15,000.

The next year there were uncovered bleachers in left field extending to the flag pole. The former bleachers to the right and left were roofed and became the "pavilions" (50 cents). When showers interrupted play, it was the unofficial privilege of the two-bit sitters in left to storm the pavilion.

In 1925 the pavilions were double-decked and extended to 20th St. on the right and on the other side clear around to the flagpole.

The first deck in left field became the shadowy roost of the 50-cent patrons. They are still called bleachers although covered. The upper deck became part of the main grandstand.

There was more improvement and seating expansion in 1928 and '30.

In the renovation of 1949, the Shibe Shack was brought to its present state. Capacity was hiked to 33,000 plus, with new seats, including 2,300 in boxes, of easy chair design. The approach to these was ramped. For better visibility, the stands in the left and right field corners were "turned."

Actually, those 1909 A's were next best to "real." The Tigers beat them to the pennant by three games.

The next year they took it all with no regrets except that the Cubs won one game in the Series. Connie stayed sore at himself for years because he let Ira Thomas tout him off a tactic that might have brought it off in four straight.

In the next year's Series the A's had their pleasure with the Giants to square off the shutout humiliation of 1905.

Bender won the clincher sixth game, 13-2—a result which moved a press box jongleur to put this lament in the mouth of McGraw:

> Break the news gently to Broadway,
> Be kind when you tell them the score;
> And tell Connie Mack that I owe him a whack
> When we meet on that beautiful shore.

In 1912 the A's were third behind the Red Sox and Senators with the cast of characters Connie has often called his best. The $100,000 infield—McInnis, Collins, Barry, Baker—were in full bloom and the hotspur Amos Strunk had come to grace the outfield as a regular. Bender, Plank and Coombs cut up 62 wins.

In 1913 McGraw owed Mack another whack when the A's took the Giants again, four games to one.

The melancholy days were in the offing, but who could tell when they won their sixth pennant breezing in 1914.

Then they were done in, four straight, by the Miracle Braves and Mack flabbergasted the sporting world by razing his team.

First to go was Collins—to the White Sox for $50,000. In three years they were all gone for a total take reckoned at $180,000—scratch money compared to later sales.

From 1915 through '21 the misfits and makeshifts trading as the A's set a major league record with seven straight finishes in the coal bin.

After 1923 the team began to live and breathe again and the money rolled in as they finished fifth, second, third and twice second to the Ruth-paced Yanks.

Happy days were near again with three straight pennants and two World championships coming right up in 1929-'30-'31.

It was harvest time for pitchers Grove, Earnshaw and Walberg and hitters Simmons, Foxx, Cochrane and Miller. Afield they were superb.

The A's were still able, but second in '32. Then Connie, sensing depression just around the turnstile, did it again—busted up that old gang of his. The times were out of joint with his payroll load.

Simmons went to the White Sox with Mule Haas and Jimmy Dykes. The next year Grove, Walberg and Bishop became Red Sox. Cochrane brought $100,000 from the Tigers. Later Earnshaw went to the White Sox.

When the checks were all cashed, Mack had approximately $275,000, of which it was surmised he owed $250,000 to the banks. This he denied.

In 1935, Foxx, pitcher John Marcum and outfielder Roger Cramer were shunted to the Red Sox. Another $300,000 came Connie's way.

From 1933 the A's were at close quarters with misery until after the war—never better than fifth through 1947. The cellar was all theirs four straight years, 1940-43.

On July 4, 1938, the Phils abandoned Baker Bowl and moved

into Shibe Park as tenants to pay the landlord A's ten cents per admission. That and the rental from the Eagles helped. The A's were cellar-bound that year and drew accordingly.

There was more help the next year when the lights went on at Shibe Park on a cold May night. Connie had been against the electroliers but he was the first American Leaguer to go for them. He saw the light when Larry MacPhail got the Dodgers out of hock with night prowling in 1938.

Among the pre-war notables who failed to brace the club in 1946, when much was expected, were pitcher Phil Marchildon, Canadian Air Force hero, outfielder Sam Chapman and second baseman Benny McCoy.

Before leaving Florida, Mack startled the home fans with the outright release of McCoy and six others.

The firing of McCoy completed the wreck of one of Connie's most spectacular investments. In 1940 he had chosen Benny from the parcel of 91 Detroit-owned players declared free agents by Judge Landis and paid him a $45,000 bonus to sign a two-year contract at $10,000 per season.

For the 1947 effort, the infield was refurbished with Eddie Joost, lifted from Rochester after slipping out of the National League, and first baseman Ferris Fain from San Francisco.

These starboys made a difference. At season's end the A's were fifth. In 1948 they put on a real show, had the fans talking pennant until the tank went dry in September and they settled for fourth.

The next year came the onset of change and decay leading to the end of the Mack era.

The family squabbling—Connie Mack, Jr., with Roy—became general fan knowledge. At a meeting of the directors coaches Al Simmons and Earle Brucker were fired.

Jimmy Dykes stayed on as coach and after the season, Mickey Cochrane and Bing Miller were hired as coaches.

Cochrane served briefly in uniform as bullpen tutor, then was promoted to general manager in May, 1950. Dykes became assistant manager to help Connie complete his 50 years as boss.

In the reorganization of September, 1950, Cochrane was given the heave. He had served less than four months as general manager.

Connie's dugout reign ended drably. The rear-end finish of 1950 was his 17th—the major league record.

Dykes took charge in '51 and got the team out of the second division once in three tries before he was fired last winter.

Over Connie's far from dead body, the park became officially "Connie Mack Stadium" last year. As long as he lived, he thundered, it would be "Shibe's Park" in his book.

From curtain-rise almost to final drop, the Mack show dripped with Connie's stage presence.

Going good, or going nearly broke, driving his bargains, or facing his worldwide public, "Mr. Baseball" was every scorecard wave a star.

Only Time, or maybe Waddell, could steal a scene on him.

BASEBALL WIFE

By Booton Herndon

From Cosmopolitan

ONE SPRING afternoon in 1952, an attractive young housewife returned home from a shopping expedition to hear a television announcer excitedly shouting her husband's name. She hurried to the set, the announcer's words harsh in her ears. Her husband had been seriously injured—multiple fractures of the left ankle. No one knew how long it would be before he could play ball again.

That was the costliest broken ankle in sports history. It belonged to Monte Irvin, the most valuable player on the New York Giants baseball team. The cost of that broken ankle to the Giants has been estimated at anywhere from $100,000 to $300,000. And it robbed Monte himself of what might have been his best year in baseball.

But Dee Irvin, standing, horrified, before the TV set, didn't give a thought to the Giants, or even her husband's career. All she knew was that Monte was hurt.

That was probably the only time in the ten years Monte has been in professional baseball that Dee Irvin has been able to forget her husband's occupation. Like every other baseball wife, she is a slave to the game eight months of the year, counting spring training. Her domestic life is patterned by the hectic demands of her husband's career. She has no social life. Even her own laughter and tears are subordinated to baseball's demands.

She can't even risk a domestic battle. She knows, along with every other baseball wife, the story of a once-great player whose decline was hastened by a shrewish wife. She is determined this will never happen to Monte.

Monte Irvin, on and off the baseball field, is a man of pride, reserve, and intelligence, with a strong competitive sense. Dee doesn't think she could interfere with his game if she wanted to. But she is taking no chances. Monte—and baseball—come first in every phase of her life.

Even the two little Irvin girls, ten-year-old Pam and six-year-old Patti, are disciplined by baseball's demands. Dee has trained them to respect their father's need for quiet when he rests during the day, without lessening their affection for him.

Though Dee and her husband are both basically warm people, she has to keep people at arm's length. Having friends drop in unannounced is simply impossible during baseball season.

Take a recent Sunday. Monte left home at ten in the morning for the Polo Grounds in New York. Practice session lasted an hour and a half, and then came a double-header. During the long, hot afternoon, Monte played eighteen innings of baseball, making several brilliant plays, including a spectacular catch and knocking out a home run. After the game, he had a rubdown, showered and dressed, then bucked Sunday-evening traffic for two hours to get back home to Orange, New Jersey.

It was eleven that night when he pulled in. Fatigue lined his face. The ankle pained him with every step. A pulled muscle in his side was a dull, throbbing ache. A sty was forming on his right eye. He hadn't eaten for twelve hours and had lost ten pounds that day, but he had no appetite. Before going to bed he had to eat, exercise his ankle a half hour on the Exercycle in the attic, and soak ankle and side in hot water another half hour.

Next morning he had to get up at nine and start all over again.

This, needless to say, was hardly the time to have people drop by for a drink.

Not only Dee's day-to-day living but her entire outlook is determined by the qualities of baseball. Monte gets $25,000 a year from the New York Giants, and additional income—for such sources as endorsements and off-season employment—brings his total earnings up to between $30,000 and $35,000. But the Irvins have been exposed to big money for only a few years, and they don't intend to succumb to its temptations. A Negro, Monte was twenty-nine before the racial barriers were dropped and he could enter the majors. Now thirty-three, Monte gives himself only two more years on the diamond. Unless he strikes unexpected gold in the business world, he will step out of the high-salaried brackets at an age when most men are just entering them. In few fields are a man's earning years so brief.

So Dee Irvin resolutely puts the figure $30,000 out of her mind when planning her household budget. The Irvins are a one-car family, and except for a woman who comes in a few hours once a week for heavy cleaning, a maidless one.

Two years ago, they bought a three-bedroom house. Though it

is a pleasant home, with gigantic rhododendrons and evergreens and a big grassy back yard for the kids, the Irvins got it for $17,-500. Eager to retire the mortgage as soon as possible, they are already two years ahead on their payments.

The furniture, in unostentatious good taste, was added piece by piece out of the budget. It was a pretty barren house a year and a half ago.

Both Dee and Monte admit they had to acquire good taste as well as money. For years now, as a star athlete, Monte has been invited to wealthy homes. And after each such visit, Dee has collared him and made him describe in fine detail every last chair and drape. Through Monte's eyes, Dee has become a home decorator once-removed.

This plush world Monte occasionally glimpses—and even their own modestly comfortable life—are remote from the harsh setting they grew up in. They were both poor kids, children of laborers, reared in the sprawling industrial area around Newark. Monford Irvin, a four-letter man in high school, was the greatest high-school athlete in New Jersey's history. He lived around the corner from Dorinda Otey.

One night, when Monte was a junior and Dee a sophomore, Monte was taken suddenly ill. He was rushed to a hospital and placed in a private room. Nobody could see him. A friend of Dee's was a nurse at the hospital, and more as a stunt than anything else, Dee got her friend to sneak her in.

Sitting in the darkened room, watching over the unconscious young athlete, Dee felt a sudden wave of tenderness. By the time Monte left the hospital, the two youngsters were in love.

Dee doubled up her two last years in high school so she could graduate with Monte. Their dream was to go off to college together, but they knew it was hopeless. They had no money. Monte got an athletic scholarship to Lincoln University, in Pennsylvania, but Dee stayed home and got a job.

In his second year at Lincoln, Monte came home one weekend with a problem. He had been offered a chance to play professional baseball. It would mean he and Dee could get married. It would also mean an end to his education.

Dee knew Monte was a superb athlete. She knew he had plenty of sense, too. But though she was only an eighteen-year-old factory girl, she realized he didn't have the cultural background to keep up with the circles his sports career would introduce him to, and she didn't think Lincoln, though it was an excellent school scholastically, was helping him polish off the rough spots. They decided on a professional-baseball career for Monte. A year later, when he had made good, they were married.

Though pay in the Negro leagues was small, it was plenty for twenty-one-year-old Monte and nineteen-year-old Dee. Besides, it meant a three-month honeymoon in Mexico City. In those days, Negro stars played baseball the year round, going to Mexico, Venezuela, Cuba, or Puerto Rico for the winter.

Although Dee has lived in Mexico, Cuba, and Puerto Rico, she can't speak any Spanish. In Mexico, a Mexican girl named Carmelita started teaching her the language. One of the first words Carmelita trotted out was the one for *town*—*pueblo*. Dee repeated it painstakingly.

"Poo-ay-below," Dee intoned. "Poo-ay-below."

That struck Monte so funny that he laughed until he couldn't stand up. He gasped for breath. Meanwhile, Dee watched coldly.

And that was her last Spanish lesson.

In Havana, Dee and the clerks at the neighborhood grocery store quickly established a routine. When she came in, the clerk stepped out from behind the counter and Dee stepped in. She circled the store, mutely pointing out what she wanted, while the obliging clerk clambered up the shelves or dived into the refrigerator to get it. It got to be a neighborhood event. As soon as she headed for the store, all the housewives dropped their work to catch the show.

One winter in Puerto Rico, Monte and Dee shared a house with Larry Doby, now with the Cleveland Indians, and his wife, Helen. Occasionally one of the monstrous bugs that abound in Puerto Rico flew into their living room in the evening. Dee and Helen would run screaming into the bedroom and barricade the door, while Monte and Larry stood outside and shouted they were going to throw the bug through the transom. Screams shrilled from behind the door.

Soon neighborhood gossip started about those crazy American baseball players and what they were doing to make their women scream so. Word about this dark speculation got back to Monte and Larry. The next time a bug flew in, they went through the same routine, then strolled out on the front porch and stood chatting despite the hysterical screams coming from inside the house. At this point, the natives gave up.

During Monte's Negro-league days, Pam was born. Dee went to college for a year, but between Monte and Pam, there wasn't time for her studies. The war came, and Monte served a three-year hitch,

while Dee worked in a Government office. Monte came home and
returned to baseball. Patti was born.

Then Jackie Robinson, the great Brooklyn Dodger, broke down
the major-league color barrier. The winter of 1948, Monte was
playing in Havana, Cuba. One morning, a long-distance call came
from New York. It was the Giants, offering him a contract. Monte
accepted, but he and Dee were too afraid something would go
wrong to let themselves get excited over it. They celebrated by
splitting a can of beer.

To Dee, the big break wasn't real until she actually saw Monte
in a Giant uniform. The first game she watched was nerve-racking
for both of them, him on the diamond, her alone in the stands—
until Monte exploded a home run.

"I was on my feet before the bat hit the ball," Dee says today,
smiling. "What do I mean on my feet—I was ten feet in the air!"

It was not until 1951, at the age of thirty, his major-league
career delayed at least five years because of his race, that Monte
Irvin came into his own. The statistics tell the story. In 1951,
Monte had a batting average of .312 and his 121 runs batted in led
the league. More than that, it was in the crucial closing days of the
season, when the Giants were battling to catch up with the league-
leading Dodgers, that Monte was most effective.

Then came Monte's first World Series. Far and away the star of
the team, he stole home in the first game, and tied the all-time
World Series record for six games with his eleven hits. He was
named the outstanding Giant of 1952. The mayor of New York
presented the huge trophy at a banquet. Dee couldn't be there to
see it. Patti had the measles.

It was a sure bet that 1952 was going to be Monte's greatest
year. The broken ankle was all the more tragic because of it. When
the baseball writers heard about the accident, their immediate reaction was, "Well, there goes the pennant." That was how much
Monte meant to the Giants.

They kept Monte in a Denver hospital for a few days, then flew
him home. Dee waited anxiously at the airport. Was this the end
of the dream? Was the house they'd been planning now an im-
possibility? The life they had still not yet dared to live, was it over
before it began?

The plane landed. The door opened, and Monte was rolled out
in a wheel chair. Suddenly the reserved Mrs. Irvin was running as
fast as she could. She threw her arms around her husband.

Monte held her for a moment, then assured her, "Dee, it's going to be all right."

People tried to commiserate with Dee in the period that followed. They wanted to sympathize with her difficult task of being cooped up with an invalid, of living with irritability, fear, frustration. Dee almost gave up trying to explain. "It wasn't like that at all," she insists. "Don't you see, Monte said it would be all right. And I *believe* Monte."

It was late in August when Monte got back into the lineup. The Giants were ten games out of first place. Monte's ankle was weak and his batting eye was out of practice, but he nevertheless went on a hitting spree. The Giants cut the Dodger lead down to four games, but Monte got hurt again and the team collapsed. Brooklyn won the pennant, but Monte had proved he was still a $25,000 ball player.

Life in a baseball player's home is a frantic struggle to adapt to the constantly shifting game schedule. There are day games and night games, double-headers and twinight games (doubleheaders starting at twilight). For each, Monte must eat and sleep at a different time. The girls, however, who are in school for half the season, live on an unchanging schedule. Dee, caught between the two timetables, is sometimes convinced she spends all her time in the kitchen.

Although she has to build her whole life around Monte's baseball career, Dee has no complaints. She has watched Monte play professional ball for over ten years now, and she knows the harsh demands it makes on both physique and nerves. Saving Monte's strength for baseball is a matter of practical necessity.

Because she is so aware of how her husband's life is dictated by his career, Dee was not overjoyed when the county Democratic party asked Monte to run for state assembly in 1952. She knew campaigning would eat into his precious rest time. But Monte, who spends much of his free time working with youth in neighborhood centers and churches, decided to run. When Dee saw his mind was made up, she did all she could to help. She even made a speech, although her stage fright was so acute she does not remember a word of it.

That was in 1952. Monte pulled more votes than any other Democrat on the ticket, but lost the election.

Being a baseball player's child has very real advantages and disadvantages. Going to Phoenix, the Giants' spring training camp, was a big treat for the two little Irvin girls. Dee was undecided about taking along Pam, who would miss several months of school. But Pam is an excellent student, and her teacher endorsed the idea of her going. Pam took along a complete study plan to cover the two-month absence.

Thanks to wide-eyed Pam and Patti, Dee and Monte found their trip went a lot more entertaining. They gave themselves time for rubber-necking. Instead of by-passing Pittsburgh, they drove through the city, and all remember vividly the Alcoa Company Building. They took a ferry across the Ohio River and Pam and Monte had an absorbing discussion with the captain. In Arizona, Pam spent three hours a day on her lessons, and Dee heard them each night. Pam was up with her class when she got back home.

Although Pam is a sweet, reliable, and likable child—the most popular girl in her class—she is sometimes the innocent victim of others' envy. When the Irvins moved two years ago, Pam switched to the Brownie Troop linked with the school district she was entering. It was an automatic move, but to the girls in Pam's old troop, it meant she was going high hat, and they taunted her cruelly. It was several months before this unhappy situation was ironed out.

Dee tries hard to keep the children's feet on the ground. One summer day she overheard a youthful conversation outside the house. A boy named Joey was proudly announcing his father was going to take him into Newark that afternoon to attend a television show.

"Oh, that's nothing," Pam said disdainfully. "My father has taken me to lots more places than any old television show."

Dee whipped out the kitchen door and hustled Pam inside.

"I'm ashamed of you," Dee said sternly. "Joey was completely happy until you chose to put on airs and ruin everything for him. Let me tell you something. Because your father is a baseball player doesn't mean you can hurt people. Your father works hard, just like Joey's father. That's why you and Patti must walk on tiptoes when your father is sleeping, because he's tired and he needs his rest. Now, when you go back outside I want you to tell Joey you hope he has a wonderful time at the television show. And when you see him tomorrow, I want you to ask him all about it. You hear me?"

Patti is a different proposition. She's as cute as a bug—but mischievous as a kitten. Many a morning Dee awakens to find Monte gone. Patti has done it again. She has sneaked into her parents' room, roused a weary Monte, and the two have gone for a six a.m. stroll.

The Irvins do not socialize much with the other Giant families, most of whom live on the other side of New York. Dee does not sit with the other wives at ball games, as the Giant management shrewdly scatters the wives over an entire section. This prevents Mrs. Pitcher from needling Mrs. Infielder when an error costs her husband the game.

Once a year Dee attends the annual party Laraine Day, movie-star wife of Leo Durocher, the Giant manager, gives for the wives. Like the other wives, Dee turns out for baby showers, wedding receptions, and the like. Dee is closest to Henry Thompson's wife, Maria. Their friendship dates back to the old days in the Negro leagues. She's also good friends with Kay Maglie, wife of pitcher Sal.

In her efforts to be the perfect baseball wife, Dee once decided to help her husband pack for a two-week road trip. She got out several suits, slacks, and sport coats, a dozen shirts, and piles of socks, shorts, undershirts, and shoes. She overflowed one bag, and moved on to the next.

When Monte's next road trip came up, Dee got out the bags again and devotedly began laying out suit after suit after suit. At this point, Monte gently but firmly took over and proceeded to do his own packing, as he had done it for years.

Actually, of course, a baseball player's uniform, in which he spends most of his time on road trips, is carried by the team. He spends three or four days in each city, always stopping at hotels with valet service. A baseball player is one of the few people who goes off on a two-week trip and returns with a bagful of clean clothes.

Aware that the golden years are coming to an end, Dee is constantly groping for self-improvement. She enrolled in a secretarial school a couple of years ago, but a baseball player and two children and a three-bedroom house were too much. She took piano lessons along with Pam.

Currently she is reading up on how to run a nursery school. In her neighborhood, there are several educated Negro families with small children. Dee believes that by taking care of their preschool children, she could achieve a double goal. She could bring additional income into her own home and at the same time free other mothers to take jobs outside the home that would mean extra advantages for their families.

And, of course, there is still one unfinished project ahead of her. For anyone who loves both kids and baseball as much as Monte does, it's a real shame not to have a boy or two around the house. At the same time, after all Monte's bad breaks—his irretrievable delay in getting into major-league baseball, the costly broken ankle —Dee wants Monte to play the two remaining years he has set himself without the complications and sleepless nights a brand-new baby would bring to the house. She is, first of all, a baseball player's wife.

DODGERS ON THE ROCKS

By Dick Young

From The New York Daily News, September 9, 1954

DEAR BOSS: Lasht year, when the Brooks were losing game after game, Cholly Dressen told the boys to go out an' have a few drinks to loosen 'em up. So, after the way the Brooksh losht to St. Louish tonight, I figgered it wash a pretty good idea. The score was . . . jusht a minnit. Hey, wha wash the score? Oh yeah, 6-5, an' that makes 'em six in back of the Giants, and two in backa Milwaukee.

Itsh not so much that they losht again, but how they losht it thash so terrible. They wash winnin' it, by . . . hey what were they winnin' it by? Oh, yeah, 5-4, in 'a ninth innin', becaush Duke Schnider hit a coupla homersh, and Roy Campanella hit one. And Carl Ershkin was wobblin' along all the way, and when he walksh a man in 'a ninth, an' anodder man hitsch a double, Jim Hughsh relievsh him wi' one out.

Thish ish Hughesh' 55th relief appearance, an' thash mor' times than any Brooklyn p'cher ever hash relieved before, and thash because he's good. Ony he wasn' sho good thish time. He made two pitches, and Brooklyn wash behin'. The firs' pitch, this here Cunningh'm hitsch to left field on a line—but deep—and this Amorosh ish playing him short becaush he's a lef' han'ed hitter, and the ball goesh over his hed for two-bashes and two runs.

An' 'en, on hish next pitch, Repulshki hitsch the ball through the millul, an Cunnin'ham comesh in, an the schkor ish . . . jusht a shecond. Hey, wha wash the schkor? Oh, yesh, 6-5.

But thash not sho terr'ble. Wha happensh after that, thash real' terrubl. Hughes has finely got the shide out, an' one a' tha guys he got out wash a pinsh-hitta fer the pishter, Gordon Jonsh. Show itsh Jerry Schtayley thash pitschin when Brooklyn comesh up inna ninth, and Campynella beatsh out a topper to the right shide a' tha infield.

An' 'nen, Moryn batsch for Hughesh, ony becaush he'sh a lefty-hann'ed hitter. They call in Harvy Haddixch to pitsch becaush he'sh a lefty-ann'ed pitscher, show the Brooksh—they're not show dum—an' they call Hoak to hit fer Moryn, becaush he's a rightyhann'ed hitter. And shur enuf, Hoke shingles to right, an' tha Brooksh have men on firsht and secon' with none out.

An' sho, itsh pretty shur tha Brooks are gonna get at leasht a ty outa thish, again, because Gilliam ish gonna bunt, an' 'nen Reesh, who alreddy hash two hitsh, a singl an'na double, ish gonna be up, an after him, Schnieder again. But Gilliam buntsh . . . not so good . . . an' Haddixh jumpsh on it an throwsh Zhimmer out at third becaush Zhimmer wash runnin' for Campy. Show thersh shtill men on firsht an secon', wi' one out. An' 'nen, Reesh, he hitsch back to Haddixsh, an itsch a doubleplay—an itsch all over, an' the Cardsh win it, by . . . Hey, wha' they win it by? Oh, yeh, 6-5.

Thersh a guy here, bosh, who jusht shaid: "Las' call fer alcohol." Sho I gotta make the resht short. Oiskin wasnt mush—jusht like he hasn' been much lately. He gave up 11 hitsch before Alson finly come an got him in a ninth. Mushial Duddle to lef helped tha Cardsh get a run in a third, but Schnider hit for two runs over the schkorbord in a nescht inning. Show, Brooklyn led by one.

But then they reeley blashted Erskine inn'a next, and three shingles shent one run in . . . and Rice doubles to left-shenter, and another run schkors . . . and if Repulski diddn' try an' schkor from firs' on 'at hit, Oiskhin wodda been outta there. But they nail Repulshki priddy good, show Oiskin's shtill in when the Brooksh get even on Campysh shot inn'a left fiel' sheats in'a seventh. Hesh lookin like the winnin' pitscher when Schnider poles another inta tha schenter sheats inn'a eighth—an befor' the innin' is over, Amoros walksh an Robinshon dubbles to left-shenter, an Shanny comes all a way home, becaush he's runnin on a hit-'n'-run.

Show, tha schkor ish . . . Just a minnit. Hey, wha wash the schkor inn'a eighth? Oh, yes, 5-3, Brooklyn. But then it wash terrble.

Thish guy here, Bosh, shays I gotta get out now, cause they're closing the joint, but before I go, I gotta tell ya. Jeht before Hughes pitchshed to Cunninghm, he waved to Amorosh to come in closher . . . an' 'nen closher . . . and shtill closher. An pretty soon, the ball was flyn' over his hed. It wash terrble.

An Bossh, that Dresshen wash right. The way I feel now, Brooklyn's gonna win the next sheventeen in a row. Make that shixteen. Thash all they have left.

"I COVER THE BIG LEAGUES"

By Arch Murray

From Real

THIS WAS an August afternoon in 1953. The Giants had hit the skids and were sliding down the chute that was to lead to a fifth-place finish, 35 games back of the pennant-winning Dodgers. In the Giant clubhouse, things were grim. The club was losing and everybody seemed to be mad at everybody else.

On this particular day I walked into Leo Durocher's office about a half-hour before game time. Leo was sitting behind his desk talking to a couple of other baseball writers. "Say," he said to me, "what did you write about Dusty Rhodes? He's really steaming."

"I can imagine," I replied, "and in a way I don't blame him. I led off my story today with the words, 'They jeered at the Polo Grounds last night when Dusty Rhodes stepped up to the plate.' It wasn't nice but you know it was the truth. You heard the going-over they gave him."

"Yeah," nodded Leo, "but if I were you I'd stay away from him for a while. He's really burnt. He came up to me when I got here today and asked me how much it would cost to slug a baseball writer. I asked him who it was. He said it was you. I said, 'For him, fifty dollars. For a guy from the AP, five hundred.'"

Everybody laughed; it was a typical Durocher gag. But it wasn't any gag about Rhodes being sore. He was. For days I could spot him across the clubhouse glowering at me. I knew he was itching to pop me. It wasn't me personally, but he was having a bad season at the plate and I was somebody he could take it out on.

He never did pop me, though. Leo put him into the regular lineup a few days after the story and he started to hit. One day against the Cards he hit three homers. Later in the clubhouse Leo was kidding me again.

"I'll bet," he said, "you don't dare go over and congratulate him."

That was all I needed. I walked over to Dusty. It was the first time I'd spoken to him since the story. He was sitting in front of

77

his locker. "Nice going, Dusty," I said, sticking out my hand. "You sure had yourself a day."

Dusty looked up. His right hand was clenched. He'd never expected this and he wasn't sure whether to belt me, refuse to say anything, or just walk away. After a long couple of seconds, he put out his paw and shook my hand.

"Thanks," he said slowly.

"Dusty," I replied, looking him right in the eyes, "don't worry. When you hit good, I'll write good."

It wasn't grammatical, but it did serve to clear the air. There haven't been any hard feelings since. The final day of that terrible season, Dusty was waiting for me as I left the clubhouse for the last time. "Look," he said, "I just want to thank you for what you wrote. I think it was sort of a turning point for me."

I thought of that last October when Dusty Rhodes became a national idol with his heroic pinch-hitting against the Indians in the World Series. I'd thought of it a lot of times during the past season when Dusty came through time and again with clutch hits that won big ball games for the Giants. Dusty had come a long way from the dreary days of '53 when the fans were on him and his batting average was gradually slipping down beneath the .200 mark.

Whether or not I actually had anything to do with Dusty Rhodes going on to become one of the game's great pinch-hitters, I don't know. Frankly I doubt it. But if I helped a little, I'm glad I got Dusty mad.

That's one more reason why, as a baseball writer swinging along with the big league ball clubs since 1943, I can honestly say I wouldn't swap jobs with any guy in the world. Baseball writers don't make much money. There's small chance of promotion. The hours aren't the soft touch they used to be before night baseball and that most fiendish of all devices—day-night doubleheaders. My wife spends at least three months of the season waiting for her husband to come home. Traveling gets tougher every year and those climbs to the press box in parks like Cleveland's Municipal Stadium and Milwaukee's County Stadium get steeper with each trip.

But you're a part of one of the greatest shows in the land. Every day brings another story and a new thrill. You are there at the big moments—the no-hitters, the tense games en route to a pennant, the flag-clinchings and the World Series. Perhaps the real fascination lies in the fact that the door is always open to you; you can go where the fan can't. You travel with the club from the day they launch spring training until they pick up their bats and go home. You see raw kids develop into great stars and then with vast regret, you see them age and fade away into the musty ledgers of baseball history.

Perhaps my own case is a bit special. I'm one of those frustrated athletes. When I was a lot younger, I was too slow, too small and had about as much coordination and grace as an aging amoeba. At Princeton University, my alma mater, I tried out for nearly every varsity sport there was—but never got as much as a small "p" (though I must say I had a lot of fun). Sports have always been my life, and as a baseball reporter I can still stay a part of it.

I'm one of those lucky guys who had a dream when he was a kid, and has been able to live it over the years. I can remember how I used to think what a thrill it would be to make a trip with a ball club. In lots of ways it still is, though I'll admit the miles and days on the road grow longer with each season.

The big thing, though, is the people you meet. People like Branch Rickey, Leo Durocher,. Cholly Dressen, Casey Stengel, Frank Lane, Hank Greenberg, Al Lopez, Stan Musial, Alvin Dark, Willie Mays, Pee Wee Reese, Gil Hodges, Sal Maglie, Gabe Paul, Eddie Stanky, Stan Hack, Birdie Tebbets, Joe DiMaggio, Jackie Robinson, Eddie Brannick, Horace Stoneham, Walter O'Malley, Ted Patterson, and many others. They all have left their mark deep on my memory book.

I'd have to say, however, that two men have left a deeper impact on me than any others—Branch Rickey and Leo Durocher. Perhaps it was because I broke in with the Dodgers in 1943 when Rickey had just succeeded Larry MacPhail as the head man in Brooklyn. Leo was managing the Dodgers then, of course, and he and I have traveled literally close to 500,000 miles together over the years.

Rickey is the smartest baseball man I've ever met. He's having a rough time in Pittsburgh these days but at 73 he's still the most tireless worker you've ever seen. Rickey developed the farm system and he turned out great ball-clubs both at St. Louis and Brooklyn, but his greatest fame will always be that he broke baseball's unwritten color line.

There are cynics who insist that he did it because it furnished him a new source of baseball talent. But I know better.

The story goes back to a night in Rickey's Montague Street offices in Brooklyn. It was the winter of 1948—the year after Jackie Robinson had broken in and, as rookie of the year, had played a tremendous role in the winning of the pennant for the Dodgers. I had gone over to get a story but now it was late, and Rickey was in a nostalgic mood. Relaxing over a fat cigar, he told me more about himself that night than in all the years I've known him. It was one of those rare moments when a reporter catches a famous man at perfect ease.

After he had talked awhile, I popped the big question: What had made him decide to make the big move and open the door to Negro ball players?

"That's a long story," he murmured through the cigar smoke, "and it goes back a long way. Back to the days when I was baseball coach at Michigan University and we went to South Bend to play Notre Dame. We had a colored boy on our team—a boy named Charlie Thomas. He was a catcher and a good one. But when we got to South Bend, the hotel clerk said that they didn't have a room for him. The reason was obvious. So I said to put a cot in my room and he'd sleep there. Otherwise, we'd move somewhere else.

"They put up the cot and I went out to dinner. When I came back, I let myself in quietly. There was Charlie sitting on the cot, his back to the door. He was picking nervously at his hands and there were tears in his eyes. 'Black,' he murmured, pulling at his skin. 'Black. If these weren't black, I wouldn't have any trouble.' "

Rickey paused a moment. You could see he was back in that hotel room in South Bend.

"I made up my mind right then," he said, "that I would some day make up to this boy and all the others like him for the indignities they have suffered because of race prejudice. In St. Louis, basically a southern city, I never had a chance. But when I came to Brooklyn I knew that here was the spot. Now the big job was to find the right guy to be the first one. Robinson was it. He answered every test. And now I feel I've kept the promise I made to myself 30 years ago."

He did, too, and it was a tremendous thing for baseball that he did. One shudders to think what baseball would have been like the last few years without the Robinsons, the Dobys, the Campanellas and all the others to whom Rickey opened the door when he came to Brooklyn. Imagine what it would have been like not to have had the thrill of watching Robinson steal home or Willie Mays catch a fly ball. That's really only a small part of it, though. The big thing is that Rickey, in one fell swoop, did more for the Negro than all the law-makers and do-gooders. As Jimmy Walker said about Joe Louis, Branch Rickey laid a rose on Abraham Lincoln's grave.

Leo Durocher has changed a lot since that first year when we started hitting the road together with the Dodgers. He's mellower now and far more polished. But, there are times when I long for the old Leo to whom baseball was everything. Now he has countless other interests.

But basically Durocher is still the same guy—kind and thoughtful and loyal, as well as the smartest manager in the business. The sense of humor is still as sharp. From the time I made my first trip with the Dodgers in '43 he has loved to kid me. There was one time when we were leaving New York for St. Louis. I had on a new suit.

"Bet," he said, knowing my propensity for falling asleep with a cigarette going full blast, "that you have a hole in it by the time we get to St. Louis."

The next morning I showed a still flawless suit and Leo shelled out a ten. He let out a yelp when I told him that I'd gone right to my roomette and taken it off the minute I got on the train. It was the only time I've ever outwitted Leo.

There was another time that first summer I'll never forget. As a rookie writer, those rollicking Dodgers loved to rib me. The Dodgers had played an exhibition game at Cooperstown and we were standing on the station platform waiting for the train to Chicago. We were singing and everybody was in good spirits. I was in the center of a little group. Around me were Frenchy Bordagaray, Dixie Walker, Joe Medwick and Kirby Higbe. Somebody started, "Keep the Home Fires Burning," and I let it rip in my usual off-key fashion. Then suddenly my foot got unbearably hot. I looked down. Frenchy had given me a hot-foot and there was a small blaze going. As Frenchy said later, "It's a wonder your pants weren't burned right off." To this day a lot of those Dodgers still hum, "Keep the Home Fires Burning" whenever they see me.

Still another early baseball memory that I can never forget was V-J Night in Detroit. The Yankees were leaving for St. Louis. These were, you know, the wartime Yankees. They didn't win any pennants and they weren't, for the most part, great ball-players. There were guys like Mike Garbark, Russ Derry, Nick Etten and Bud Metheny—wonderful guys who did their best while the stars were away. And they provided their share of thrills.

On V-J Night, Detroit was a howling madhouse with strangers dancing arm-in-arm in the streets and motor cavalcades rolling steadily and seemingly aimlessly. The Yankees were in their Pullmans waiting to leave. Nick Etten burst into one car holding a

late paper in front of him with the headlines, TRUMAN AN-
NOUNCES JAP SURRENDER.

"Take a good look at Cadillac Square, boys," roared Etten. "We
won't be seeing its like again. It's back to the bushes for us. The
big boys are coming home."

There was a poignancy to that moment that I'll never forget.
All of a sudden I didn't feel like celebrating. In a way it was terribly
sad. The guys who had carried the load would go back to the
minors and the bus-rides and make room for the DiMaggios, the
Fellers, Reeses, Mizes and Coopers who were coming home.

Maybe I've talked too much about moments off the field. But
those are the ones you remember most. All baseball remembers, for
example, the double that Cookie Lavagetto slashed off the right-
field wall at Ebbets Field, breaking up Bill Bevens' no-hitter with
two out and two on in the ninth inning of the fourth game of the
1947 World Series. Not only did Cookie's blow ruin the no-hitter,
but it won the game for the Dodgers, driving in two runs, and
tying the Series at two games apiece.

I was assigned to the clubhouse brigade that year. That's the
group that has to leave the press box at the start of the ninth inning
and get down to the clubhouse to record the epic utterances of the
athletes upon their arrival—the manager's explanations, the jubila-
tion in victory and the grim misery in defeat.

Now it was the last of the ninth. A radio was going and Red
Barber was telling the story of that memorable frame as it developed. There were two out with Al Gionfriddo on second base
and Eddie Miksis on first. Lavagetto was up swinging for Eddie
Stanky. Bevens was within one out of the first no-hitter in Series
history. Hal Gregg, the Dodgers' pitcher, was standing in front of
a mirror, shaving. His face was coated with lather. Clustered
around the radio were the newspapermen, and the players who had
been in the game.

"Here's the first pitch to Lavagetto," Barber was saying. "He
swings and he misses. Strike one." Gregg's razor was poised at his
right temple.

"Bevens is ready now," snapped Barber's voice. "Here comes
the pitch. Lavagetto swings . . . It's going out toward right field
. . . up against the wall . . . it bounces away from Tommy Henrich.
Here comes Gionfriddo around with the tying run . . . here comes
Miksis around third. He's trying to score . . . here comes Henrich's
throw . . . it's too late! Miksis scores! The Dodgers win!"

Nobody ever heard any more that Barber said. Gregg, one half of his face shaved clean and the other still heavy with lather, threw his razor up in the air and started dancing around the room. The other Dodgers were doing the same. Pandemonium was rampant. Twenty minutes later, when we had to leave to write our post-game stories, Gregg was still dancing around the room with the lather on his face.

There are so many memories over the years—some vivid, others a bit hazy in the mists of the receding years. There was Jim Tobin's no-hitter for the Braves against the Dodgers on a cold gray April afternoon at Braves Field in 1944. Old Jim had his knuckler working to perfection that afternoon and the Dodger hitters were thoroughly shackled.

There was Ed Head's no-hitter two years later almost to the day against the same Braves at Ebbets Field. It was the last good game—but one—he pitched for the Dodgers: then his arm went bad. And there was the one that ill-starred Rex Barney pitched against the Giants at the Polo Grounds in 1948. I can still see Bruce Edwards slithering through the mud to catch the foul pop that ended it in the drizzling rain. And I can remember Rex later that night drinking water like mad and telling how a hot dog—he'd eaten it when he thought the game wouldn't be played—had bothered him in the early innings.

There was the day in 1945 that the Cubs clinched the pennant at Forbes Field when Paul Erickson, the big fireballing right-hander, struck out Tommy O'Brien to end the game. Later he came storming into the clubhouse with his uniform shirt open and the ball held high in a grimy fist. "It was a curve ball," he was yelling, "a big curve ball that I got him with. They told me to stick my curve ball in my pocket, but that's what I got him with." The victory party that night at the Schenley Hotel was one of the greatest ever staged, and I'll never forget being hoisted on high by big Paul Derringer, who was just winding up a great hurling career.

There were the three weeks in '49 when I covered the Cardinals down the stretch of a tough pennant race. The last Sunday at home, they had won while the Dodgers lost, putting them two games in front. Under the stands the St. Louis fans were celebrating madly. But Dizzy Dean, the old pitching great of the fabled Gas House Gang of '34, stood there watching and shaking his head. "They're not home yet," he said. "They're about out of gas. I think the Dodgers will win it."

He was right. The Cards lost four in a row to the Pirates and Cubs, while the Dodgers were beating the Braves and Phils. One vivid memory of that final week—when a great Cardinal club ran out of steam and just about broke Manager Eddie Dyer's heart—came on the final day in Chicago. The Cards' Howie Pollett was beating the Cubs, and the Phils were giving the Dodgers a tussle. I can still see Ted Wilks down on his knees salaaming at the scoreboard when the Phils knocked out big Don Newcombe and came up with five runs to tie up the game. But the Dodgers won it—and the pennant—in the tenth inning.

There was another day at St. Louis in '44 when the Browns beat the Yankees on the final day of the season to clinch the only pennant they ever won. The biggest crowd ever to see the Browns play was in the stands, and Sig Jackucki, a house painter by trade, beat the fabled Bombers while Dutch Leonard was beating the Tigers to kill off Detroit's last hope. The two teams had been tied that morning and a special train had been arranged to take players and press to Detroit for a play-off in case of a tie. Late that night, at a victory party at Jimmy Conzelman's house, Bill De Witt, the Brown's traveling secretary, suddenly sat bolt upright in his chair.

"Holy smoke," he roared, "I forgot to cancel the special."

There was still another final day of a pennant race that I can never forget. That was in 1950 when the Dodgers had to beat the fading Whiz Kids from Philadelphia to get a tie. They almost did it in the ninth but Richie Ashburn nailed Carl Abrams at the plate as he tried to score the winning run. Then, with the bases jammed, Robin Roberts got Carl Furillo to hoist a feeble pop and Gil Hodges to fly out. The Phils clinched the pennant in the tenth on Dick Sisler's three-run homer.

But what I remember most about that day was a scene in the clubhouse later. Burt Shotton, the Dodger manager who'd been feuding with several of the baseball writers, stalked angrily out of the dressing room, muttering, "I suppose those blinking writers will be saying I should have had Furillo bunt." There was no reason for such thinking, of course, but the memory stands out vividly because they were the last words I ever heard Burt Shotton say. I'd given him a rough ride myself, and I've always felt a bit guilty. He was fired a few weeks later and Cholly Dressen hired to take his place.

No man who was there, of course, can ever forget Bobby Thomson's epic homer that climaxed the Giants' incredible miracle run of '51. I can still remember forgetting my dignity as a supposedly impartial observer and throwing a headlock around the neck of my boss, Ike Gellis, sports editor of the New York *Post*—the paper that has made all these thrills possible. I can remember, too, Eddie Stanky on the phone in the clubhouse calling the girl who is now my wife and screaming, "Pat, we won . . . we won . . . we won!" He swears to this day that he doesn't remember it, and so great was the emotional furor of that day, I can believe it.

These are just a few of the thrills I've had over the years. But they show why I wouldn't swap jobs with anybody. The life, as I've said isn't as easy as it sounds. I've heard so many people say what a soft touch we have. But let them try to get a new story every day and keep on top of the news every second of the time. Let them battle sour-pussed losing managers and grumpy, tight-lipped players. Let them cover those long, drawn-out night games into the wee hours of the morning and then write a story under the gun when it's over.

A writer usually gets to the park about an hour before game time and, depending on whether he's an evening or a morning paper guy, he's not finished from anywhere up to four hours after it's over. Then there's the game on a getaway night, when you have to cover the clubhouse after the game and still catch a train. Sometimes that's humanly impossible, but more often than not we make it.

So it all adds up to a lot of headaches to go with the thrills. For me, though, the thrills have more than made up for the headaches. As I said, I wouldn't change jobs with anybody.

TEARS, COUNTRY STYLE

By Whitney Martin

From Associated Press Newsfeatures, April 14, 1954

New York—

HERE WAS this picture showing rough, gruff and cowhide tough Enos Slaughter weeping like a baby, and suddenly you felt a surge of sympathy for this new Yankee, and also an even greater admiration for him.

You knew with finality that his professed love for baseball was no pose, and that the rich financial returns are, to him, secondary.

For here was a man somewhat less than elated that his chances of a World Series cut were vastly improved by his transfer to the practically perennial world champions. He wanted to play his baseball where he has been playing it for 13 years, man and boy, and the prospect of more money didn't interest him.

We'll skip the guesswork as to the possible hidden factors in the deal, other than to say it is our belief that, despite denials, it is in some way connected with the Vic Raschi transaction. It is inconceivable that the Cardinals would send away the still able veteran and get plenty of nothin', as one headline writer put it, in return.

We'll just concentrate on the human element involved; the effect of the deal on Slaughter. It is not difficult to put yourself in his place, and in so doing you can appreciate the cause of his shocked unbelief, and sudden flow of tears.

You can appreciate the mental turmoil involving injured pride and the realization that he abruptly was being torn away from associations of a baseball lifetime. It is as if a home-loving man was evicted without warning and forced to start a new life in distant places.

For the Cardinals represented home to him. Every inch of Busch Stadium is familiar, from the blades of grass in the outfield to his old locker in the clubhouse.

Nobody else could give the impression of "belonging" so much as Slaughter gave as he clomped into the low-slung clubhouse at St. Petersburg, his bass voice booming out in sheer exuberance in the joy of living and doing what he would rather do than anything else.

You cannot peer into anyone's mind, but the rugged veteran would be less than human if his thoughts didn't drift back to those vibrant days of spring training, and the memories of the long parade of players, some great, some who flashed briefly and faded, who blended their voices with the battered old phonograph that was as much a part of the locker room as Doc Weaver and his rubbing table.

The associations of a baseball lifetime aren't easily dismissed from the mind. They are as tenacious as fixed habits, and no matter how hard you try to forget them they rise to haunt you.

We have an idea Slaughter's pride was sorely injured by the announcement he had been shipped away in exchange for players who may never even be major leaguers. If the Cardinals had received a great sum of money, or players of recognized talent, it would not have been so bad. But to be discarded for practically nothing, that was just too much.

He'll give the Yankees all he's got. He's always given everything, and always will, even if he were assigned to the Elm Street Tigers. That's the only way he knows how to play the game.

Those were manly tears "Country" was shedding; the tears of a he-man whose great competitive heart found room for genuine sentiment.

EVERYTHING HAPPENS IN THE BULLPEN

By *Arthur and Milton Richman*

From Collier's, July 9, 1954

THE SUDDEN, frantic wigwagging from the dugout 290 feet away informed Washington pitcher Chuck Stobbs one day in Philadelphia that it was time to go to work. Unbuttoning his windbreaker, the handsome young Senator southpaw arose from his seat in the bull pen and moved toward the warmup mound. As he did so, a note tossed from the adjacent grandstand landed almost at his feet.

Stobbs glanced up toward the stands. A flustered young woman, doing her best to register the proper maidenly modesty, smiled coyly at him from the first row. The pitcher unfolded the note and skimmed over the contents.

"Dear Chuck:

"I'm 26 years old, not hard to look at, and awfully fond of baseball. My sister is afraid I'll become an old maid. She keeps telling me to go out with ballplayers because they are nice fellows and make a decent living. You are my favorite ballplayer and I think we'd get along swell together if we went out on a date."

The girl supplied her name, address and phone number, and added a precautionary postscript.

"P.S. If you think I'm a crackpot, please pass this note along to some of the other single fellows on the team. But be sure to tell them I prefer pitchers, and I work late on Tuesdays and Thursdays."

Stobbs smiled as he recalled the incident recently. "I learned long ago," he said, "not to be surprised by anything that happens in the bull pen."

Only the "mop-up brigade"—that weary-looking group of seven or eight players who trudge out to the bull pen a few minutes before the start of each game—can testify to the laughs, the pranks, the heartbreak and the hard labor which are daily crammed into the back room of baseball. To others, the bull pen is a mystery—not only to the majority of fans, but even to such established stars as Stan Musial, Ted Williams, Pee Wee Reese and Al Rosen, who rarely have any reason to set foot in it.

Even the name "bull pen" is a mystery. Some baseball historians say it owes its origin to the Bull Durham tobacco signs which provided the backdrop for unlimbering reserve hurlers in baseball's early days. Others trace the word to the similarity in the roles of baseball's relief pitchers and the reserve bulls in the sport of bullfighting, who are kept available near the bull ring in case the starting *toro* proves to be a dud.

Whatever the source of the name, there's no confusion about the modern definition. Essentially, the bull pen is a specially designated plot of ground at least 65 feet long in some distant part of the ball park, where relief pitchers, reserve catchers and, occasionally, utility players go to warm up. There are two pens in each park, each with two sets of home plates and pitching rubbers—except in St. Louis, where, for unexplained reasons, there is only one set.

Owing to the varied constructions of different parks, the width of any given bull pen is never identical with that of another. At Yankee Stadium, for example, the bull pens are huge runways separating the bleachers from the grandstands in both right and left field. But the bull pens in Brooklyn and Philadelphia, far out along the right- and left-field foul lines, are so narrow that they cramp any two pitchers who must warm up side by side.

"The average bull pen," says Cub relief pitcher Turk Lown, "is about as glamorous as a chicken coop, and twice as uncomfortable."

A hard wooden bench is usually standard equipment. The bull pens in Milwaukee, Cleveland, Boston, Philadelphia, Comiskey Park, Ebbets Field, Cincinnati and Pittsburgh also have drinking fountains. Those in Cincinnati, Comiskey Park, Cleveland, Pittsburgh, Boston, Milwaukee and the Polo Grounds boast overhanging shelter for protection against the sun and debris from the stands. Baltimore bull pens have recessed player dugouts—and Brooklyn has also protected the visitors' area to avoid any repetition of last season's near-tragedy, when Pittsburgh catcher Sam Narron was struck in the eye by a lighted firecracker.

Some players look upon the bull pen as an ideal spot to hold a buffet picnic, kindle a fire during a cold snap or grab a sorely needed nap. On the other hand, Bob Lemon, Cleveland's converted third baseman-outfielder, absorbed the ABC's of pitching as a reliever in the bull pen; Jim Konstanty of the Phillies used it to salvage a fading mound career, while ex-catchers Birdie Tebbetts and

Paul Richards made it a springboard to future managerial jobs. Richards, a one-time Detroit bull-pen receiver who now pilots the White Sox, firmly believes "pennants can be won or lost in the bull pen."

"Some fellows just go down there to fool around," he says. "In the visitors' bull pen in Washington, the players are so close to that refreshment stand near the left-field line that they sometimes swap an old baseball for two hot dogs and a soft drink. The bull pen isn't supposed to be a bartering place or a convenient spot to play Twenty Questions. Its chief purpose is to prepare a pitcher for an emergency."

When he was managing the Athletics, Jimmy Dykes, now the Baltimore pilot, once fined three members of his bull-pen crew $50 each for sneaking in soda pop on a humid afternoon. Satchel Paige occasionally used to smuggle in bottles of beer in a water pail covered with a towel when he was with the St. Louis Browns, and two Red Sox pitchers concealed a portable radio underneath a warmup jacket one night to hear a Rocky Marciano title fight.

Once shunned as a baseball Siberia, the bull pen now attracts more and more reserve players who regard it as a welcome refuge from cranky managers and a perfect place to relax. Normally, a manager sends five or six relief pitchers, a reserve catcher and a coach, who acts as the noncom in charge, to the bull pen. Sometimes a utility player also is dispatched to help warm up the hurlers or get ready himself for possible duty in the late innings. But during the first and last months of the season, when each club is allowed to carry 40 players instead of 25, many of the reserves who can't find a seat in the dugout head for the bull pen.

"Everybody and his brother makes a beeline for the bull pen these days," growls Cass Michaels of the Chicago White Sox. "You practically need a union card to get in the joint."

Those players who do get in spend considerable time heckling rival outfielders. The Cardinals' reliefers, for example, love to tease Cub outfielder Ralph Kiner because he doesn't move around much. "Get some circulation in those legs of yours," they razz him. "You're killing the grass out here."

Ted Williams, the lanky Red Sox slugger, is a favorite target of the Detroit bull-penners, who are aware of his passion for fishing.

"The fish are really biting down in Okeechobee, Ted," they yell. "Bet you wish you were there."

Ordinarily Williams is hard to distract. But even as he crouches in the outfield, his hands on his knees and his eyes on home plate, he's willing to gab about fishing. When the Tigers in the bull pen become too annoying, though, he lets them know it.

Cleveland outfielder Vic Wertz, recently traded from Baltimore, says, however, that the players in the bull pen occasionally display a warmer attitude.

"Many's the time my tongue has been hanging out from chasing Yankee base hits," he says. "But I can usually depend on Charlie Silvera or Ralph Houk (both reserve catchers) to slip me a cup of water from the Yankee bull pen."

Usually each pitcher sent down to the bull pen is entrusted with a definite assignment. Those hurlers designated as the "long men" must be prepared to pitch as many as seven or eight innings, if need be. The "short men" are most likely to be called upon in the late innings. The "stoppers," usually the most dependable on the staff, are apt to get the nod most any time.

Some sample assignments:

Indians—Art Houtteman and Ray Narleski, long. Don Mossi, long or short. Bob Hopper, short. Early Wynn and Mike Garcia, stoppers (both double as starting pitchers). Giants—Don Liddle, Jim Hearn or Marv Grissom, long. Johnny McCall, short. Hoyt Wilhelm, stopper. Yankees—Tom Gorman and Johnny Sain, long. Bob Kuzava, long or short. Allie Reynolds, stopper. Phillies— Steve Ridzik and Thornton Kipper, long. Jim Konstanty, long, short and stopper. Orioles—Howie Fox and Lou Kretlow, long. Marlin Stuart, stopper. Dodgers—Bob Milliken and Clem Labine, long. Jim Hughes and Ben Wade, short.

Managers rely on two methods to summon help from the bull pen. In Washington, Baltimore, Boston, Cleveland, Brooklyn, Philadelphia, St. Louis, Cincinnati, Milwaukee, Comisky Park, Yankee Stadium and the Polo Grounds (where the bull pen is believed to have originated in 1905), the manager can speak with the relief crew by telephone. Where there are no phones, however, a coach will climb out of the dugout and signify the manager's pitching choice by means of hand signals.

When the Phillies want Karl Drews to come in from the bull pen, for example, coach Eddie Mayo may imitate a swan dive with his hands because Drews throws a sinker. If the bespectacled Konstanty is desired, Mayo puts his hand up to his eyes as if he's looking through binoculars. Kipper, who walks with a peculiar gait, knows he's wanted whenever Mayo touches his knees.

Early Wynn of the Indians and Harry Dorish of the White Sox, both inclined toward stoutness, start ambling in from the bull pen when they get a hands-across-the stomach sign, while Cub coach Ray Blades gets the message across to Dave Cole by imitating a man shoveling coal.

We spent an afternoon in the shadow of the bull pen studying the White Sox relief crew during a game at Yankee Stadium early this season, just to see what goes on. Manager Richards had sent eight men out there: right-handers Mike Fornieles, Sandy Consuegra and Harry Dorish, left-handers Al Sima, Jack Harshman and Tom Flanigan, reserve catcher Carl Sawatski, and coach Ray Berres.

The players sat on a long bench, talking, with their feet propped up on the bull-pen barrier. Each time the White Sox took the field, Berres tossed a ball out to left fielder Bill Wilson, who used it to play catch with center fielder Johnny Groth until it was time for the game to resume.

Don Johnson, the White Sox starting pitcher, held the Yankees hitless through the first three innings, so for a while there was virtually no activity in the Chicago bull pen. Harshman and Sawatski ducked under the bleachers in the top of the third to grab a quick puff on a cigarette.

When Enos Slaughter got the first Yankee hit in the fourth, Flanigan, a rookie, asked Sima, "What kind of pitch did he hit?" Sima replied, "It's hard to tell from here whether it was a fast ball or a slider."

An inning later, Minnie Minoso of the White Sox lined a long drive that headed for the left-field stands. Consuegra, a native of Santa Clara, Cuba, jumped up from his seat and shouted, *"Arriba, arriba!"*—the Spanish equivalent of "Up, up!"—trying meanwhile to influence the flight of the ball with body English. The ball landed in the sixth row of the stands for a homer that gave Chicago a 4-0 lead. Dorish turned to Fornieles and said, "It looks like an easy day for us, eh, Mike?"

Joe Collins hit a pinch two-run homer for the Yankees in the fifth, cutting the margin to 4-2, but still there was no action in the White Sox enclosure. Everything was so quiet that Sima's wife and little daughter came through the stands to wave hello.

But with two out in the sixth, Yogi Berra singled for the Yankees, and as Eddie Robinson strode up to the plate, Chicago coach Lum Harris suddenly rose out of the dugout. Ignoring the phone—that new-fangled gadget—he pumped his hands up and down in a herky-jerky motion that meant he wanted the fidgety

Consuegra to get hot. Consuegra began warming up with Berres, then quit when Robinson ended the threat by flying out.

Upon two separate signals from Harris in the eighth, both Sima and Consuegra got up to throw.

"Maybe I talked too fast," Dorish said, keeping his eyes on home plate.

Sima was called into the game in the eighth and Fornieles started to unlimber alongside Consuegra. While he was hard at work, three teen-age girls walked up to the bull-pen railing in left field and asked him, "Where is Gene Bearden playing now?" Without bothering to look their way, Fornieles, who is also from Cuba, answered, *"No comprendo."* When the girls had left, he said to Consuegra in perfect English, "Have you ever seen such pests?"

Although Consuegra and Dorish both were summoned into the game in the ninth, the White Sox won, 4-3. The moment the game was over, the remaining bull-penners hurdled the barrier and headed for the clubhouse. Starting pitcher Johnson, who was credited with the victory, received most of the clubhouse congratulations. But the bull-penners didn't squawk. To them it was just another day's work.

Coach Jim Turner, who handles the Yankee pitchers for Casey Stengel, calls the bull pen the key spot of every major-league club.

"Twenty years ago, they put anyone in the bull pen," Turner says. "But today you have to pick out relievers more carefully than you choose your starting pitchers, or you're in trouble."

Stengel feels he's an authority on the bull pen. "Who should know more about that place than me?" he asks. "I sure hadda use it enough in my time. When I managed the Braves and Dodgers, I'd get cramps in my arm from wavin' the pitchers into so many ball games. But it's been different with the Yankees. They've always had a dependable guy like (Joe) Page or Reynolds in the bull pen."

Allie Reynolds is one of those pitching rarities who is equally effective whether he starts or relieves. Virgil Trucks of the White Sox and Russ Meyer of the Dodgers, however, are only two of many hurlers who simply can't do both. "As a rule, I just can't seem to get anyone out in relief," Trucks says. "Maybe it's because I'm used to starting games and my pitching rhythm is thrown out of kilter when I'm called in unexpectedly."

Like Trucks, the thirty-one-year-old, right-handed Meyer is considered a top-notch starter but a poor man to have in the bull pen.

Called into the fifth game of last year's World Series, Meyer gave up a grand-slam homer to Mickey Mantle on his very first pitch.

"When I was with the Phillies in 1949, I did pretty well in both starting and relief assignments," Meyer says. "But when you get a little older, it takes you longer to get loose, I guess. There's never any problem about getting loose when you start a game; you have at least 15 minutes to warm up."

The odds are generally stacked against the pitchers in the bull pen and they know it. "Whenever you get called in to relieve," explains veteran Murry Dickson of the Phillies, "the other club usually has men on base, and you're in a hole before you even start." To make matters worse, the relief pitchers find little chance to pick up a victory because their teams generally are trailing by the time they're called in. It's a discouraging situation, but not necessarily hopeless, says Ellis Kinder, the forty-year-old stopper of the Red Sox who broke an American League record by appearing in 69 games last season.

"I do a lot of thinking out there in the bull pen," Kinder says. "I make up my mind that if I'm called into the game, the hitter at the plate isn't going to be glad to see me. First of all, I'll build up the tension before pitching to him. I'll get the sign from my catcher, stall around and then walk off the mound. I know, too, that the most important pitch could be my first pitch. That's the one they're anxious to swing at. If they have men on base, I'll make that first pitch low, so I can get the batter to hit the ball on the ground for a double play."

Veteran relievers like Kinder and Al Brazle of the Cardinals are accustomed to warming up almost every day for long, indefinite stretches.

"In a well-pitched game, the guy out on the mound will make anywhere from 95 to 120 pitches," Brazle says. "Yet in one double-header last year, I threw 230 pitches in the bull pen and never got into the game. At the end of the day I was so tired I could hardly move. I've thrown up to 3,000 pitches in one month—enough for 25 full games."

Relievers know in advance they'll be bouncing up and down in the bull pen when pitchers with erratic control, like Marion Fricano of the Athletics or Lou Kretlow of the Orioles, start a game. But they expect a breather when control specialists like Robin Roberts of the Phillies or Eddie Lopat of the Yankees take the mound.

Bull-pen pitchers also are affected by the idiosyncracies of their managers. The Giants' Leo Durocher and Al Lopez of Cleveland make repeated trips to the mound before taking a pitcher out, thereby giving their bull-penners plenty of time to warm up. But Bucky Harris of Washington and Jimmy Dykes of Baltimore, who normally go with their pitchers a long time, act quickly once they've made up their minds to take out the starter.

Naturally, most bull-pen complaints center about the manager. "Don't tell me that slave driver wants me in there again today?" one pitcher will moan. "This is the fourth time he's called me in a week." Another pitcher may beef about not getting any work at all.

The salary disparity between relief pitchers and starters is another source of irritation to the bull-pen crew. "Until Joe Page came along with the Yankees, relievers got little credit and even less cash," Frank Smith, Cincinnati's number one fireman, declares. "Ball clubs have learned to appreciate a good reliever since Page, but they're still not paying 'em what they deserve."

Konstanty, voted the Most Valuable Player in the National League in 1950, when he won 16 games for the Phillies and helped them to a pennant, feels the same way. "No matter how much work you do in the bull pen," he says, "it isn't appreciated unless you're with a winning ball club. If your club isn't a contender, it won't mean a nickel in your pocket the next year."

Even if the bull-pen salaries haven't skyrocketed (most relief pitchers average between $7,500 and $9,500 a season), working conditions have improved during the last five years.

The Cleveland management provides an auto to shuttle Indian relief pitchers from the bull pen to the mound. For a time, White Sox hurlers made the trip by station wagon at Comiskey Park. General manager Frank Lane admits it was difficult to find a chauffeur with the proper temperament for the job. "We had one fellow who drove as if he was on a speedway," Lane says. "I had to get rid of him before he killed some of our pitchers."

Ultimately, Lane had to get rid of the bull-pen taxi, in turn, before the fans killed the chauffeur (they were using him as a target for debris), but while it was in operation the service was available to visiting teams as well as the White Sox. The Yankees, however, preferred to walk the 345-foot distance. Once when a couple of Yankee pitchers said they traveled only in Cadillacs, Lane tried to accommodate them: he hired a big, black Cadillac hearse and placed it at their disposal. The Yankees turned down the lift.

The Pittsburgh bull-pen brigade unquestionably is the most

active in the majors today—first, because the Pirates' starting staff isn't too strong, and second, because manager Fred Haney has a standing rule that a reliever must begin warming up any time the opposition gets two men on base during the first seven innings. After that, a reliever goes to work as soon as the opposition gets a single man on.

"On my ball club," Haney explains, "the bull pen often is more important to me than our pitchers who start the game." However, Haney has had trouble driving home that theory to some of the young, inexperienced players on his club. "One young catcher came to me before a game last season and asked me which pitchers I wanted in the bull pen," Haney recalls with a smile. "I told him Roger Bowman and Johnny Hetki. Halfway through the first inning, though, I looked down the bench and saw Bowman there. 'What are you doing here?' I asked. 'Don't you know I'm using you in relief today?'

" 'No one told me,' he said.

"I took the rookie catcher aside after the game and asked him why he hadn't sent Bowman to the bull pen.

" 'I'm sorry, sir,' he said, 'I forgot.' "

Rookies who enter a big-league bull pen for the first time occasionally are subjected to practical jokes by way of initiation. When Bob Miller, an eighteen-year-old bonus hurler, reported to the Detroit bull pen last summer, he discovered two dead mice and a collection of spiders stuffed inside his glove. The Senators' Sonny Dixon put his glove down on a ledge during his first trip to Washington's bull pen. While his back was turned, a cup of water was placed in his mitt, and when he reached for it he got an unexpected shower.

Time passes most slowly in the bull pen during long doubleheaders. At such times, Don Johnson of the White Sox chases boredom by describing the game as if he were a radio sportscaster, spicing his accounts with station breaks, commercials and urgent news bulletins. One Phillie pitcher of last season, rarely used and no longer with the club, used to pick out a remote corner of the bull pen during night games in Philadelphia, pull his cap over his eyes, take off his shoes and fall sound asleep. Each time he was awakened, after the game, his first words always were, "Who won?" They claim he didn't see a single night game in Philadelphia all last year.

Veteran bull-pen men agree that the best relief pitchers require about four minutes to warm up (Konstanty and Reynolds are examples), but the length of time varies with the individual.

Lew Burdette of the Braves, Jim Hughes of the Dodgers, Howie Judson of the Redlegs, Sonny Dixon of the Senators, John Hetki of the Pirates, Hoyt Wilhelm of the Giants and Frank Smith of the Redlegs are ready to go after a brief warmup; but Steve Ridzik of the Phillies needs eight to 10 minutes, and Ned Garver of the Tigers, when he's used in relief, requires at least 15.

On some occasions, a pitcher will have no time to warm up at all. Hal White, former Cardinal reliever now with Oakland, once decided to shave in the clubhouse a few minutes before the start of a game. But the starting pitcher was blasted from the box before he could retire a man.

When the call came back for White, he bolted out of the clubhouse and past the bull pen in such a hurry that he neglected to wipe all the shaving cream off his face. Spotting the lather still clinging to his cheeks, an inquisitive bleacherite hollered, "Hey, White! How ya fixed for blades?"

OLD SATCH

By Tex Maule

From The Dallas Morning News, February 21, 1954

MAYBE HE WAS the greatest pitcher who ever lived.

When he was young—and he was young a lot longer than most —he could throw a baseball faster than any man alive. His curve came off the same long, easy delivery as that unbelievable fast ball and it broke a foot. His control was uncanny.

Only one thing kept him out of the major leagues and it wasn't a thing his speed or his curve or his courage could whip. For a long, long twenty years he pitched summer and winter and in the spring he'd strike out the best the major leagues had to offer. Then he'd finish out the year pitching in tank towns during the summer and Mexico or South America or Cuba in the winter and it wasn't until the twenty years were over that he pitched in the big league parks where he had belonged all the time.

"Man, ah was like Samson back in thos days," he said the other day. "Didn't know mah own stren'th. Pitched twenty-eight days in a row one time and mah ah'm felt jus' as good as ever when ah got through."

He was raised in Mobile and his talk is slow and soft and South and underneath it is the sad humor of his kind.

He finished his brief career as a major leaguer last season. He played in an All-Star game and he was with a World Series team and he did pretty well. Twenty years in the bushes had left his fast ball just fast and his curve didn't break a foot anymore. He still had that unerring control, but it wasn't enough.

"Figger ah could have won twenty-five games a year for twenty years up there in mah prime," he said the other day. "Coulda gone up there ten years before Bob did and lasted just as long. Reckon ah was as fast as Feller, too."

He never pitched with an old ball, although many pitchers prefer a scuffed one because it's easier to do tricks with. Maybe a measure of his stature as a man is the gentleness in him. He used new balls because once, in Cuba long ago, an old, lumpy ball got away when he fired that whistling fast one and beaned a player.

"Ah'd like to teach kids how to play now," he says softly. "Man, they's lotsa things they got to know. Can't teach like you useta, either. All that hollerin' and cussin' at 'em don't do 'em no good and makes lots of 'em lose their enthusiasm and quit. Got to teach 'em control. Put a couple of l'll ol' sticks 'bout this far apart— eighteen inches—then give 'em a prize when they stays inside 'em. Ah know how to teach. Ah never have done any but Ah want to so bad Ah'm sure Ah can."

That's how he learned control way back when he went to high school in Mobile. That pinpoint control kept him pitching in the majors when the incredible hop on his fast ball had died with the years and the curling break had gone from his curve.

As he talked, you remembered the tall, skinny figure he made out there on the box in the autumn of his pitching years. He had a sort of quiet dignity that underlay the comic effect of the long, pipestem legs and sad face and he threw with as much heart as he had in his youth and with as much head. All he lacked was the speed and the break on that curve and finally they began to murder him every time he threw the ball over and he was through.

He pitched for a little while longer even then, getting by on all that baseball knowledge behind the sad eyes, but the whiplash right arm was gone after lasting longer than any other arm ever did.

"Never babied mah ahm," he explained. "Never had it rubbed over three, four times. Finish pitching, ah'd put hot water on it to ease the muscles but tha's all. Pitchers nowadays don't exercise enough, way ah figger. Man got to keep movin' all the time, year 'round. You set all day on a stool, you can't even git off the stool come sundown. Average man likes a nice, easy job lak that, quite naturally. But it's twenty times better for a pitcher to keep moving. Don't play baseball in the winter, he should go huntin', or chop wood or shoot some pool, jes' so he keep movin' and keep loose."

He didn't use much besides the fast ball, the curve and his control when he had all of it.

"Got pitchers now so's they think they got to have twelve pitches to get by on," he said. "Don't need but two. The fast one and the curve and always that control. Tha's what ah want to teach kids— show 'em how to throw and work 'em on that control. Don't make any difference where ah teach—south or north or east or west."

He grinned the slow, wide grin that erases the sadness on his face.

"Shuah talked a lot, didn't ah?" he asked. "Man get in the mood, he go on an' on."

He walked off with the effortless shamble that carried him through all those years of hot afternoons in small towns.

Leroy (Satchel) Paige had all it takes, but he was born twenty years too soon. The unwritten ban against Negroes playing in organized baseball was broken when Jackie Robinson joined the Brooklyn Dodgers, but for Satch the break came late.

There's no way to tell now, but you can't help feeling maybe he was the greatest pitcher who ever lived.

THE ARTFUL O'MALLEY AND THE DODGERS

By Milton Gross

From True, May 1954

THE LEGEND goes that Brooklyn is a place where anything can happen and Ebbets Field is where it usually does. It is a durable piece of folklore, accepted without reserve by those sympathetic to baseball, perpetuated by those to whom baseball is their bread and butter. That is why the elevation of Walter F. O'Malley to the presidency of the Dodgers seemed so incongruous a move when it happened in October 1950 after the Dodgers had blown a pennant.

Here was a man who, for twenty-five years, had been a successful engineer, attorney and Tammany politician. Here was a man also with a fabulous business background. Besides owning 37 percent of the Dodgers, O'Malley also: (1) is sole owner of the New York Subway Advertising Company, worth roughly $6 million; (2) is co-owner of J. P. Duffy & Company, a $5 million firm making building materials; (3) is one of a syndicate of seven which owns the Brooklyn Borough Gas Company, a $7½ million public utility; (4) owns 6 percent of the stock in the Long Island Rail Road, making him the Pennsylvania Railroad's only partner in the suburban line that carries more commuting traffic than any other in the world; (5) is half-owner of a $200,000 building block company in Port Jefferson, Long Island; (6) is a director of several banks and corporations.

With that bit of drapery, you would have a perfect right to expect O'Malley to instill some reason and sanity in a ball club steeped in the lore of the eccentric and perverse. But you would be dead wrong.

Since assuming control of the Dodgers from the Bible-quoting Branch Rickey, O'Malley has seen to it that things have been utterly normal in Flatbush, which is to say, as topsy-turvy as ever. The Dodgers have gone through two managers and are working on a third. O'Malley fired Burt Shotton, a manager he admitted he should have kept. He replaced him with Chuck Dressen, a manager he admitted he should not have hired, then fired him when he was ready to keep him. This season there is Walter Alston, an

101

obscure but successful minor-league manager, who was plucked from the bushes to defend the Dodgers' good name, National League leadership and, if humanly possible, to win a World Series.

One other thing about O'Malley's reign. In his three full seasons with the Dodgers, the team won two pennants. They missed a third in 1951 by the width of Bobby Thomson's bat, in the dying seconds of a post-season playoff.

A 50-year-old 200-pounder, whose face is running to jowls and multiple chins, O'Malley looks like and actually is a caricature of himself. His bulging middle testifies to his appetite for rich and abundant food. He is a poker player who will not cash in his chips while a card is left to be turned. He is a party-goer and party-giver who will not leave while the conversation and company last. He also moves swiftly when he thinks he is being taken.

Which brings us to the Chuck Dressen case, a clinical gem if you would observe O'Malley at his active best.

Did Chuck fall or was he pushed? In three seasons under Dressen the Dodgers compiled a better won and lost record than under any previous manager. His teams were the first to win two straight pennants. Attendance, which had fallen off 448,648 in Rickey's last season, climbed steadily during Dressen's regime. Everything seemed in Dressen's favor. But all the while, at least from that 1951 day of infamy when the Dodgers were beaten by Bobby Thomson, O'Malley was waiting for the opportunity to fire his manager. When it came, he didn't miss.

The reasons O'Malley had hired Dressen in the first place were threefold. First, Dressen had a solid reputation as a baseball tactician. Second, his predecessor Burt Shotton was a friend of Branch Rickey's—and any friend of Rickey's was no friend of O'Malley's. But Dressen had one other important attribute. He was an exhibitionist and the Dodgers needed color badly. Their reputation was suffering from the noiseless, if efficient, Burt Shotton administration. Burt managed from the bench in civilian clothes. When Dressen took over, not only did he take over the third-base coaching box, but also all the credit when it seemed certain the Dodgers would spreadeagle the field. When Ralph Branca was called in from the bullpen to toss the home-run pitch to Thomson that blew the flag, Dressen passed the buck to Coach Clyde Sukeforth, his bullpen keeper.

O'Malley cannot abide an alibi, but there were other irritations, too. For one, he would have liked to have won a World Series from the hated Yankees. For another, he would have liked Dressen to administer dressing downs to his players in private, not in public, as he did with pitcher Erv Palica, calling him a "quitter" loud enough for every baseball fan in the country to hear it. But O'Malley's hands were tied. He found himself in the position of having a manager whom he no longer wanted, and had to keep. How could you fire a manager who had just won two pennants in a row for you? It was Dressen, himself, by virtue of his famous letter-writing incident, who put the noose around his own neck.

The letter, which Charley's wife, Ruth, helped compose, was Dressen's demand for a three-year contract. It mentioned that Leo Durocher of the Giants, Eddie Stanky of the Cardinals and Charlie Grimm of the Braves, managers of teams finishing below the Dodgers, had long-term contracts. A compromise might have been worked out on this had O'Malley been so inclined. There was, however, a further demand from Dressen for a tax-free $10,000 expense account over and above his yearly salary.

Dressen was adamant on this point. He is a man who gambles on the field and off it and he staked his future on the conviction that O'Malley had to bow to all his demands. He could not conceive O'Malley's letting him go. It was a major misconception in Brooklyn history.

"You are no longer the manager of the Brooklyn club," O'Malley said in so many words.

"I was afraid you'd say that," Dressen said.

While O'Malley moves quickly and ruthlessly when pressed, he can be just as decisively lovable under the right conditions. Walter Alston, for instance, was not the Dodger president's personal choice to succeed Dressen. His two vice-presidents, Buzzy Bavasi and Fresco Thompson, and two top scouts, Andy High and John Corriden, were Alston men. O'Malley had another man in mind but he went along with the majority. Then he promptly set Alston's mind at ease.

"I want you to feel," he said to the new Dodger manager, "that the job is yours as long as you are happy with it and we are happy with you. There will be no looking over your shoulder while you are doing your work. This is no interim job. No Brooklyn manager was ever fired by us for losing."

This formula of sweetness has paid off for the Dodgers since O'Malley took over the club. It's paid off at the box-office where the per capita paid at the gate rose from $1.07 to $1.29 without an increase in ticket prices. It's also paid off in player-management-fan relations.

How does O'Malley do it? Harold Parrott, the team's business manager, puts it this way: "He's wrapped up the Dodger rooters and their heroes in one emotional sandwich."

One of O'Malley's first moves as Dodger owner was the elimination of two-admission, twi-night doubleheaders instituted by Rickey as money makers. Another was a new policy of ticket distribution which put 12,000 seats on sale the morning of the game no matter its importance in the pennant race. Group-plan ticket sales were broken down so that the ordinary Joe could raise the cash to buy in without going to a bank or going broke. Ladies Days were increased and baseball clinics were set up at department stores where the female fan could learn more about the game.

Some shrewd O'Malley promoting has also helped the gate. Once, in 1951, he received a letter from Glasgow, Scotland. The writer, 23-year-old Alistair Forbes, explained that he had become a Dodger fan while listening to broadcasts of the games beamed to American troops in Europe. Alistair asked for an autographed Dodger yearbook. O'Malley did much better. He had Forbes flown to Brooklyn to meet him, get the autographs personally and watch the Dodgers in action.

Perhaps the biggest and most profitable promotional stunt of all was Music Appreciation Night on August 31, 1951. Typical of O'Malley's luck (and cunning) he turned a labor difficulty into a publicity bonanza that was carried on front pages all over the country.

Among the Dodger fans is a group of seven men, two of them professional musicians, who parade through the park during games serenading the spectators, playing salutes to the Dodgers and ragging the opposition eight to the bar—or worse. They call themselves "The Dodger Sym-Phony Band." Except for being allowed free admission to the games, they are not paid.

The two pros are card-carrying members of Local 802, Musicians' Union. The union protested their playing in a unit with nonunion members. O'Malley met the crisis by reducing it to such an absurdity that the union pulled in its French horns in sheer embarrassment.

What he did was schedule a "Music Appreciation Night." Any fan bringing a musical instrument was admitted free to the park. On a platform erected in leftfield, Mayor Vincent Impellitteri and members of the New York City Board of Estimate sang, *Take Me Out to the Ball Game,* accompanied by the most horrible cacaphony ever perpetrated in the name of music. The mayor, in an official proclamation, declared it, "Music Depreciation Night." Immediately after, Local 802, fearful of its own good reputation, withdrew its protest and the "Dodger Sym-Phony" was back in business.

Another O'Malley innovation has been the bringing of the player and fan closer together. In most parks the customers are separated from the player by a cordon of police. At Ebbets Field, an alleyway runs from the Dodger dressing room to their dugout. Formerly, the players walked in full view of the customers but were separated from them by a high grille iron fence. When O'Malley took over, he had windows cut into the fence and established regular autograph days. Each player was asked to spend some time at the windows to talk to the fans and autograph anything for them except blank checks.

He also felt that baseball could be used as a social agency in helping to fight juvenile delinquency. He supplied free tickets for the children's court to distribute among the kids who appeared before them.

The same informality that has attracted the customers is O'Malley's prescription in player relations. He tries to make their family problems his own. He arranges for baby sitters, apartments, theater tickets and bridge luncheons for the "baseball widows" when their husbands are on the road.

O'Malley is distinguished for the happy climate in his own home. He appreciates that a player unhappy in his home may be unproductive on the field. In Florida during spring training Dodger families are welcome in the sprawling Vero Beach training base that was once a naval training station, but has been converted to the Dodgers' conditioning camp.

During the year, O'Malley shows the same kind of personal interest in his hirelings. When Roy Campanella decided to open a package store, O'Malley helped him get his retail liquor license. When Jackie Robinson went into a real-estate deal in Brooklyn, he came to the boss for legal advice. When Robinson ran into trouble with major-league commissioner Ford Frick, it was O'Malley who stepped in between.

Frick, concerned about some of Robinson's outspoken public statements, warned the Dodgers to handle Robinson or he would do it. O'Malley had a quick reply ready. "I have no reason to be dissatisfied with Jackie Robinson, his conduct on the field or his spirit. He has the full support of the organization."

If O'Malley mixes with the help in one sense, he avoids it in another. On most clubs the president or general manager keeps salary negotiation with the players as his own province. O'Malley takes no part in them, leaving the headache to Buzzy Bavasi. In three years the Dodgers have had only two salary disagreements Bavasi felt required the boss's attention.

One was the case of Duke Snider after the 1951 season. Another was Billy Cox a year ago. O'Malley needed all of his charm to get Snider to accept a $2,500 raise. Duke felt he had had a bad season and wanted to take the full 25 percent cut allowed under major-league rules.

Cox was a different matter. He refused to sign and refused to tell Bavasi why. The rest of the Dodgers were already in training when Bavasi asked O'Malley to contact Cox.

"What's troubling you, Bill?" O'Malley asked. "If you're not satisfied with our terms, just tell us what you want and we'll make an adjustment."

"I need more time to think about it," Cox said.

"You're building a new house, isn't that it?" O'Malley asked. "Do you want a little more time to stay around and see it go up?"

"Well," said Cox, "I could use some more time."

"Tell you what, Billy," O'Malley suggested. "Sign your contract, send it in and if you feel you need more time to get the house ready you have my permission to take it."

That's the way O'Malley works. Those who have seen him in action and know enough about him to pass judgment say that he is a rare combination of Rickey and Rickey's predecessor, Larry Mac-Phail. They say that Walter has their best features without some of their glaring faults, that he has the shrewdness of one and the business acumen of the other, plus the singleness of purpose and the ruthlessness of both.

Rickey was the son of a farmer. MacPhail was the son of a banker. O'Malley is the son of a hustler, who was a salesman and a New York City politician and became Commissioner of Public Markets under Mayor John F. Hylan.

O'Malley's father failed in the dry-goods business when he put too much stock in petticoats. Walter, who also classifies himself as a hustler, never waited for any venture to die. He became a financial adventurer whose risks were always gilt-edged. He never failed in any business or profession—and he's made a career out of a half dozen.

His work for Todd and Brown alone during World War II might be considered a lifetime of labor for most men. O'Malley took over 110 Indiana farms equal in area to 32 square miles, or approximately the size of Manhattan Island. In one year the farm land, which had been under cultivation, was converted into an arsenal and began a steady delivery of ammunition to U. S. Ordnance.

You might say that O'Malley was literally born to get ahead. Even as a Bronx youngster he was the neighborhood leader. When his family moved to Hollis, Long Island, O'Malley became a Boy Scout leader. At Culver Military Academy, he ran the school paper.

O'Malley is remembered by Frank Murdock, a classmate at the University of Pennsylvania, as a born politician and promoter. "He built the strongest political machine ever on the campus," Murdock recalled.

"The Turk," as O'Malley was nicknamed in his college yearbook, set a precedent by being elected class president in his junior and senior years. He was Spoon Man, highest honorary award open to members of the graduating class; chairman of the undergraduate council; undergraduate member of the university council on athletics and of the baseball committee; and salutatorian at the commencement exercises. He was, in short, big man on campus.

After graduation in 1926, O'Malley entered Columbia Law School but transferred to Fordham Law for night classes when his father's business collapsed. At Penn, O'Malley had studied engineering. He wanted to become a city surveyor but needed five years of experience in field survey parties. He got a job as an assistant engineer with the New York subways system, getting the needed experience during the daytime and learning about law at night.

From the subway job, O'Malley moved on to do tracings for Thomas F. Riley, a practical driller. By this time the elder O'Malley had become part of Mayor Hylan's staff and soon after his son was made Riley's partner.

The new firm began drawing juicy contracts for subways, tunnels, highways and bridges. Riley and O'Malley did geological surveys and foundation reports for a 100-school building program sanctioned by the Board of Education, and they did the same thing for a series of twenty New York Telephone Company exchanges and a Wall Street building.

This background came in handy when it came to constructing the Dodgers training camp at Vero Beach. Holman Stadium, where Brooklyn plays its exhibition games, is an ingenious, economical, engineering monument to O'Malley. The total cost of building the park was $30,000, or $6 a seat. By usual methods of construction these days a ball field with 5,000 seats would run between $100-$125 a seat.

But O'Malley conceived the idea of constructing dirt mounds as a foundation over which the concrete was poured for stands. The mounds also encircle the outfield as a fence, which is topped by a semicircle of royal palms.

Bulldozers dug a six-acre hole adjoining the field for the dirt to build the mounds. The hole gave O'Malley another idea. He had it filled with water and stocked with trout. Thus the players have a private fishing preserve for their off-hours in camp.

The team of Riley and O'Malley was going strong until they agreed to disagree about a job. O'Malley estimated a contract for New York City to build fifteen artesian wells on Long Island would be profitable. He felt that a proffered contract to build a water tunnel from upstate New York into the city would be unprofitable. Riley felt otherwise and took the tunnel job. O'Malley, starting his own engineering firm, took the well job. He was now W. F. O'Malley Engineering Company.

The tightening effects of the depression, however, were already beginning to be felt. The well job was to have been the first of fifty such but instead it became the last. As succeeding contracts were cancelled, O'Malley began to seek in a new direction. He had a law degree, but had not completed his clerkship. Just as he had planned to become a city surveyor, he now laid the foundation for active practice of law. He found a practicing, but officeless attorney, gave him space in his engineering office and thus satisfied the requirements of the bar. One day a sign painter changed the names on the door to Walter F. O'Malley, Attorney-at-law.

Cases did not come easily and for once O'Malley began to doubt himself. Then, when he had been without a client for weeks, his phone rang.

"Do you do wills?" a voice asked in a thick Irish brogue.

"I do," said Walter, thinking the question had concerned wells.

"I was getting desperate," O'Malley recalls. "I didn't understand the caller but I'd have dug a well or written a will."

O'Malley asked his caller's name. He was told it was Barrett.

"I can see you in my office tomorrow at 2, Mr. Barrett," O'Malley said, putting up a brave front.

"Not Mr. Barrett," the caller corrected, "Father Barrett, and it's got to be right away and in my rectory. A parishioner is dying. He has no will."

O'Malley hurried to St. Bernard's Church on 14th Street. His curiosity led him to ask how Father Barrett had picked him as the attorney.

The priest explained that his pastor, who was experienced in such legal matters, had recently died. He was the assistant and knew no lawyers. He checked the names off in the phone booth until he came to O'Malley's, which read as though it originated in County Mayo, Ireland.

"I'm a Mayo man myself," the priest said.

This chance choice projected O'Malley into a relatively unexplored legal field. The parishioner's will, in addition to property in Ireland, included several mortgage bonds in default. The mortgage reorganization law was vague and inadequate, particularly for depression times when so many issues were going under. The practice of law was bad, but reorganization work could be good. O'Malley grasped the immensity of the practice which could be developed if the laws were revised, brought up to date and he could get on the ground floor.

He saw to it that the laws were changed. In collaboration with George Brower, a judge of the Supreme Court and the State Superintendent of Insurance, O'Malley prepared a program of new legislation and the laws were passed. Thus, from an attorney who would take any case, he became one who commanded legal fees as high as $100,000 for a single case. At one time his practice was so vast O'Malley represented nine large banks.

Association with the officers and directors of these banks brought new contracts and opened fabulous avenues of investment. Out of it also came a lasting friendship with George V. McLaughlin, president of the Brooklyn Trust Company, which held the paper for the Dodgers' indebtedness.

McLaughlin was both a banker and the kind of baseball fan who would watch a semipro team, the Bushwicks, play Sunday doubleheaders when the Dodgers were out of town. O'Malley accompanied him to the games. He became a baseball fan himself. In 1943 when Rickey replaced MacPhail, McLaughlin arranged for O'Malley to replace Wendell Willkie as the Dodgers' attorney.

The early war years brought hard times for baseball teams faced with rising costs, restricted personnel and the threat of limited travel and schedules. In 1944 the Edward J. McKeever Estate advised the Brooklyn Trust Company it wished to sell half of its 50 percent interest in the Dodgers. McLaughlin counseled O'Malley to take an option on the stock. He did, forming a syndicate for its purchase at close to $300,000.

The following year O'Malley's syndicate, equal partners under agreement to vote their shares as a unit, bought the Ebbets' half for $850,000, giving O'Malley, the late John Smith, president of the Pfizer Chemical Company, and Branch Rickey equal 25 percent shares. The fourth quarter still is owned by Mrs. James A. Mulvey, heir of Frank McKeever. O'Malley and Mrs. Smith share control in the 75 percent they accumulated after buying Rickey's holdings.

Rickey became O'Malley's business enemy in 1950. As the Dodgers were about to blow the 1950 pennant to the Phillies on Dick Sisler's tenth inning homer in the season's final game, Rickey was completing the sale of his stock.

He had arranged with William Zeckendorf, a real-estate broker, to sell out for $1 million. Under the pooling agreement of the syndicate O'Malley had formed to hold the controlling interest, no partner could sell without giving the other partners prior choice to meet the price. In meeting it, however, they would also have to stand Zeckendorf's "expense" in appraising the deal.

Mrs. Smith's husband had recently died. For inheritance purposes his share had been assessed at $300,000. But with Rickey's million-dollar offer, the internal-revenue people revalued them. If any amity was left among the one-time partners after this additional tax bite, none was discernible when O'Malley had to pay Zeckendorf a $50,000 commitment fee.

The cancelled check that was returned to O'Malley was first endorsed by Zeckendorf and then by Rickey.

O'Malley took this brush with Rickey in stride, as he does with most things about his life. Despite the variety of his interests, great wealth and political power as an intimate of the Kings County Democratic bigwigs, Walter makes no show of ostentation. His only visible displays are the heavy Havana cigars he smokes through white holders and the chauffeur who is employed by the Dodgers to drive him daily in a Buick from his Amityville, Long Island, home to the team's downtown Brooklyn offices. At one time O'Malley also maintained law offices in mid-Manhattan, but since becoming president he gave up the active practice of law. The same informality exists inside the 30-year-old four-bedroom frame house in which O'Malley lives with his wife, Kay; 20-year-old daughter Terry; and Pete, his 16-year-old son. No domestic help is employed. The O'Malleys do their own chores. They share the cooking and grow orchids in a 32-foot greenhouse, which adjoins the property.

"We prefer it that way," O'Malley explains. "Kay and I like an informal life. So do the children. We have a woman in once a week to clean up the place and we spend a lot of time out of doors when the weather's right."

Theirs is a waterfront home with a small swimming pool and a private dock on Great South Bay. When the family skiff needs its bottom painted or its barnacles scraped, the O'Malleys do it. They are all sailing and fishing fans and O'Malley is one of the originators of the U. S. Atlantic Tuna Fishing Association.

As O'Malley is good to his associates, so is he to the fans. For the most part they are unable to hold out against his charm. Sample the two gentlemen who were drowning their grief in an Amityville bar after the playoff loss in 1951. One said to the other, "Let's go see O'Malley and make him get rid of Dressen for calling in Branca to throw that home-run pitch to Thomson."

The idea was passed unanimously and a terrified bartender, seeing the two lurch off in the general direction of O'Malley's home, called the police.

When the police arrived, O'Malley invited them in to join his two friends in a "wee drap." The pair were sitting quietly, sipping Scotch, being hypnotized by O'Malley and agreeing that Dressen was blameless for the pennant loss.

"They came to him to do him harm and now they're as harmless as a couple of puppies," one cop said in amazement.

"How," asked the other, "can you stay mad at a man who talks the way he can and gives you a drink while you listen to him?"

Football

HE DIES FOR DETROIT

By Stanley Frank

From The Saturday Evening Post, November 13, 1954

A SILENT, solitary brooder, like a silent wife or a solitary drinker, is an emotional time bomb likely to explode more violently when the big blowoff comes than folks who flaunt the wound stripes of their troubles. By this token, Buddy Parker is long overdue for an eruption of Bikini proportions. Parker constantly seethes with aggravation, but he keeps it completely bottled up except in the privacy of his own quarters. He has masked himself so successfully that many sports addicts would have trouble placing him as coach of the Detroit Lions, professional football champions for the last two years.

Parker has been forced to swallow as few defeats in recent seasons as anyone in the business, a circumstance that merely makes losing more indigestible. Only three other coaches, George Halas, Curly Lambeau and Greesy Neale, ever have duplicated Parker's feat of winning two successive National Football League titles. During the three years he has been masterminding the Lions, a deficit of $221,000 has been turned into a net profit of $66,287 for 136 stockholders. Parker's take-home pay is close to $30,000 a year, and he seems entrenched in Detroit as solidly as Cadillac Square, yet he carries on at home as though his dear wife and child are headed for destitution if he loses an unimportant exhibition game. To forestall the catastrophe he always morosely anticipates, he kowtows to superstition like a witch doctor in the deepest jungle.

Such behavior is so typical of football coaches that it would not be particularly noteworthy in anyone but Parker. His case is striking because he gives such a strong outward impression of being one bloke who takes the game calmly. The most lenient disciplinarian in the league—in contrast to his Detroit predecessor, the late Bo McMillin—he doesn't have training rules or a curfew for his team. Shortly before a game with the Rams in Los Angeles last

112

year, Parker ran into a covey of players prowling the Sunset Strip, Hollywood's hot-spot center, after midnight.

Another coach would have fined the heroes a hundred dollars apiece and attributed every defeat in the next two years to that breach of training. Parker did not penalize a man or even mention the incident after the game, although the Lions played their worst football of the season in taking a 37-24 licking from the Rams.

It is standard operating procedure in pro football for coaches to direct their teams with signals from the bench or by sending a steady stream of substitutes into the game with orders for the quarterbacks. Parker lets Bobby Layne, the Lions' No. 1 field general, call the shots as he jolly well pleases. "There's no use telling Layne what to do, because he doesn't listen to me," Parker says laconically, an admission that couldn't be drawn from his colleagues on the rack.

The photogenic face Parker shows the public always is composed, his voice rarely rises above the conversational drone of a Texas drawl and he moves in the shambling, relaxed fashion of a bear that has just made a successful raid on a honeycomb. That impression is as misleading as a process server's smile. In the two and a half hours between the kickoff and the final whistle of a game, he smokes two packs of cigarettes. After the Lions beat the Cleveland Browns by 17-16 for the title last December, the Parkers gave a party in their home at 23051 Lodge Lane, in Dearborn, Michigan. The company left at a decent hour, but the host was so keyed up that he washed the dishes at five o'clock in the morning. He did not unwind sufficiently to go to bed until noon.

In 1951, the Lions missed a crack at the championship by losing their final game to the San Francisco Forty-Niners in the last four minutes. A party had been arranged to celebrate Parker's thirty-eighth birthday and an expected victory. The coaches and players gave the backs of their necks to a huge seventy-five-dollar cake and concentrated on the liquid refreshments. Presently, feeling only occasional twinges of anguish, one and all cut the crowns off their hats to indicate they had blown their tops.

Parker played along with the gag to demonstrate he was a good sport, but just before leaving the hotel to board a plane for Detroit, he retired to his room and hurled his expensive watch against the wall, smashing it to bits. Having expressed his true feelings, Parker rejoined the gang and went back to impersonating a graceful loser.

"When the team loses, Buddy has a routine that never varies," says his wife, Jane, who has managed to keep her sense of humor in spite of everything. "He flops on an ottoman in the living room and pulls out a pocketknife he's been carrying for thirty years. He raises the knife to his throat slowly and cuts his tie at the knot. Until I hear the material rip, I'm never sure it's the tie, not his throat, that he's cutting. He bends down and slashes his shoelaces with two quick strokes. Then he literally tears his shirt off his back without unbuttoning it.

"After that, there's a deep silence around the house until Tuesday. The only sound Buddy will tolerate is music. He can't carry a tune, he doesn't know a classical from a popular number and he doesn't care if the needle sticks on the record. He says the music relaxes him. Malarkey. Nothing brings him out of his black mood until he wins one.

"Maybe I'm saying too much, but he should act like a rational person if he doesn't want me to talk about him. Friends avoid us like the plague after a defeat. It's amazing how peaceful it is around the house between January and July. Nothing ruffles him then, but things begin to pop as soon as the team goes to training camp. Our son, Bobby, and I would be more comfortable living in a cave.

"I suppose you've heard what a maniac he is on superstitions. He collects hairpins and hits the roof if I move them an inch. If somebody throws a hat on a bed, he'll harp on it for months and trace all his bad breaks to it. I know I'm making him sound like a moron, but his brainstorms will drive me out of my mind yet.

"The worst is his horror of the number thirteen or any combination that adds up to thirteen. During the war, when Buddy was with the Chicago Cardinals, I came up from Texas to join him. It was almost impossible to find accommodations in a residential hotel, but I finally got a room in the Ridgeland Apartments. I naturally thought Buddy would be anxious to see me for the first time in six weeks, but he refused to come home when I told him we had Room 319. 'Do you want to ruin me?' he yelled over the phone. 'Three and one and nine equal thirteen. Move out or I'll sleep in the park.' The upshot was that we had the only hotel room on the third floor in America numbered 711. Mrs. Reinard, the manager, saved me from becoming a football widow by nailing those numerals on the door."

The whole thing is not quite so amusing as it sounds. To establish accord with son Bobby Parker, who is going on seven, I asked him whether he wanted to play football when he grew up. The answer was an education in two words.

"No, sir!" Bobby said vehemently.

Parker's single-minded intensity on winning is a trial even to his aids, who are dedicated nuts themselves. The business of preparing for a dozen games a season is, quite incomprehensibly to laymen, a year-round grind for all pro coaches. All devote a good deal of the time to studying movies of previous games with forthcoming opponents, but no one does it more exhaustively than Parker.

Most other men put in a couple of hours a day analyzing plays in slow motion. Parker averages six hours a day at this during the season. He examines the film one frame, or still picture, at a time. It sometimes takes him two days to review a single quarter, during which the ball actually is in play perhaps five minutes.

He may stare at a frame for twenty minutes in stupefying silence, jot on a blackboard the cabalistic crosses and circles of a formation, then sink into another deep trance while he scrutinizes the diagram. Mealtimes come and go, his assistant coaches squirm in an agony of boredom, but the boss does not let them leave until he has charted a play to his satisfaction. These seances frequently break up after midnight—and commence all over again at nine o'clock the following morning.

Football is an all-absorbing passion with Parker. He never has worked at anything else since graduating from Centenary College twenty years ago. He once made a pretense of helping his father operate a small lumberyard in Kemp, Texas, during the off season, but he hasn't been near it since he was appointed head keeper of the Lions. He is an ardent bettor on horses, but from the moment the team assembles in training camp until the final game is wrapped up he will not look at a form chart or lend an attentive ear to a tip. Last spring a neighbor, Walter Scott, persuaded him to take up gardening as a hobby. Scott put one pepper, two cabbage and four potato plants in the Parkers' back yard. Parker watered the patch once.

Everyone associated with Parker professionally must play ball with his superstitions. Three years ago, while waiting for an appointment with a friend at the Hotel Seward, in Detroit, he dropped into the barbershop for a haircut. The Lions won the next game. Parker religiously has had his hair cut at the Seward ever since, although there are many barbers more convenient to his office. He is apprehensive flying in planes unless Bob McClelland, sports editor of the Detroit Times, occupies the window seat alongside him for good luck.

Last January, a unique record was broken in the Pro Bowl at

Los Angeles when Parker's Western all-star team was beaten by the Eastern all-star squad, coached by Cleveland's Paul Brown. It marked the first time in eight meetings, including two championship battles, that Parker ever had lost to Brown, who is rated by many people—Parker among them—the best strategist in the business.

Although the affair was a meaningless exhibition, Parker was disconsolate. "I knew we were cooked as soon as I walked into that room you gave me," he groused to Nick Kerbawy, general manager of the Lions.

Kerbawy, who is thoroughly familiar with Parker's fear of the thirteen hoodoo, had checked with an abacus before assigning him to Cottage 46C at the Ambassador Hotel. "What's the beef?" Kerbawy demanded. "Four and six equal ten."

"Yeah, and three more for C, the third letter of the alphabet, are thirteen," Parker snapped.

Indulging one of Parker's idiosyncrasies costs the Lions $3500 a year. In 1952, after a 28-0 shellacking from the Forty-Niners in Briggs Stadium, Parker wondered out loud why the Lions played better on the road than they did at home.

Kerbawy, a good straight man, threw him the line he was fishing for. "Would you feel better if we follow the same routine in Detroit that we have on the road?" Kerbawy asked.

Parker allowed it would be a splendid idea. So thirty-three players, five coaches and a trainer check into the Sheraton-Cadillac Hotel at seven p.m. on Saturday six times a year, go to the movies in a massive body, retire at eleven p.m., reassemble at the feeding trough for a steak breakfast at ten a.m. Sunday, then ride to the ball park in a chartered bus. Going into the current season, the Lions had lost only one home game since the management began picking up the tab for the week-end socials.

The Detroit bench generally is cluttered up during games by a retinue of odd characters to whom Parker ascribes a mystic affinity with luck. In 1949, when he was co-coach of the Chicago Cardinals, Parker fell with loud, gladsome cries upon the neck of a Negro shining shoes in the Los Angeles airport. It developed that his long-lost chum was Wallace (Boots) Lewis, who had been the campus handy man in the days when Parker was a student at Centenary.

"This guy is the luckiest crapshooter in the world," Parker explained. "Whenever we were broke in school, we'd scrape together quarters and give them to Boots. He brought back a fistful of folding money every time. I can't lose when he's around."

Boots was on Parker's bench for the ensuing Cardinals-Rams game. The Cardinals, trailing the Rams by 27-10 going into the fourth quarter, scored three touchdowns, the last one on the final play, and won, 31-27. Since then, with Boots in attendance, Parker's Lions have taken two out of three in Los Angeles from the Rams, usually the team to beat for the division title.

Parker also has sublime faith in the hexes cast on the opposition by Larry Gersh, a Chicago tailor, and John Francis Burke, a Hollywood florist. Their spells are not so powerful as Boots', but Parker is not an ingrate who forgets past favors. They brought him luck once. They may bring it to him again.

For all his superstitions, Parker is essentially a down-to-earth, meat-and-potatoes type of coach. He resorts to less technical double talk than practically any other coach you are likely to encounter. The Lions have only twenty basic plays, or about fifty in all with variations, and they seldom use more than half their repertory in any given game. At the other extreme, the Chicago Bears, for example, have a grab bag of some 300 plays, and dip into it constantly.

"If you pull too much razzle-dazzle you confuse nobody but your own men," Parker says. "All plays wind up with blocking anyway, so why get fancy? A guy can't remember a couple of hundred plays. His execution on assignments is bound to be sloppy if you load him down with details. Another reason I keep my system simple is that it's easier for a rookie to break in. Players get old awfully fast in this racket. You've got to have four or five new regulars in the lineup every year to keep rolling.

"I'm called an old-fashioned coach because I emphasize defense, but I haven't noticed that winning has gone out of style. Go back over all the great teams and you'll see they were outstanding defensively. We scored only seventeen points against Cleveland in each of the last two championship games, but we won them by holding the Browns to one touchdown both times. I figure my club will be all right if we limit the opposition to 21 points a game. That was a lot twenty years ago, but passers and receivers are so good nowadays that touchdowns come in bushels.

"I'm not setting myself up as a great big authority because I happen to be on top temporarily, but I think all teams are throwing the ball too much. You've got to put on a show in the pros to draw the customers, but they're getting fed up with passing on almost every other play. The fans get their biggest kick from a running game—watching the blocking develop and seeing the ball carrier brought down in the open with a hard tackle. That's football. The other stuff is imitation basketball.

"The big idea is to win, and to do it a team has got to have a good balance between running and passing. There never was a greater passer than Sammy Baugh, but the Redskins won titles only when they had runners like Cliff Battles and Dick Todd. You can't win by stressing one thing. Versatility is the pay-off. Look at my own club. We didn't have a man who led the league in any major department last year. Instead of a few stars, we had a lot of guys who could do many things well. A club that depends on one or two key men is up the creek when they have an off day or they're hurt. There's another important angle. Spirit is to football what pitching is to baseball. It's the decisive factor. You have better morale when everybody on the club knows he's sharing in the credit for winning."

As Parker says, the Lions' two championships were essentially team triumphs. Last year Doak Walker was third in the league in scoring, Bobby Layne was fifth in passing, Bobby Hoernschemeyer was ninth in ball carrying, Bob Smith was seventh in punting, and Walker was nineteenth in pass receptions. As a team, the Lions were fifth in gaining yards, and fifth in yielding them. Parker obviously did a first-class job of sustaining his players' efficiency and spirit at a high pitch, a coach's prime function.

An accurate indication of a team's morale is its performance in the second half of the season, when the stalwarts have been separated from the panty-waists, and the survivors, nursing large lumps, welts and abrasions, find strenuous exertion an onerous chore. In the last two years the Lions have dropped only one game after midseason, a 24-23 brawl with the Bears. Parker keeps his men driving down the stretch without exhorting them to break a leg for the greater glory of Detroit or the dear old stockholders. His locker-room oratory is confined to one warning, "Don't lose your poise," and technical analyses of the games.

Parker's only approach to an inspirational pep talk was made in his first year as head coach. "My main job was eliminating the team's defeatist complex," he confides. "I thought that licking Cleveland, the champions, in an exhibition game at Detroit would give the players the confidence they needed, so I told 'em it was the one game they had to win. There could've been a bad kickback if we'd lost, but I had to take my chances on getting away with it. I did. Cleveland wasn't ready for a big effort and we pulled out a 21-20 squeeze. Paul Brown was sore about losing and told me,

'You're going to be sorry for getting your club so high so early in the season.' We faded out at the end, but at least we were contenders for the first time in a dozen years, and we went all the way the next season."

Parker holds himself aloof from the team, but he gives his men aid and comfort by going to bat for them when they appreciate it most—in money matters. Last year Jim Doran, who was paid $5000 as a rookie in 1952, was given a raise of only $500. Doran said he couldn't afford to leave his farm in Iowa for less than $7500. Parker went over the head of the front office and agreed to the terms. Doran reciprocated handsomely by scoring the winning touchdown in the championship game with Cleveland.

When a man is willing to go all out to win, Parker ignores occasional violations of the team's honor system on training rules. He may soak a culprit twenty-five dollars for missing a workout, but he invariably returns the fine after running the wretch until his tongue is sunburned.

"It's more to sweat out the beer than to punish him," he remarks. "I assume everyone who plays pro football loves hard body contact and wants to win. If he doesn't, this is a helluva way to make a living. There isn't enough money in the world to pay for the beating he takes. If I have to fine a man to make him keep in shape to stand the gaff, he's too dumb to play good ball and I don't want him around.

"You've got to make allowances, though, when young guys under nervous tension blow off steam now and then. Casey Stengel gave me a good tip last winter for keeping them out of trouble. You know how Casey talks. 'When your fellas do a little night explorin', make sure they go in pairs,' he said. 'If a fella goes alone, he meets strangers, and one thing leads to another. If six go out together, one fella buys the first round, then everybody else has to set 'em up, and pretty soon they're loopin'. When two fellas go out, they have two beers apiece and everything is O.K.' "

Stengel's formula is not sure-fire protection for the team or, for that matter, the players. In October a year ago, Layne, Hoernschemeyer, Smith and Gedman went out for dinner in San Francisco and ran into two citizens who gave them a verbal going-over. The flannelmouths became so abusive that the Lions invited them to step outside and repeat their comments. The chumps accepted. One swung at Smith and was flattened by a counterpunch. Hoernschemeyer grabbed the other pest by the seat of the pants and tossed him over a stone wall. The fracas was splashed all over the newspapers, but Parker did not question his men about the incident. They played well in beating the Forty-Niners, 14-10. That was his sole concern.

Some people who know Parker intimately think that his recent five-to-one winning ratio is not sufficient compensation for the black depression he suffers after a defeat. "I suppose they're right," he admits. "I'm a bad loser. But I hope I never change. You're through the minute you take losing complacently."

Had Raymond (Buddy) Parker been content to accept things as they came, he would still be in Kemp, Texas, a small town forty-five miles south of Dallas, where he was born on December 16, 1913. There was no money in his family to send him to college, and there seemed little chance of his getting an athletic scholarship at obscure Kemp High. Parker applied himself so diligently to football, baseball and basketball, however, that in his junior year he received a bid from North Texas, a junior college. When he finished there in 1931, he was courted by a number of southwestern senior colleges. Uncle Billy Disch, the famous baseball coach at the University of Texas, wanted him because of his promising hitting, but Parker preferred to belt football players and joined his older brother, Bob—now coaching at San Marcos Teachers—at Centenary College in Louisiana.

Centenary was putting on a drive for the football headlines and made no bones about the fact that it was going out and proselyting large, muscular youths. Parker got room, board, tuition, twenty dollars a month and an occasional suit of clothes from Bonneau Peters, a local booster. He was a bargain at the price. In three years Centenary lost only two games. As a senior in 1934, Parker ranked among the leading ground gainers in the country and accounted for a stunning upset with an 18-yard field goal—the first and last he ever attempted—that gave Centenary a 9-6 victory over Texas, which had defeated Notre Dame two weeks previously.

In those days there was no draft rule in pro football governing the competition for college players, and Parker had his pick of half a dozen offers. He sought the advice of Cal Hubbard, now the supervisor of American League baseball umpires, who had played football at Centenary before going on to dismember pro linemen. Hubbard told him to go with George (Potsy) Clark in Detroit. Parker signed to play for $1200 a season, less than some of his stars now average per league game.

Parker was given an unmerciful ribbing when he arrived at training camp with a battered trunk containing all his belongings.

He naively thought his contract guaranteed him a full season's salary. He discovered that it was contingent upon his making the squad, as pro contracts still are, and that he would get nothing more than best regards if he failed to win a berth.

The odds against him were overwhelming. The Lions in 1935 were loaded with fine backs, including Earl (Dutch) Clark, considered by many experts the all-time pro quarterback, Ernie Caddel, Ace Gutowsky, Glenn Presnell and Frank Christensen. There was only one vacancy in the backfield, and it was earmarked for Steve Banas, fresh out of Notre Dame with a big reputation. Banas was released after the first game. Parker strewed Philadelphia gladiators all over the arena and nailed down a job as a blocker and line backer on the team that won the title.

Parker was not a fast or shifty back. He was serviceable rather than spectacular, a rugged gent who could go sixty minutes in the days when the pros had the single platoon. He was fearless about bouncing off Bronko Nagurski, the twentieth century's answer to the Neanderthal man, Clark Hinkle, Tuffy Leemans and other celebrated hard rocks in the National Football League.

In the romantic league, on the other hand, he was a wallflower who practically disappeared into the woodwork. "Buddy was a big man on the Lions, and I was just a sixteen-year-old girl in high school when we started to go together," Jane Parker relates now. "He was so shy that he sent his sister, Peepsie, to ask me for a date. I never saw much of him, even during the off season, until one day late in May of 1940. I was sitting in front of the one drugstore in Kemp looking like a fright. My hair was in curlers and I was barefooted. Buddy came up, dropped a little box in my lap and said, 'I bought you something. Tell me how you like it tonight.' Then he ran off. There was a lovely diamond engagement ring in the box, and a few days later I had a wedding band to go with it.

"I used to worry about him getting hurt when he was playing," Mrs. Parker says. "I hoped he would get a job as a coach. What a fool I was!"

Parker was traded to the Chicago Cardinals in 1937 and played with them until 1943, when he ended his active career after nineteen years of football. He then became an assistant to Jimmy Conzelman, the best barrel-house piano player in America and one of the most imaginative coaches in the game. Parker was an ideal lieutenant. He kept in the background, he was a bearcat on details and a horse for work. The Cardinals reflected his painstaking labor in winning the championship in 1947 and narrowly missing the next year, but he did not impress anyone as having the personality or the creative flair for a head coach.

When Conzelman resigned from coaching in 1949 to take a lucrative advertising job at a time when the club's affairs were in a state of flux, Parker and Phil Handler were designated co-coaches. The team won half its games, but Parker was dissatisfied with the setup and went to Detroit as Bo McMillin's aid in 1950.

The Lions had become chronic losers both on the field and at the gate. No improvement was in sight. It is now agreed that McMillin laid the foundation for Detroit's current success by drafting or acquiring in trades most of the team's key players. But he had to function as both head coach and general manager, an arrangement that seldom works out. Opposition to McMillin developed among the Lions' many important stockholders, among the players and, it was said, even among members of the coaching staff.

To cap it all, the team kept losing. When home attendance fell to 151,600 in 1950—it was 315,549 last year—the stockholders paid off McMillin and gave the job to Parker. The Detroit public had been expecting a big-name coach, and Parker hardly answered that description. However, fans have been slow to realize that pro football has bred a new species of coach. He is, paradoxically, often a fellow who would be lost in the collegiate shuffle—an easier tactical branch of the game. The successful college coach today generally is a personality kid who can charm alumni, sell himself to high-school prospects and lift his team to emotional peaks for traditional games.

None of this enters into pro football. It is like major-league baseball in demanding a sound grasp of mechanics and strategy. Teams meet so frequently and the turnover in personnel is so comparatively slow that a coach becomes thoroughly familiar with the opposition's strength and weakness. That puts a premium on his ability to analyze and improvise plays, and that's right down Parker's alley. The interminable hours he spends looking at movies and diagramming formations have pulled a succession of crucial games out of the fire in the second half.

"It's not unusual for a team to change its entire offense and defense between halves," he says. "You've got to anticipate the other coach's moves and outsmart him by springing some new stuff yourself. The trick is to hold a surprise for the proper spot, because you can't get away with it more than once."

One bold strategic stroke a game was enough to beat Cleveland two years in a row with the title on the line. Both times the decisive points were scored by a man who had not made a touchdown all year. In 1952, Doak Walker, who was injured most of the campaign, was shaken loose by the only split-T play the Lions used all season and ran sixty-seven yards. Last year Jim Doran, who had been exclusively a defensive end, caught a thirty-three-yard pass in the end zone with two minutes to go and Cleveland leading, 16-10. Early in the game Parker noticed that Tommy James, the Browns' defensive halfback, was coming up too close to the line of scrimmage on passes. He knew Doran, a fast man, could get behind James and outrun him. The temptation was strong to exploit the opening immediately, but he did not lower the boom until time was too short for Cleveland to launch a long counterdrive down the field.

In shooting for a third straight championship this year, Parker is having to exert saintly self-control to maintain the tight rein on his temper. The draft, the Canadian league and retirements made severe inroads on the Lions' manpower. A couple of prospects were lost through highly unusual circumstances. The team's No. 1 draft choice, Dick Chapman, a 230-pound tackle from Rice, decided to give all his attention to nuclear physics. The second draft choice, Michigan State's Jim Neal, married a girl who is a member of a sect which frowns on Sunday sports.

"The losses have hurt, but we'll have a good team," Parker was saying before the season started. "We can win it again with a little luck."

"That's what he says for publication," Jane Parker retorted. "I'll probably be up to my hips in shreds of ties, shirts and shoelaces. Mamma will put her foot down, though, if he starts to cut up his suits. He's got only three suits. He'll be arrested for indecent exposure if the team loses more than two straight."

SO YOU WANT TO BE A QUARTERBACK?

By Oliver Kuechle

From The Milwaukee Journal

"WEST-2-right-48-fly-Ed-Grace-A blocking-on 4."

Gibberish? Ramblings of a guy hit on one side of the head by an arithmetic and on the other side by a dictionary?

Not at all. Just a pro football quarterback's designation in the huddle for a simple sweep around right end by the right halfback. And you call the guy who has to call these plays and 50 or 60 others in the heat of battle a bum? You want to be a quarterback?

Signal calling in professional football has reached such a state of complexity that only a man with a high forehead and thinning hair should even attempt it. It is far beyond anything that the average fan in the stands or in front of his TV set imagines.

Back in the dinosaur days of football, the quarterback would say, "Joe, you take it. We'll all push."

And then in the stone age of football, Joe had a play number like "16" which meant he would carry the ball over right tackle, and the quarterback would bark out: "53-16-43-17-12." Joe would get the pass from center and go over right tackle with all of the roughly organized blocking help his side could achieve.

And then in the kerosene days of football, refinements having entered the game, it was that the quarterback would say "formation left, 42 on 2." Here was progress. The deployment of men was designated, the play, the hole which the ball carrier was to hit, and the signal at which the ball was to be passed by the center.

But it was still kerosene football. A team with such signal calling now, and what it stood for, would probably finish in last place.

The signal caller in professional football today carries the complete responsibility of directing the move of every man on his team. He must call the formation from which the play will be run, the play number, the ball carrier, the exact point of attack, the defensive alignment of opponents, the exact blocking assignment of every man and the starting signal—the signal at which the center will pass the ball. And he must do it in a matter of seconds in the huddle.

A few college coaches have come to burden their quarterbacks even as the pros do, but only a few. The responsibility, most feel, is too great. They take a lesser course. They divide the responsibility. The college quarterback at most schools will call the formation, the play number, the ball carrier, the point of attack and the starting signal, but the tackles, having taken their position in the line after the huddle, will call the blocking assignments as dictated by the defense which confronts them.

To understand the professional quarterback's gibberish in the huddle, a few arbitrary designations must first be explained.

Thus, the quarterback is always the No. 1 back, the left halfback the No. 2, the fullback the No. 3 and the right halfback the No. 4. Thus, also, definite lanes of attack are set up and numbered from zero to nine, the odd numbers, 1, 3, 5, 7 and 9 all to the right of center, and the even numbers, zero, 2, 4, 6 and 8, all to the left of center. And thus also certain words or combination of words, or combinations of words and numbers are established to describe basic and unchanging assignments.

"Fly" always means that the fullback fakes in the opposite direction from the one the ball carrier takes. "Bill" that the halfback blocks the end. "Fire" that the fullback blocks the line backer. "West" that the right end splits 12 or 15 yards out from the right tackle. "East" that the left end splits similarly from the left tackle. "West-2-right" that the right end splits 15 yards from the right tackle and that the No. 2 back takes a flanking position just inside the split end.

"A" blocking in the line means that the strong side guard always pulls and the other men in the line, unless otherwise specifically assigned, block the men nearest them—inside. "B" blocking means that the tackle similarly pulls and that others in the line, unless assigned, block the men nearest them. "AO" blocking means that the weak side guard pulls and "BO" blocking that the weak side tackle pulls. The list of arbitrary blocking assignments or combinations of blocking assignments is longer than space permits.

To help, further, on very specific blocks in these arbitrary designations, the linemen all receive names—those on the side of the line at which the play is directed, boys' names, and those on the other side girls' names. Thus on the strong side, the side at which the play is directed, "Ed" is at end, "Tom" at tackle, "Gill" at guard and on the weak side "Eve" at end, "Tess" at tackle and "Grace" at guard. The poor center has no name. Neuter gender.

Each name involves a specific assignment. "Ed" in the huddle signal means that the strong side end blocks the line backer. "Tom"

that the strong side tackle takes him, and "Gill" that the strong
side guard takes him. "Eve" means that the weak side end takes
the halfback, "Tess" that the weak side tackle takes him and
"Grace" that the weak side guard does the job.

Conceivably, of course, the tackle on one play will be "Tom"
and on the next "Tess." The direction of the play determines the
"sex" of all—and the assignment.

The first number in the gibberish which the quarterback gives
designates the play and it is always a number of two digits. The
first indicates the ball carrier and the second the point of attack.
Thus, 24 would be the No. 2 back, the left halfback, over the No. 4
hole, 36 the No. 3 back, the fullback, over the No. 6 hole and 48
the No. 4 back, the right halfback, over the No. 8 hole.

So much for the arbitrary designations and procedures learned
like ABC's—and you still want to be a quarterback? You still call
the guy a bum when he stays in the huddle a second too long and
draws a five yard penalty?

In the huddle itself, the team may line up in different ways.
Generally, so his lips may not be read, the quarterback has his back
to the defensive team as he calls the play, or if he does not, he stoops
low in the circle to conceal the movement of his lips.

"West-2-right-48-fly-Ed-Grace-A blocking-on 4" he orders, then
hurries the men to their positions in an upright stance.

But the play has only begun—and the quarterback's work only
begun.

"Set" he orders next and all men except himself go down to a
three point stance. He himself, with hands between the center's legs
to receive the ball, looks over the defense. And here occurs a very
important point in the play. What is the defense? A five? A six?
A seven?

What the quarterback sees here determines the exact blocking.
His original signal as given in the huddle had "A" blocking to be
used, but "A" blocking has variations, depending upon the defensive alignment. The signal here, then, informs of the variation.
And having signalled the exact variation, he swings into the ca-
dence leading up the signal on which the ball will be passed.

"Forty-seven, 62, 87," he will bark, and then "Hut-one," "Hut-
two," "Hut-three," "Hut-four." How long he will continue this
apparent nonsense of "Huts" has already been determined by the
original gibberish back in the huddle.

The last part of the huddle signal, the "on 4," determines at
what exact point in the signal calling the center will pass the ball

"On 4" means that the ball will be passed on the fourth of the Huts."

And why the prefix of the "Hut"? Why not just "one, two, three, four"? Oh, just a little trick. The charge by the line and backs both will not be made on the "four" part of the signal but on the "Hut" before it. It is a legitimate bit of cheating, so to speak.

And what happens when good old "West-2-right-48-fly-Ed-Grace-A blocking-on 4" has been called and the quarterback has finished with his "Huts"?

Everything should now fall into place.

"West-2-right" indicates the formation with the right end split 5 yards and the left halfback just inside him. "Forty-eight-fly" tells that the right halfback will carry the ball, that the point of attack will be lane No. 8, around right end, and that the fullback will fake the opposite way. "Ed-Grace-A blocking" reveals that the left end "Ed" will block the line backer, the right guard "Grace" will pull out of the line and block the defensive halfback and the "A" blocking that the right guard "Gill" will also pull out of the line and block the defensive right end. All others, unless assigned, take the men nearest them. "On 4" means that the center will pass the ball on the fourth of the quarterback's "Huts."

Simple? And you still want to be a quarterback?

Suppose, though, as the team has hurried from its huddle with the quarterback standing over center surveying the field, that the defense has deployed itself in such a way that good old "West-2-right-48-fly-Ed-Grace-A blocking-on 4" appears doomed.

At once the signal caller, in those numbers which precede his "Huts," exercises a check. Everything which has gone before is nullified with a single word—"Blue" or "green" or "red." The original play is canceled and a new arbitrary play, described by the single word, is substituted. The "Hut-one," "Hut-two," "Hut-three" and "Hut-four" complete the signal as usual.

A team may have eight or ten arbitrary check plays of this kind, described by a single word, to take advantage of the defense.

The college coaches who do not feel that a quarterback should be burdened with the immense responsibility of calling every player's move, have their tackles call the line blocks.

"Eighty-six, 62, 45" the left tackle will call. "Seventy-seven, 62, 24," the right tackle will call. Depending on the play as originally called by the quarterback in the huddle, only one of the signals will be heeded. The other will be meaningless.

It's a tricky business, this signal calling.

128 *Oliver Kuechle*

And you want to be a quarterback?

Well, anyway, the next time you want to call the quarterback
bum, just count 10 on your fingers. And the next time you want t
fire the coach count 10, too. Perhaps he lost the game, the big game
only because his battered quarterback said "East-2-left-43-fog
Tom-Tess-on 2" when he should have said "West-2-right-48-fly
Ed-Grace-A blocking-on 4."

THAT TEAM NAMED DESIRE

By Frank Cashen

From The Baltimore News-Post, November 28, 1954

Philadelphia—

UNDERDOG NAVY, its proud line continually pierced by the cavalry charge of Army's slashing backs, kept a date with destiny here in cavernous Municipal Stadium this sunny, cool afternoon as the Middies blasted from behind to unend the Cadets, 27-20, and insure themselves a berth in the Sugar Bowl classic January 1 in New Orleans where they will meet Mississippi.

Trailing 20-14 late in the second session, the Tars showed their undeniable class by thundering back to score the go-ahead touchdown in two minutes and eight seconds as they moved 63 yards and sent quarterback George Welsh crashing over from a yard out on the sixth play of the sustained march.

That knotted the tally at 20 apiece and a stadium full of people stood screaming on their feet as halfback Johnny Weaver calmly booted his third straight extra point to put the Tars in front for keeps.

In the third session, the Sailors added another touchdown but it was icing on the cake. Navy's defense which appeared befuddled through the wild first half, was its old indomitable self in the third and fourth session. And the vaunted Army offense never hit pay-dirt.

Thus did the Middies, which looked like the weakest Navy team in a decade before the season opened, win their seventh and most important game of the season and post their 23rd victory in this storied tradition-steeped series. Army has won 28 games down through the years, including last year's 54th renewal.

Navy needed this win today to get the Sugar Bowl bid. Actually, several other post season bowl committees were interested in the Middies but in a ballot of the players shortly after the game the Middie gridders decided on the New Orleans offer.

It will mark the first bowl appearance of a Navy team since 1924 when the Middies went to the Rose Bowl and played Washington U. to a 14-14 standoff.

This Army-Navy test was billed as the best game in the long series between the service clubs. Army led the nation in offense going into this one and Navy was the number one club in the country in defense.

Besides that, the Middies ranked number two to Army on attack. And, as if the game needed any more spice, the Cadets were working on a seven game win streak. After losing their season opener to South Carolina, they came through the rest of the schedule unscratched.

Even after such a buildup this was all that 102,000 fans could have expected. Both clubs played wide open football, the tackling was savage and the running tremendous.

Army did not go down easy. It fought to the end, bitterly and full of the precision that hall-marked its season. Even in defeat, the Cadets never lost their poise.

If Navy lacked Army's precision, it made up for it in uncontrolled fury. Even when Navy fumbled, which it did six times, they fought savagely for the ball. Such spirit was not to be denied.

If Navy had one hero this afternoon it was George Welsh, the precocious quarterback who passed for three Sailor touchdowns and personally banged over for the other.

But Welsh very nearly put the Tars in serious trouble in the final half when, with his club leading 27-20, he passed on third down while deep in his own territory. Fortunately for the Middies, the pass was incomplete but Tommy Bell, Army's hard-hitting halfback, came close to intercepting it.

Two of Welsh's flips were taken by sophomore end Bill Smith who started the season as fourth string quarterback and wound up as first string end. The other, which accounted for the initial Tar tally, went to halfback Bob Craig.

The payoff counter for the Middies was put in motion when the Cadets kicked off after going into a 20-14 lead. Ralph Chesnauskas' flat boot bounded to the Middie 47 where tackle Hugh Webster fell on the ball for the Middies.

On first down, Welsh pitched out to Craig who turned the right end for 27 yards and first down on the 26. Welsh then sneaked for two and fullback Joe Gattuso pounded out seven more.

A backfield in motion penalty cost the Middies five and a Welsh to Weaver pass fell incomplete. But on fourth down, Welsh, faking beautifully, whipped a pass to second string end Jim Owens and the latter stumbled out of bounds on the one. Welsh went over on the next play to produce the tie and Weaver converted to put the Middies in front, 21-20.

An Army fumble set up Navy's first touchdown. Bell bobbled the ball on his own 27 and Jim Royer, big Tar tackle, recovered.

Welsh got 15 on the keep play as the Tars went to first down on the 12. After three plays it was fourth and four and Welsh poked a short screen pass to Craig, who got stunning blocks from Royer and center Wilson Whitmire, and tight roped his way down the sidelines to the end zone.

Army got the touchdown back the next time it got the ball but it didn't get the point. From its own 31, the Cadets moved 69 yards in 16 plays, all but one of which were on the ground.

During the sortie, Pat Uebel, Army's workhorse fullback who scored all three of the Cadet tallies in their 20-7 win over the Middies here a year ago, carried the ball eight times and got 32 yards.

But when the West Pointers arrived at the eight they sent Bell charging over for the TD. Chesnauski's boot was wide and for a large part of the afternoon it looked like a most important miss.

Following Army's pattern, the Middies took the kickoff and didn't let up until they hit the Promised Land. This advance started late in the opening period but wasn't culminated until the second session when Welsh chucked an 11-yard flip to Smith. It was a nine play, 59-yard march, a pitchout play from Welsh to Weaver, good for 24 yards was the big gainer during the drive.

At this point, the Cadets produced their long awaited explosion. From the kickoff they went 55 yards to the 15 where the drive fizzled. Navy gave the ball right back when Dick Guest fumbled and Army, after trying two running plays, also gave up possession when Pete Vann, the Cadets' wondrous quarterback who played the entire 60 minutes of the bruising battle, lost the ball in taking the pass from center. Lenny Benzi, who was one of four Middie players to go all the way, recovered.

The Tars couldn't go and Guest went into kick formation. He fumbled the pass from center and the ball went tumbling back to the three yard stripe where Don Hollender, Army's All-American end, covered the ball for the Cadets.

From here, Uebel knifed over on one crack. Uebel, like Vann, went all the way for the Cadets and was easily the best running back on the field as he personally gathered 133 of the Cadets' 265 rushing yards, or one more yard than the rest of the West Point backs gathered all afternoon.

An intercepted pass set up the third and final Cadet score. Uebel committed the act of leaping larceny as he pulled down a Welsh shot that was intended for Beagle. The Cadet fullback smacked up to the Middie 42 before being unended and Army set out from that point.

The Cadets went all the way in one play, Vann tossing to halfback Bob Kyasky, who took the pass on the eight and raced over.

That set the stage for Navy's comeback center and the Middies went to rest at the intermission on the long end of a 21-20 situation.

The ball changed hands only once before the Middies were in the end zone in the third stanza. This time they moved 59 yards in ten plays, a 19 yard pass from Welsh to Smith producing the final payoff. Weaver missed the upright for the first and only time of the afternoon but it didn't matter. It was all over now.

Early in the final chapter, the Middies threatened again, as they moved to the Cadet 11 only to lose possession when Bill Chance, Army center, intercepted a Welsh pass on his own three and came out five yards to the 8.

From there Army drove all the way down field to the Tar 8 but here Vann couldn't unfurl his famous passing arm as Ronnie Beagle, Navy All-American flankman, twice bulled through to smash him down with ferocious tackles.

Beagle, Benzi, Weaver and Craig played 60 minutes for the Tars as Eddie Erdelatz went with his best all the way.

Gattuso, who was Navy's leading ground gainer throughout the season, was again a stickout as he produced 72 yards in 13 trips, including a clutch first down to keep Navy in possession of the ball when the clock was nearing the end of its tour.

Welsh completed five of 11 passes for 75 yards and, as mentioned before, three touchdowns. Vann hit with five of 10 for 98 yards and one TD.

The final statistics give mute testimony to this beautifully played game. The Middies got 21 first downs to Army's 20 and picked up 259 yards rushing to Army's 265. There just wasn't much to choose from between the teams except for a little thing that Coach Eddie Erdelatz of Navy, calls desire.

His outfit, which he fondly calls, "a team named desire," was on the right track this afternoon.

FATHER IS A FOOTBALL COACH

By Jean Butts Jones and Furman Bisher

From The Saturday Evening Post, November 20, 1954

WHEN I ANNOUNCED to my family last year that I planned to marry a high-school football coach I had been dating a few months, everyone was pleased except my father, who went up in a puff of smoke. "Marrying any football coach is bad enough," he said in a volcanic mood, "but to marry a high-school coach, that's going too far."

My father, Wallace Butts, has been a football coach since 1928, the last sixteen years at the University of Georgia, in Athens. I consider him an authority on matters of football, and on the field he has an extensive reputation as a taskmaster. But he found out you can't coach love, and, to prove it, a few weeks later he marched down the aisle of the First Methodist Church in Athens to give me away to that high-school coach.

First, let me set the record straight. My husband, Frank Jones, is not an ordinary coach. His teams at Decatur High School, in a suburb of Atlanta, have won three region championships in a row and three times got to the Georgia state semifinals playoff, where they lost by close scores. In two seasons his team lost only one regularly scheduled game. Actually, I think my father was flattered that, after observing a coach's life from the inside for the greater part of my twenty-one years, I should still be brave enough to marry one.

I've heard him say many times, "I know the futile feeling of a high-school coach. I was one myself for ten years, and when I found I was on a deadend street, I happened to get a college break. But there are still only a hundred good coaching jobs in the country. The field is too limited. You meet a lot of nice people, but you never make any money."

My father is a renowned pessimist, but really, I don't think that coach Wallace Butts or any member of his family has any grounds for complaint. If I had a chance to start over again, I'd still choose to be the daughter of a football coach and the wife of one. I didn't marry Frank Jones because he was a football coach, but it didn't

133

hurt his chances any. When I thought about marrying Frank, I remembered something important. Daddy was installing the split-T formation at Georgia, and Frank had coached the split-T several years, so I knew they'd have something in common.

It worked out just beautifully. It's awfully pleasant to sit around and listen to the menfolk talk about overshifting and the option play and brush-blocking and such. A lot of wives wouldn't appreciate it, but when you're raised in a football family it comes just as naturally as matters of the church come to a preacher's family.

A football family doesn't live or die with each victory or defeat, but winning does improve the atmosphere around the house considerably. It isn't, however, quite so serious as Frank made it out to be just before we were married. His team had lost heavily by graduation, and the material looked rather poor for the 1953 season.

In a very serious mood one day, he said to me, "I'm awful sorry our first year will have to be a losing year." As it turned out, it wasn't, but I still chuckle inside when I think of this coach-husband being so greatly concerned about how many games he would win for his bride.

I got my indoctrination early in the vagaries of the coaching family's life. Here's something they say happened when I was only three years old—I remember little about it myself.

Daddy was coaching at Male High, in Louisville, Kentucky, at the time. The big game with Manual High was coming up, and already in those days the name of Wallace Butts was becoming synonymous with pessimism. He had been moaning low around the house all week, telling anybody who would listen to him, "Well, if we lose this one, I guess we'll have to pack up and get out of town."

Male High did lose. I was too little to go to the game, and when they came home and I heard the bad news and saw the sorrowful expressions on their faces, I went up to my room in tears. When my mother came up she found me packing my dolls and clothes. I had taken my pessimistic papa at his word. I was getting ready to get out of town.

We have been a rather fortunate family as football fortune goes. There has been none of the gypsy life for us, here one year and there the next, none of the continual moving and living from one job to the next that is the lot of some coaches. But there have been rough times, like 1951.

That was one of daddy's hardest seasons. The Georgia squad was inexperienced and slow. Some businesses he had an interest in, including a restaurant in Athens, took a bad turn. Everything went wrong at the same time, except a sophomore quarterback named Zeke Brathowski. Fortunately Zeke came through in a spectacular way, and eased the pain of a season that ended with five victories and five defeats.

In 1953, daddy experienced another season of depression, though by this time I was gone from the family circle and had the problems of my own coach on my mind, too. Georgia won only three games and lost seven, the worst record in daddy's whole coaching history. But this distressing season had a positive rather than negative effect. It was plainly evident that Georgia just didn't have the material. Instead of starting a fire-the-coach campaign, Georgia supporters rallied together in the biggest wave of college spirit the state has ever known.

We Buttses have been lucky like that from the start. The game that sent me to my room packing at three was the only one daddy lost to Manual High in three seasons in Louisville, where his record was so impressive that he was hired as an assistant coach at Georgia in 1938. He was appointed head coach in 1939, and since that time his teams have won 104 games, lost fifty-two and tied seven. They have played in seven bowl games and won the Southeastern Conference championship three times.

Daddy was born and grew up in Milledgeville, Georgia, and in February, 1929, he eloped with his home-town sweetheart, Winifred Taylor. He was just out of Mercer University, where he had been a 165-pound end, and was on his first job at Madison A. & M., in Madison, Georgia. He returned to Milledgeville in 1932 to coach at Georgia Military College, a prep school. With the family now increased by two—my older sister, Faye, and myself—we moved to Louisville in 1935. There the third daughter, Nancy, arrived. Then came the final move, back to Georgia and the state university, and here the four Butts women seriously began the process of bringing up father.

There's a tradition, it seems, that football coaches never have sons—they lean predominantly toward the production of daughters. You might think these daughters would have easy access to the manly beasts their fathers coach, but it doesn't work out that way. Being a coach's daughter can be an awful millstone on a girl's romantic life.

A coach's daughter is the last girl in the world a football player is likely to show any interest in, for fear that the other boys will accuse him of playing politics. But if one does happen to be so bold, he is (1) afraid to come around to the house, (2) watching himself like a hawk to keep from violating training rules, and (3) about as much at ease as an escaped convict calling on the sheriff.

On the practice field, you see, my father is as intense as a drill sergeant. He expects his players to work as hard as he is willing to work. The players expect him to be just as tough around home, which is a laugh. We Butts girls always have had him under control, and the tough-taskmaster characterization seems unreal to us.

I have always been a worshiper of the handsome, heroic athlete, but as I grew up, my romantic opportunities with members of the football team were seriously limited by fear of the coach. On bowl trips or away from home, dates came easily with them. But in Athens the players kept their distance, because it meant coming to the house for me or bringing me home.

If they could come around in a group, players were much more at ease, although this didn't always work either. One night I had a little party for some girl friends and their dates, most of them football players. As daddy came in simply to say hello in his most polite manner, one of the boys was so frightened he jumped over a sofa and ran out into the yard to escape.

It hasn't been so hard on Nancy, the youngest, for she has had the benefit of observing her two older sisters. Besides, she's a brash teen-ager who says what she thinks and flinches before no one. Daddy has often said that she is his best critic.

"What do you think about your sister marrying up with a football coach, Nancy?" he asked her, driving to town one day.

"Well, we've had to put up with you," she said, "and it hasn't been too bad."

"How do women go around picking a husband, anyway?" daddy said. "Don't you think she could do better? That fellow wouldn't win any beauty contest, you know."

"Well, look who's talking! You're a good daddy, I'll give you credit for that, but you're no raving handsome beast yourself. Besides, you wouldn't know anything about love and romance, so why don't you leave those things to the women in the family?"

Nancy has had her trying moments, though. A couple of years ago she was beauty queen of the sophomore class at Athens High School, but on the day of her selection she came home in tears. One of the judges had been Bob West, the captain of the football team, and some of the catty numbers around school had been whispering that Nancy won it in a "fix." She was grief-stricken.

Daughters can be a coach's asset in the process of player recruiting. A constant battle goes on the year round for the high-school football stars who have college ability. All of us have pitched in to give daddy a hand, though I can't honestly say that we have ever been the lone determining factor.

Once I thought I was going to be, and I threw myself into the case with enthusiasm. The player was a handsome young tackle from Ohio. He played the piano beautifully and he had wonderful manners. Mother thought he was something sensational, and daddy thought so, too, though their perspectives were miles apart.

Finally, the boy smiled across the piano at me, like Liberace, and said he'd come to Georgia if I'd promise to date him. I did my part. I promised, and the tackle came to Georgia, but something happened that was entirely out of my hands. They found out he was ineligible for some reason or other, and the tackle eventually transferred to a school out West.

Many times I've wished I had been born a boy, so I could have played football and helped daddy. I've always done the next best thing. I had an awful scrap with a boy when I was in the fourth grade. He said some things about daddy that weren't nice and I popped him. They sent him to the principal's office and let me go free.

When I was a student at Georgia—Faye and I both attended the university, and Nancy will too—I was a cheerleader. I majored in journalism to help him with his propaganda. Now, on the Atlanta Journal, I'm on the city staff rather than in the sports department, but I do write a series of features each fall weekend about bitter rival Georgia Tech. These pieces take the form of "scouting letters" to daddy.

Right after my wedding, Bobby Dodd, the head coach at Georgia Tech, quipped at a banquet, "Coach Butts is using unfair tactics. He's training his daughters to be newspaper reporters to get all the people on his side, and marrying them off to football coaches to get all the players." I hope it works, I might add.

Football coaching is a twelve-month grind that hits a peak of pressure in September, October and November. We have always tried to make life around the house as easy and as pleasant for our coach Butts as possible, but it's difficult with daddy. Relaxation never has been a natural thing with him. He works as hard at relaxing as some people do at work.

We did get him off to St. Simon's Island on the Georgia coast last summer, and each morning at the miserable hour of four o'clock we arose to go deep-sea fishing with him. He got sick every time he went out, and we wound up doing most of the fishing.

After a few days of these predawn sleep wreckers, we began to investigate. We found out that he really didn't give a hang for deep-sea fishing. He had been showing enthusiasm for it just to please us. That ended the deep-sea excursions and we all resumed our delightful sleep, with which the vacation became a vacation again.

He isn't much for swimming either. Once we gave him two dazzling new swim suits for Father's Day. A bright high-school prospect hit town that same weekend. I asked the prospect if he'd like to go for a swim, and when he said he didn't have a suit with him, daddy gave him both of his new ones.

Once, about five years ago, mother decided that he needed a new hobby that would completely captivate him. She selected golf for him, and gave him a set of the finest new clubs she could find. This was not a good idea, for he doesn't like to do anything he can't do well, and so he played with feverish intent at becoming a good golfer. He was knocking himself out, working on his woods, practicing his irons, haunting driving ranges by day and night. Finally, after six or seven months, mother convinced him he should give it up. It had ceased to be a hobby any more. It had become his master, and he was a slave to his passion for the game.

There is no escape for any football coach from the natural hazards of his profession, such as antagonistic alumni, ticket moochers, anonymous telephone callers, doting parents of players—especially mothers—and sidewalk quarterbacks. In that terrible 1951 season we tried to get him to have an on-and-off switch installed on the telephone or to have an unpublished number, but he wouldn't have any part of it.

"Part of my job is talking to the people who are interested in football at Georgia," he said. "They wouldn't be calling if they weren't interested. I can spot the phonies and I can hang up on them, but I'll still give them the chance to call."

Another big problem is last-minute calls for game tickets. Often close friends are just as guilty as anybody. A couple of years ago an old acquaintance who should have known better phoned the day before the Georgia-Georgia Tech game, the state's football World Series, and asked for twenty-two tickets. There not only wasn't an extra ticket at our house, there wasn't one in town. Daddy told the man, an influential Georgia alumnus, that asking for twenty-two tickets was one of the best jokes he'd heard in a long time, but if the man would settle for twenty less, he could take care of him.

Then he came begging to the women in his life. Only Faye had

extra tickets and she'd been planning for weeks to take two friends
with her.

"But this is important," daddy pleaded. "This is for———,
and it might be bread and butter in our mouths. You don't want to
see your poor old daddy cold, hungry and penniless just because
you wouldn't let him have two little old football tickets back in
1952, do you?"

"I'll let you have them for twenty-five dollars," Faye said.

"But that's scalping," daddy hollered, "and you know I don't
approve of scalping!"

"I don't approve of fathers' taking advantage of defenseless
daughters either. I think I'm being quite reasonable. I know of
some tickets that are selling for fifty dollars a pair. Twenty-five
dollars is my price. Take it or leave it."

Reluctantly daddy dug into his pocket and shelled out the
twenty-five dollars; then turned around and let the "influential
alumnus" have them for game price. We have never let him forget
the time he was ticket-scalped by his own daughter.

Game days are always hectic days at our house, a twelve-room
red-brick place on a large, shady block of Highland Avenue in
Athens. Every bed is always filled, and relatives and friends drop
by in a steady stream from Friday night until late into Sunday
morning.

The football Saturday usually begins with daddy arising at
6:30 a.m. He never sleeps very well the night before a game.
Mother gets up and has breakfast with him, but there isn't much
conversation. Some days he is uncommonly cheerful—this mood
usually coincides with games which Georgia has been picked to lose
decisively. He'll read the morning paper—he follows the newspapers avidly—then drift away without saying good-by to anybody. We won't see him again until we arrive at the stadium, and
then our view of him is no better than any other spectator's.

After the game we never know what to expect. If Georgia has
won, usually droves of miscellaneous people show up to offer congratulations. If Georgia has lost, only the people who were invited
to dinner show up, and they are customarily full of patronizing
condolences.

I can't rightfully say that the family suffers as hard through the
actual game as daddy, for he is one of the worst sufferers in the
coaching business. For the longest while he had a habit of chewing sprigs of grass during the game, like Nebuchadnezzar, the king
of Babylon. His stomach began to bother him, and while daddy

thought it was being caused by defeat, his doctor told him it was grass. Then he switched to chewing gum. He breaks up the sticks into little pieces and eats—not chews—them during a game.

While he is having his troubles on the field, his family every so often is having trouble of its own in the stands. The worst of these occasions took place while Georgia was losing a heartbreaker to Alabama, 14-7, at Athens in 1949. Everything seemed to go wrong for Georgia that day, and a very fat man sitting directly in front of me decided it was daddy's fault.

"Let's get rid of Wally!" he hollered. No matter what happened, that was his cry. "Let's get rid of Wally!"

Now I realize, of course, that neither my father nor any other football coach ever will achieve universal popularity, even if he should win them all, but it does grate somewhat on the tender nerves of a loving daughter to hear her old man attacked like a baseball umpire. All the while this fellow was bellowing at my father I'd been eating peanuts and placing the hulls on his hatbrim. When he took his hat off, the hulls fell down his back and inside his coat and in his eyes, and he turned furiously on me.

"Yes, I did it," I told him, "and I'm glad. That's my father you've been shouting at, and we love him. Besides, we like to eat, and we can't if he hasn't got a steady job."

He really was a very nice man. He spent the rest of the afternoon apologizing to us. "It isn't that I don't like coach Butts," he said, "but it's just because I love Georgia so much I hate to see them lose." And I guess that's the way it is with most football fans. It's still pretty hard on a coach's family in a losing season, though.

As you can imagine, daddy is very sensitive to defeat. After the Orange Bowl game in 1949 daddy just wouldn't budge from his room. Georgia had won the Southeastern Conference championship and had been favored to beat Texas, a three-time loser, on New Year's Day. With no pressure on, the loose Texas team won, 41-28—the only major bowl game daddy ever lost. Daddy was simply crushed. They always throw a big postgame party for the players and coaches at a night club in Miami, but daddy refused to go. While mother dressed in her prettiest evening gown, daddy crawled into bed, and nobody could reason with him.

After a while there was a knock on the door, and when mother opened it, there stood Frank Leahy, of Notre Dame, one of daddy's closest friends, and two Catholic priests. They were so appropriately solemn that it looked as if they had come to administer last rites. Mother started laughing, and then daddy, and then all of us.

That broke the spell. Daddy got up and dressed and went off to the party to face the music.

Many of his players think of him only as a football coach. If they could see him around the house, those Georgia Bulldogs would never believe it. While he has never washed a dish in his life and couldn't fry an egg without an instructor, he is otherwise a well-domesticated animal.

He loves to show up at mother's teas and stand in the receiving line. When I had parties, he always joined in to help with the serving. It gave him a chance to act cute. He has always lavished gifts on us, and I must say that he's much better about sizes than mother.

There seems to be something magnetic about his personality that attracts characters of all types and all descriptions. This is perhaps native in all football coaches, but in coach Butts and family the characteristic appears to be overdeveloped. Even our cooks have been characters, such as the one who had to resign to have her ninth child without benefit of a husband.

For years and years the leading symbol of undying loyalty at Georgia has been a flap-mouthed Negro waterboy-trainer named Clegg Stark, who doesn't know his own age or how long he has been there. They say that Clegg once was able to throw a football the length of a field. The late Grantland Rice prevailed upon him to demonstrate his mighty arm when Georgia played New York University in New York some years ago. He so amazed the sports writers that several of them wrote at length about the fabulous Negro waterboy from Georgia.

Clegg is held in such esteem by past Georgia football players that they raised a fund to buy him a new house. Then came time for the touching presentation, and old Clegg, wearing his red-and-black Georgia sweater, stood there with his head bowed in humility, occasionally wiping away a dripping tear. Then he stepped forward to make his acceptance speech.

"I sho' do appreciate this from you boys," he said. "But who's gonna pay the tax on it?"

Daddy has had his player characters, too, not the least of whom was a flat-footed, slope-shouldered halfback from Ohio. This player had great talent, but he almost drove daddy wild with his flightiness.

Now, a player's problems are the coach's problems, too, no matter how personal they may be. Romance-stricken Georgia players have come by home many a time to tell daddy they wanted to get married. I've seen the terrified bride-elect sit in the parlor while daddy grew furious with the player in the den. He has always maintained that marriage and college don't mix, mainly for financial reasons. Sometimes daddy has been able to restrain romance, but more times than not he has been the loser.

One day in the spring of 1941, this flat-footed, slope-shouldered boy came by daddy's office and told him he was quitting football. "I want to live a normal student's life," he said. "I want to have some time for a girl friend, like the other fellows on the campus."

This set off another explosion by coach Butts. Spring practice opened without the boy among those reporting, and daddy was resigned to losing him. About a week later, though, the boy came sidling into his office and wanted to know if he could rejoin the team.

"I don't know," daddy said. "I'll have to take a vote of the squad to see."

I'm not sure of this, but I've got a hunch that when the boy went out one door, daddy rushed out the other to hold his ballot. And when the players elected to take the boy back, I'm sure it saved daddy from having a heart attack, for the boy was Frank Sinkwich, in daddy's own estimation the greatest player he ever coached.

Another great one was Charley Trippi, the big star of the only perfect season—1946—that Georgia has had in modern times. Trippi, now with the Chicago Cardinals, was a cold-blooded businessman both on and off the field. But he was a tremendous athlete who could do everything well, and that season he was an overwhelming All-American selection.

Looking back on it all, I can't contend that I've been especially blessed by being a football coach's daughter. Coaches don't make the best fathers in the world, because you don't get to see enough of them.

The months from September to December you may as well scratch off. If you are with him, he's got his mind on 600 other things and seldom knows you're alive. But I don't care to trade my pessimistic papa in on a new model.

Life in a coach's family, with all its hazards, has given me something extra. We've had our trips to the Rose Bowl, to the Sugar Bowl, to the Orange Bowl; and we've had our parties and rubbed shoulders with celebrities.

I got one of the greatest thrills of my life when Joe E. Brown introduced me to some friends in New York as "Miss Butts, whom

I met in Atlanta." If I hadn't been the coach's daughter, he'd never have remembered me. Other children envied us and our "connections" and "influence" with the coach, and I always felt the envy was justified. I'd have envied them if they'd been in my place.

As a coach's wife now, I find myself living through many of the same joys and agonies I saw my mother experience. She suffered silently with Georgia, but I die violently with Decatur High School. I'm a nervous bundle of screams and hollers and other assorted noises during a game. In football matters my father's nature dominates me. We're both pessimistic. We both feel that anybody who isn't fur you is agin you. We both hate to lose, passionately. They call him "The Little Round Man" and me "The Little Round Girl."

Eventually, though, I feel that the lady in me will take over and I shall become the exemplary wife of a football coach. I have been exceedingly well trained for the position.

POP PASSES

By Harry Borba

From The San Francisco Examiner, September 8, 1954

Copyright, 1954, San Francisco Examiner
Reprinted by permission of copyright owner

ANOTHER FRIEND has passed and the evenings will be bleak again. Priceless evenings reminiscing with Glenn Scobey Warner have passed, too. Old Pop, a deliberate man with a deliberate manner of speech, loved nothing more than companions who would hear his tales of the Carlisle Indians, Pittsburg Panthers and Stanford Reds. These were all teams he raised to eminence in collegiate ranks.

Pop deftly promoted the little arguments that made 2 o'clock in the morning arrive before you barely had sat down.

Warner would sit awhile talking about today's problems and about the new formation he would spring on the Stanfords on the morrow. Out would come the stub of pencil and he'd grab an envelope off his desk. The design of crosses and ciphers always looked pretty intricate but reasonably sound. Nine times out of ten he'd discard the new formation after trial the next day. With his laboratory mind, Pop always was questing for new bafflers.

The new formation adequately explained, Pop would remark gruffly:

"Maybe you could stand a little drink?"

He'd hobble painfully, because of his sore hip, to the kitchen. Back he'd come with a drink of rare old whiskey he had saved for his friends or perhaps a sip of elderberry wine he had made ever so many years before.

Pop, a man who always gave in to his Scotch instincts, had picked the delicious berries in Pennsylvania during a late summer training camp. He made them into juice, sent them to his then New York home. During the winter he fermented them into wine as savory as any made by skilled vinners.

These preliminaries finally completed, the "bull" session would begin in earnest.

Yea, that wobbly pass that Herb Fleishhacker threw to Louie Vincenti for a touchdown to get a 13-13 tie with Southern Cali-

144

fornia in 1927 wasn't wobbly. The Indians were in Trojan territory with time running against them.

"I'll never forget what Fleishhacker said to the referee," Pop
would recall. "He was excited when he replaced Biff Hoffman at
fullback. He said, 'Fleischhacker for Hoffman and let Fleischhacker pass.'

"The pass Herb threw was devised for an occasion. Vincenti
came around behind his line. The Trojans barely were blocked
as they thundered through to tackle Herb. He hardly could see
Vincenti but knew about where he should be. Herb had to waft the
ball over the Trojan heads. That's how it got that falling leaf
effect."

Then there was the one day cure for George Bogue, a moun-
tainous halfback of the late 1920s who could run like a deer and hit
you like a fullback but seldom felt like it. Large George was lazy.
Pop finally lost his temper and halted practice.

"Bogue," he drawled, "you're like the handle on a pitcher.
You're always around it but never in it."

Bogue got in it immediately thereafter. He got so mad that Pop
had to call off scrimmage before he ruined the rest of the squad.

Pop's lawyer mind helped him out of one predicament. In the
early winter of 1932 with the searing breath of Southern California's unhappy old Stanford grads scorching his neck, Pop decided to move to Temple University in Philadelphia.

Temple provided a challenge Pop couldn't resist. The man who
had built football at Carlisle, Pittsburgh and Stanford evidently
was expected to get new Temple U. on the schedules of Harvard,
Yale, Princeton, et al. That never developed and is somewhat beside the point.

Two of his sports writing friends hit his living room at the same
hour one evening. Each was playing a hunch that the hour of decision had arrived. It had.

Old Pop had considered everything and he announced he was
quitting Stanford to take the Temple offer. Both men argued that
he was foolish and begged him to stay. They lauded the freshman
team that later was to become the famed Vow Boys. Pop was determined. No alumni group was going to tell him how to run his
football team.

Came then the question, which newspaperman was to get the
scoop. One was an afternoon writer, the other a morning paper
man with his presses poised to run. Pop pondered this while the
newsmen sat uncomfortably but hopefully.

"You," he said to the morning paper man, "can't you write a story saying that you know that I am leaving? Make it your own story but with no verification from me. Go as strong as you like.

"Then I'll write out a resignation for the afternoon paper feller. He can have an engraving made for his first edition tomorrow morning and he'll have his scoop, too."

That worked fine. The other morning paper went sound asleep, disbelieving the opinionated piece by the rival writer. So did the afternoon opposition. The Examiner and the News both had clean scoops on the same story, probably one of the few double morning-afternoon exclusives of record.

Small wonder that I loved the Old Fox?

"Warner had more color than any man I've ever met in football," says Don Liebendorfer, publicity man for the Indians since 1923. "He'd be invited to an exclusive fishing place in the mountains by one of his rich friends.

"Pop would spend days repairing old fishing rods. They probably lasted him fifteen minutes against tough trout. He'd spend hours in his workshop patching old tires. But let an old gridder of his show up broke and he'd dig down for a hundred or a thousand and never ask for a note or interest."

That workshop under the elevated garage at his first Palo Alto home was something to see. There the Old Fox worked on his inventions as well as salvaging broken javelins, concocting new golf clubs, painting pictures and generally relieving his restlessness.

One day, according to Liebendorfer, big "Horse" Reynolds, the giant tackle who played three complete games in the Rose Bowl without relief, showed up. He was accompanied by a buddy named Newman who played football, too, but stood only about five feet six. Liebendorfer trundled them off to see Pop. Warner, incidentally, never bothered to proselyte for himself. The alumni sent them, his reputation attracted them or he went with what showed up.

Pop was in his workshop when the trio entered. Liebendorfer found Pop fitting a head to one of his rare golf clubs. "Here are a couple of boys who want to meet you," he said.

First over the threshold was the peewee Newman. Warner looked up from his chair with some disinterest if not disgust. Behind came the red-haired Horse, about six feet six and 250 pounds of man. Pop's celerity getting up undoubtedly surprised his aching hip. The Old Man liked the big guys—as what football coach doesn't?—particularly big men who can move.

Yet Pop went away and left Reynolds, Bobby Grayson, "Bones" Hamilton, "Monk" Moscrip, et al., because "nobody is going to tell me how to coach my football team."

Warner liked to recall the first time he ever took the Carlisle Indians off their reservation and into a hotel in a big city. One of the Indians—I believe it was a fellow named Mount Pleasant— was enthralled by his first ride in an elevator. He said to the elevator man as he got out:

"Mr. Warner, he will pay my fare."

Unlike the present day coaches with their high power methods, Warner never drew up a plan for the afternoon practice. Undoubtedly he had one in mind or just let one develop. Pop worked the boys hard and scrimmaged often. The broken noses the guards inflicted upon one another pulling out the wrong way still are legend. His players all declared they loved the gruelling going, the long hours under Warner.

Pop probably got that way during his undergraduate days at Cornell.

"I always looked forward to playing a game on Saturday," he growled. "That was the easiest day of the week."

The "Old Fox" concealed his sentimental side to all but a few. Occasionally he would be overcome by sentiment and then he'd growl. Persons who sat with him on the occasion of his eightieth birthday some three years ago and watched him read hundreds of telegrams, letters and postcards from all over the world say he didn't growl that day.

ROUTE TO THE ROSE BOWL

By Leo Fischer

From The Chicago American, November 21, 1954

Columbus, O.—

THIS FOOTBALL-CRAZY town is whooping it up tonight to celebrate a pulse-stirring 21-7 victory over Michigan that gave its beloved Ohio State team the Big Ten title, the national collegiate championship, and unbeaten 9-0 record and the trip to the Rose Bowl.

They're singing the praises of the Battling Buckeyes, who came up off the floor to beat their ancient rivals from Ann Arbor. They're giving the supreme accolade to Coach Woody Hayes, whom a year ago these same fans were trying to get fired after a fairly unsuccessful year.

Somewhere, however, in all this singing and whooping and hollering, they'd better reserve a verse and chapter for a kid named Jack Gibbs, a 22-year-old third-stringer who turned the game around about the time the Buckeyes were back on their heels and Michigan was ready to put over a KO blow.

It was Gibbs, a senior whose playing time in his previous seasons probably didn't total five minutes, who intercepted a pass with the Wolverines leading 7-0 and driving for another touchdown, ran it back 45 yards and put his team in position to tie the count and then go on to win.

A tie game was all Ohio needed to take the Big Ten title and clinch the Rose Bowl trip. A decisive victory was needed to hit the rest of the jackpot, and credit for that goes to a young All-American named Howard Cassady who has never had to worry whether folks knew he was on the squad.

Cassady's 52-yard run from scrimmage was the payoff play. It came early in the third quarter after a great Ohio goal line stand had stopped Michigan only a ball's length from a touchdown.

Hoppy's long dash rubbed out more than half the yardage on what ultimately turned out to be a 99½-yard march and set the stage for Dave Leggett's second and winning touchdown pass.

Leggett, too, deserves a little of the cheers and glory they're tossing around with such great abandon here tonight. His direction of the Ohio team was magnificent, particularly since he was forced to operate most of the way with what in effect was a three-man backfield.

Bobby Watkins, Cassady's partner in the great Buckeye offensive, was hurt shortly after Michigan scored midway in the first period. Jerry Harkrader, who took his place, carried the ball just four times.

That left it up to Leggett, Cassady and fullback Hubert Bobo, who did so well they made 188 of the 196 yards Ohio gained from rushing.

When the game finally came to its thrilling end before a crowd here of 82,428 and millions more over the national television network, all bedlam broke loose.

The players rushed over and hoisted hefty coach Hayes on their shoulders and carried him nearly around the field before they headed for their locker room.

The crowd swarmed out of the seats for a mass assault on their own steel-pipe goal posts, which they finally succeeded in ripping out as the Ohio band tooted encouragement for them and marching music for the hundreds of others who joined in a massive snake dance.

From the stands also came what looked like tons of shredded newspapers and programs, swirled into the air in a manner reminiscent of the blizzard four years ago when another Michigan team won its game and kept Ohio from the Rose Bowl.

Then, as an added touch of drama, the sun came out—its first appearance after a morning of heavy rain and a full game played under gloomy skies and a raw chill breeze.

Michigan, a 13-point underdog, was magnificent in defeat—but just couldn't match the poise and personnel of its championship foe.

The Wolverines, thanks to their first-half domination, had the edge in all the statistics except the final score, and the satisfaction of knowing that they gave the Buckeyes and their hopeful rooters a worrisome afternoon until the final clinching Ohio touchdown with just 44 seconds to play.

Commented losing Coach Bennie Osterbaan:

"We played as well as at any time this year. Ohio was a worthy representative of the Big Ten. I wish them well."

Hayes added:

"In that first half we were out-smarted, out-fought and out-played. In the second half, it was the reverse. The luck came our way. Whenever you go through a season undefeated you have to be lucky. We're looking forward to spending the holidays in Pasadena."

Actually, Ohio doesn't get the Rose Bowl bid until the Big Ten votes tomorrow, but its designation as the conference representative is just a formality.

Michigan wound up with 15 first downs to Ohio's 13, after holding an 11-3 edge at half-time. The Wolverines also made 303 yards from scrimmage to Ohio's 254, but at the end of those first two quarters Ohio had gained only 42 to 190 for its keyed-up foe.

The Wolverines showed the big crowd early that they meant business. They took the opening kickoff on their own 33 and didn't yield the ball until 12 plays and about six and one-half minutes later, when Dan Cline scored from their seven at the tag end of a triple pass strangely reminiscent of "Old 83" which Fielding Yost used for so many years.

Throughout the rest of the first period Michigan was in command, taking the ball back on a pass interception after Ohio's only chance to handle the pigskin.

The second period started with the Wolverines just as impressive. In one stretch they received a punt on their own 14, then went 74 yards to Ohio's 14 in a dozen plays, with Fred Baer carrying most of the load, in addition to a pair of passes by Lou Baldacci to Ron Kramer and one by Cline to Baldacci.

There the drive stalled, mainly because of an offside penalty. Kramer's attempted field goal missed, but Ohio couldn't get anywhere after taking the ball out to the 20.

The crowd groaned when Johnny Borton got off a weak punt which went only to midfield, and even more when Ohio was penalized five for delay of the game.

Then came the break. Jim Maddock, who had replaced Baldacci, tried a pass to his right. Gibbs, playing only because Bobo had been hurt and Don Vicic, the No. 2 fullback, was ill, grabbed the ball and away he went.

When he was finally caught from behind on Michigan's 10 after a 45-yard return, it was apparent that Ohio's drooping spirits had suddenly been revived. A 5-yard penalty for offside moved the ball back to the 15, but on the next play Leggett hit sophomore end Fred Griss, son of an Ohio hero of a generation ago, with a touchdown pass.

Thad Weed, playing his last collegiate game, tied the score at 7-7 with the first of his three conversions which gave him a record of 24 out of 25 for this season.

Michigan was far from beaten, thanks to a 27-yard run by Baer shortly after the third period began. The Wolves moved to Ohio's 23, but lost the ball on a fumble. Then Kramer rushed in to block one of Bobo's punts and Michigan recovered on Ohio's 14 to set the stage for the great Buckeye stand.

Using straight line plays, Michigan finally achieved first down on the four, Dave Hill hit the line for a yard, Cline was stopped for no gain, Hill picked up another yard and finally, when the pile was untangled on a fourth-down smash, Hill was still not over a foot from the line.

Leggett had run the ball out to the 10 when the third period ended, and made it a first down on the 11 to open the final quarter. That's where Cassady did his stuff. Contained more or less by Michigan's great offense up to then, he finally broke loose for those all-important 52 yards.

Ed Hickey finally caught him on Michigan's 37 and tackled him outside the field, drawing boos from the crowd. Cassady was unhurt, although Leggett and Bobo took over from there. Between them they carried the ball seven times for 29 yards. Then Leggett pitched one to Dick Brubaker in the end zone for what proved to be the winning point.

Nearly 11 minutes of the final period remained but it was apparent to all concerned that only a miracle would prevent an Ohio victory.

The Buckeyes did give the ball back once to Michigan on a fumble near midfield, but recovered it soon thereafter when Cassady intercepted a pass on his own 39.

From there, with Bobo's 28-yard run as the big noise, the Buckeyes drove to their final tally. Leggett's 9-yard pass to Harkrader let him get into the picture and put the ball on the 1, from where Cassady took it over.

That left just 44 seconds between Ohio and its most cherished victory, during which the crowd built up its enthusiasm for the big blowoff as soon as the final gun sounded to indicate that the Buckeyes had won everything in sight.

FOOTBALL—ARMY STYLE

By Til Ferdenzi

From The New York Journal-American, October 21, 1954

FOOTBALL—ARMY STYLE—is for men only. Strictly for young men. You have got to love the game on a dedicated level to play it here.

To ferret out what makes the sport tick so effectively on the Plains, I spent the last 24 hours shadowing Cadet Robert G. Farris, captain of the Army team. In addition to discovering muscles fortyish reporters forget they have, I found football players at West Point get up early, go to bed early and during the hours in between never have to worry about an idle mind being the devil's workshop.

There are no special privileges granted for being on the Army varsity. No faculty favors. No padded academic courses. No big-man-on-campus routine for services rendered in the touchdown department. Everybody registered here in the Cadet Corps is taking a military engineering course. It drips with such brain heaters as calculus, physics, chemistry and electricity. There are no credits for horsemanship, pathfinding and star gazing.

The Cadets you see Saturday afternoons going about their business in gold helmets and black shirts do things at West Point exactly like every one of the 2,294 future generals quartered on the reservation.

You truly need a scorecard to identify these football players. At reveille—in the damp gray of 5:50 a.m.—Farris, Pete Vann, Tommy Bell, Pat Uebel, they all look alike. Sleepy. Just the way everybody looks who has been routed out of a warm bed at the crack of dawn.

"No one really enjoys getting up in the morning," Farris said, "but how else can you start the day?"

It is this philosophical approach that softens the annoyance of meeting a rigid time schedule which starts at 5:50 and ends with taps at 10:15.

With the exception of an hour's study break in the morning, and another in the afternoon, the football Cadet is on the move. In the

words of Second Classman Farris, "We are either going somewhere, coming from somewhere or getting there."

"Going somewhere" with Farris means plenty—especially if
you're not used to getting there in a hurry. After reveille at 5:50
and assembly at 6:00, there's a half hour for shaving, cleaning up
the room and making the bed before it's time for breakfast.

The academic schedule Farris and I followed today ran from
7:55 through 3:15, including appropriate study breaks in the
morning and afternoon.

For a reporter who found it hard to forget he had been up since
dawn's early light, it was a lulling and confusing day at school.

The classroom session started with a solid helping of "mechanics
of solids." This portion of the discussion period probed such
mysteries as statics and trusses.

Next came a session in electricity, touching on sine waves,
powers and RM's current. Farris and Howie Glock, a 206-pound
tackle from Pittsburgh, contributed their share of the classroom
recitation conducted by Major Joseph Waterman.

A seminar on social sciences topped off the academic day.

Getting ready to play is as much a double time operation as getting to class on time. Trainer Rollie Bevan says there is no other
football team in the country held to such a time schedule as these
Cadets.

"We have five trainers who have to get over 100 football players of assorted grades ready for practice," Bevan said. "That
means taping, bandaging and the other things that have to be done
before a boy is ready to scrimmage. All we are allowed for this are
45 minutes."

Football practice runs from 4:00 to 5:30. Supper is 6:20. Call
to quarters to study is 7:15.

"When taps are sounded," Farris said, "we usually are ready
for bed."

OWLS OVER ALABAMA

By Bill Rives

From The Dallas Morning News, January 2, 1954

RICE'S DICKY MOEGLE, a pink-cheeked teen-ager equipped with jet propulsion and a one-track mind, rolled back the Crimson Tide Friday with one of the great exhibitions of football history.

He scored three touchdowns, on runs of 79, 95 and 34 yards and gained a total of 265 yards as the Rice Owls swamped Alabama, 28 to 6, in the Cotton Bowl.

The 19-year-old stop-twist-and-go artist, who made his first letter this season and who was left off the All-Southwest Conference team, had more to contend with than eleven opponents.

On his second touchdown run, one of the weirdest events in Bowl history occurred when Alabama's "twelfth man," Fullback Tommy Lewis, leaped off the bench as Moegle was roaring past it along the 45-yard line, and downed him with a fierce block.

At the time, Moegle was steaming along with only one man having a chance—and that a doubtful one—of stopping him.

Lewis, under a sudden compulsion which he could not deny, came off the bench like a rocket and cut down Moegle with a perfect block. Then the Alabaman, who is alternate captain of the Tide, retreated quickly to the spot he had vacated and sat there with his head down in acute embarrassment as Coach Red Drew stood before him and looked at the crushed youngster in disbelief of what he had seen.

Referee Cliff Shaw ruled that Moegle should be credited with a touchdown. The play had started on the Owl 5-yard line and thus was good for 95 yards.

Moegle, who is a junior and who certainly must have established himself as a unanimous preseason All-American in 1954, delighted a jammed bowl of 75,504 fans as he produced his record-wrecking bowl performance.

Statistics of individual Cotton Bowl stars have not been compiled but it makes no difference. No back ever achieved more in the bowl's history and, probably, no back ever will.

There simply was no stopping Moegle, who broke the game

wide open after Alabama had taken a 6-to-0 lead in the first period on a lightning-like, 49-yard drive which brought the score in only six plays and one penalty.

On the first play of the second period, Moegle broke over right guard for 79 yards and a touchdown. Six minutes later, he made the 95-yard dash which was halted halfway by Lewis' illegal block, the oddest play in a bowl game since Roy Riegels of California made his memorable wrong-way run in the 1929 Rose Bowl game.

In the third quarter, Moegle sizzled through right tackle and went 34 yards to score.

In the final period, he almost did it again as he raced 20 yards down the right side line. Center Ralph Carrigan caught the Flying Kid from Taylor by a heel to prevent him scoring again.

Substitute Quarterback Buddy Grantham put the frosting on the cake Moegle had baked by scoring the final Rice touchdown in the fourth quarter when he bolted through a big hole at right tackle for 7 yards.

Moegle, who still found time during his whirlwind afternoon to sit on the bench for about eighteen minutes, compiled a fantastic average 21.4 yards on his eleven carries.

Naturally, he was voted the outstanding back of the game; in fact, he was the only nominee. End Dan Hart was the outstanding lineman, winning by the slim margin of three votes over his Rice teammate, Tackle Dick Chapman.

Once Moegle revved up his motor and made up his mind to tour the other end of the field, the contest became onesided. The Owls gained a total of 448 yards to Alabama's 225.

Moegle was the difference in the game. Except for his unbridled running, the affair might have been close.

Rice was hampered by the early loss of its All-America fullback, Kosse Johnson, who went out in the first period when his ailing ankle was sprained again.

The Owls preserved their perfect bowl record. This was their fourth straight victory. No other major college now has such a bowl history. For proud 'Bama, bowlingest team in the nation, it was their worst defeat in twelve post-season contests.

The game, played in near-perfect weather, began mildly enough, with the teams exchanging punts.

The scoring action began when Quarteback Bart Starr, a great defensive player as well as a shrewd offensive performer, stole a Rice pass to put the ball in Alabama's possession on the Owl 49.

Lewis, later to become the goat of the Tide's defeat, surged through the middle of the Rice line for 15 yards. On a keeper play, Starr got 12 through left tackle. Lewis got 13 more in two tries to put the ball on the 5. Rice was offside on the next play, the one in which Johnson was hurt and removed from the game.

With the ball on the 1, Lewis managed to get the ball to within inches of the goal line and then leaped high for the touchdown. The Rice line rolled him back but he had crossed the line with his forward motion. The extra-point try of Halfback Bobby Luna was blocked and Alabama led, 6 to 0.

The crowd was stunned by this sudden explosion, but Moegle remedied the situation for the partisan fans.

Just before the second period started, Starr kicked to the Owls on their 18 and Fullback Gordon Kellogg pushed the ball to the 21.

The teams traded territory for the second period and on the opening play, Moegle hit right guard. Just past the line of scrimmage, he cut to his right, faked a tackler silly, did the same thing again on a brief swerve to his left and then cut back into the clear, racing down the right sideline as Halfback Bill Oliver made a futile chase.

Quarterback Leroy Fenstemaker kicked the first of three successful extra-point tries. Sammy Burk, halfback, kicked the last one.

Midway through the period, Moegle cranked up his machine again. Alabama, principally on the strength of a 54-yard run by Oliver, was threatening seriously. Oliver's shot through left guard put the ball on the 22 and two plays later, from the 20, Starr started to pass, changed his mind, ran to his right and got to the 10 before he fumbled. Mac Taylor, Rice halfback, recovered the ball.

The Owls drew a penalty, back to their 5, for illegal motion. Behind great blocking, Moegle bulleted around right end and aimed for the goal line. As he swept by the 'Bama bench, out of nowhere came the Tide's twelfth man, Lewis, to throw that from-the-bench block.

Moegle was cut down and knocked out temporarily. Lewis was permitted to stay in the game—such a violation of the playing rules has no automatic disqualification penalty—and some of the crowd booed.

In the third period, Moegle capped a 67-yard assault by breaking through right tackle, faking three tackles out of position, and going 34 yards without being slowed up until he was a step from the goal line. There, he managed to fall across for his third and last touchdown.

Substitutes made the final Rice score, which came on a 75-yard drive. Three passes from Grantham to a junior end, Lamoine Holland, did most of the damage. Grantham scored on a 7-yard keeper play through right tackle.

In the second period, Rice moved to the Alabama 18 but had a pass intercepted, and to the 21, where the Tide held for downs. Alabama's only serious threat aside from the touchdown was stymied when Starr fumbled on the ten.

Boxing

BOBO AND THE KID

By Jesse Abramson

From The New York Herald Tribune, April 3, 1954

Chicago—

HAWAIIAN-BORN Bobo Olson, of San Francisco, retained the world middleweight title in his first defense of it by decisively outpointing Cuba's Kid Gavilan, the welterweight champion, in fifteen rounds before a near-capacity crowd in the Stadium and a national TV audience of millions tonight.

In a furiously fought battle between two clever, able, shockproof titleholders, the bigger man beat the smaller man to make a ring axiom stand up.

There was not a knockdown in it, never a truly perilous moment for either despite repeated all-out exchanges. Olson came out unmarked and fresher, looking the winner he was, while Gavilan suffered a small cut on the right cheekbone late in the ninth round, complaining to the referee as he went to his corner that he had been butted.

The action was clean, hard, interesting all the way, with no conspicuous turning point. The twenty-five-year-old but balding Bobo beat the ambitious, cocksure, high-talking Kid every which way, by outflurrying the champion flurrier, hitting him shorter, sharper, cleaner punches and blocking many of Gavilan's wilder swings and most particularly, blocking completely the heralded bolo which the Cuban unleashed three times, twice in his desperate try to salvage a losing fight in the closing round.

Olson, a rising 12-to-5 favorite at post time, won rightly enough to everyone's satisfaction with a masterful, solid performance that entrenched this perfectly-trained, well-grounded ring mechanic as the rightful holder of the title he won, in succession to retired Sugar Ray Robinson, by whipping England's Randy Turpin in New York last October.

Nevertheless, one judge Ed Hintz managed, by a mathematical

158

reak, to come up with a draw vote under the ridiculous N. B. A.
ystem of computation whereby the winner of each round gets ten
oints with nine or less to the loser, ten each for an even round.
Distributing 288 points on his ballot, the figure-juggling Hintz
ad 144 for each. The round-by-round scoring as such didn't count
ut Hintz had it 6-4-5 for Olson.

But the two other officials saw it correctly. Referee Bernard
Weissman scored it 147 points to 141, and Judge William O'Con-
ell scored it 147 to 139, both for Olson. All three officials found
t difficult to split the two warriors apart in many of their heated
ounds. In rounds, O'Connell had it 7-3-5 for Olson, while Weissman had it 6-3-6 for Olson.

Most of these rounds the officials call even, I scored for Olson
y a shade because he poured in the more accurate fire, forced the
ace, controlled the tactical duel between two keen ring wits, made
Gavilan back up ever so little from the torrid barrages. The Herald
Tribune scorecard had it eleven rounds to four, giving Gavilan
only the second, third and fourth and the twelfth.

Olson weighed 159½, exactly what his levelheaded horse trader
of a manager, Sid Flaherty, said he would weigh. Gavilan came in
surprisingly heavy at 155 pounds, his highest poundage for an important fight, eight pounds over the limit in the class he now goes
back to rule.

Gavilan had said all along he would weigh 153, and there was a
rumor, as accurate as all other rumors before this fight, that
Gavilan was secretly training down to 150½ for speed. At 155,
Gavilan was no whit stronger than he ever was, not, anyway, that
it showed against a rugged foe like Bobo. And he may have sacri-
ficed some speed.

In his dressing room Gavilan, who always has his own score in
his mind, so he says, didn't reveal what it was this time.

"I thought I won," the frustrated Kid said, but not with any
great conviction and with no complaint.

He praised Olson.

"My toughest fight," said the twenty-eight-year-old Cuban. "He
has more class than Robinson. Robinson run, run, run all the time.
I fight him one handed."

Gavilan, indeed, fought the fight of the left-hooker and jabber,
his best weapons any time, using the right in flurries but almost
never as his big power punch. He did not say his right hand was
sore, another pre-fight rumor.

Gavilan, who said Olson was made to order for him, learned

differently and learned his lesson the hard way. Gavilan is n
longer among those who underestimated the ability of this ligh
hitting but point-collecting boxer-puncher.

The phlegmatic, sallow-complexioned, almost sad-looking Olso
took this fight in stride, just another episode in his business caree
Like any business man long away from home, Olson, having di
played his wares, sold his goods, took the first plane after midnigh
out of here, and was due back with his wife and four children i
San Francisco at eight in the morning, in time for a breakfas
celebration with the family. Bobo is a homing pigeon.

In his dressing room, the unmarked Bobo said he wants to figh
anyone, say, Joey Giardello, with whom he can draw the mos
money. His purse for this one was more than $120,000, his firs
hundred grand, as he took down 35 per cent.

The gate receipts, $334,730, paid by 18,582, were augmented b
$100,000 in TV revenue. Lumping the revenue together, gate an
TV, the total $434,730 exceeded the sum of $422,918 drawn b
Tony Zale and Rocky Graziano here seven years ago for an indoo
record below the heavyweight class.

Gavilan, who succeeded Robinson as welterweight champior
could not emulate Sugar Ray's feat of dethroning a middleweigh
champion. Of six welterweight champions who have now tried thi
trick, Sugar Ray, who knocked out Jake LaMotta here three year
ago, was the only one who succeeded.

Gavilan, who had lost only one previous bout in the last thre
and a half years, met his master because he did not have the punch
ing power to damage Bobo, met a man who could meet his flurrie
and get in the last clean blow and the better one in most of the ex
changes, met a man who could react and think as fast as the Ki
and often a shade faster. Nothing bothered Bobo.

Gavilan did his best scoring with his explosive left hooks, bu
in the two-handed firing Bobo was superior. The main differenc
between them, besides the weight in Bobo's favor, was that Gavi
lan in his flurries is a wide swinger with many of his punche
blocked by Olson's elbows and arms while Olson hit inside Gavi
lan's swings, hit as fast in the clutch and hit more on the target
head or body. It was Olson's thirteenth straight victory sinc
Robinson narrowly beat him for the title two years ago.

One of the most curious incidents occurred as the principals en
tered the ring. Olson came into the ring through Gavilan's corne
wearing an orchid-colored lei around his neck. On an impulse, "be
cause it is done in Hawaii," he took off the lei and draped i

round the Kid's neck. Trainer Mundita Medina seemed about to
throw it off wrathfully, but the Kid accepted it gracefully, went
into a rhumba step in his high white shoes by way of acknowledge-
ment.

Then Olson proceeded to lay about him with vigor and continuing steadiness. They felt each other out for most of the first
round, short with leads, but Olson got in the few clean rights,
blocked Gavvy's returns to win the round.

Then Gavilan took over for his only consistent surge. Jabbing
and circling, in a strategic retreat, he jabbed smartly, won the
long-range boxing and got off with his excellent hooks. He exploded these often in the third and fourth, kept the action at long
range and seemed to have found the winning formula.

Gavilan continued these tactics at the start of the fifth. But Olson, admittedly a slow starter, had now warmed to his task. Olson
met fire with fire in the increasingly hard exchanges, and beat
Gavilan with hooks and combinations. Locked in clinches, they
were both too smart to be hurt. It was when Olson moved into
short punching range that he was at his best with his short-armed,
accurate attack. Gavilan had no combinations to mach Olson's one-
twos to the head or body and head. He could not beat two hands
with one.

From the fifth all the way through the eleventh I kept scoring
the rounds for Olson. Mostly the edge was small but unmistakably
in Bobo's favor.

Many of Gavvy's swings and the bolos must have looked good
on TV, but at the ring's apron it could be seen how expertly Olson
blocked them, how quickly he retaliated with short punches on the
inside. But most of all he was the man in charge.

The ninth was perhaps the best round of action in the fight,
with sustained, smashing exchanges. The referee warned both
simultaneously for low blows. Gavilan suffered his cut. Olson said
it wasn't from a butt, but from a solid left hook. Gavilan backed
off from three of these changes, but Olson was always willing to
keep on slugging it out.

The tremendous exchanges went, and as they went on, it became
more and more evident that Olson, was winning and Gavilan could
not salvage the lost cause, even with his desperation slugging in
the last round.

Of the judge who scored it a draw, Manager Flaherty said,
"nice fellow."

BROCKTON'S BOY

By W. C. Heinz

From Cosmopolitan, June, 1954

ON SEPTEMBER 23, 1927, in Brockton, Massachusetts, Mr. Fred
Denly, of Eighteen Everett Street, succeeded in bringing to bloom
a two-headed dahlia. Twenty-five years later, to the very day, Mr
Rocco Marchegiano, of 168 Dover Street, same city, distinguished
himself in still another field. In Philadelphia, he hit Mr. Arnold
Cream, of 1020 Cooper Street, Camden, New Jersey, on the chin
and won the heavyweight championship of the world.

Whatever the implications of Mr. Denly's botanical accomplish
ment held for Brockton, they have been lost in the years. It is safe
to say, however, that as long as there is boxing and a Brockton
twenty miles due south of Boston, the impact of the punch with
which Rocky Marciano (*ne* Marchegiano) knocked out Jersey Joe
Walcott (*ne* Cream) will be felt.

In Brockton today, for example, there is a young man named
Nicholas Rando, who lives at 69 Bartlett Street—the street, in
cidentally, where Rocky delivered the Brockton *Enterprise-Time.*
as a boy—who will forever be lacking the first joint of two fingers
of his right hand. When Marciano, with his own right hand, flat
tened Walcott, the excitement that raged through Brockton'
Ward Two Memorial Club reached such a pitch that Rando, then
fourteen years old, fed his hand into a ventilating fan.

In the state of Virginia lives Mrs. Dorothy Brown Therrien
widowed nine days after the victory over Walcott. Her husband
fifty-four-year-old Frederick J. Therrien, manager of the Brockton
office, State Division of Employment Security, and former drum
major of Brockton Post Thirty-five, American Legion, had been
warned by doctors not to overexert himself. When it was an
nounced there would be a parade to welcome home the new cham
pion, however, he couldn't resist and dropped dead in front of the
Y.M.H.A. on Legion Parkway, Brockton, while marching as a
marshal's aide.

At St. Colman's imposing field-stone Roman Catholic Church

Wendell Avenue at Lyman Street, Brockton, the Very Reverend LeRoy V. Cooney, who married Marciano and Barbara May Cousins there on December 30, 1950, will not forget Marciano, either. Just before the second Marciano-Walcott fight, televised from Chicago on May fifteenth of last year, he was directing the uncrating of a thirty-inch television set, a gift to the church by the fighter and a friend, when he stumbled off the stage in the recreation hall and fractured his right leg.

Despite such occurrences, however, the effect on Brockton of Marciano's rise to the most coveted, most romanticized throne in the world of sport is hardly a tragic one. A manufacturing city of 62,862 residents, many of whom, or their progenitors, came from Italy, Ireland, Lithuania, Poland, Sweden, and French Canada to work in its shoeshops, Brockton has benefited by what has happened to Marciano in ways that can hardly be measured.

Last year Brockton exported 12,384,378 pairs of shoes as well as unrecorded tonnages of carpet tacks, storage batteries, sausages, and burial vaults. It is the unchallenged opinion of the manufacturers that no matter what the product, sales were helped immeasurably by the fame that has accrued to the city through the fistic prowess of the thirty-year-old son of Pierino Marchegiano, ex-shoe worker.

"Why, Rocky Marciano has done more to make this city famous than all the shoes ever made here," says Perley Flint, president of Field and Flint, shoe manufacturers. "Now they've heard of Brockton in places they don't even wear shoes."

"Anybody who travels out of Brockton and only carries one line," says J. W. Mahoney, assistant sales manager of the same firm, "also carries Rocky. In Chicago, at the National Shoe Fair last year, they expected anybody from Brockton to be able to predict not only Rocky's next opponent but who would win."

Brockton's delegates to the 1952 political conventions in Chicago found themselves faced with the same questions and so did the thirty-seven Boy Scouts from the Brockton area who attended the National Jamboree, near Santa Ana, California, last July. And the Brockton *Enterprise-Times* reported that Brocktonians visiting New York TV studios found themselves plucked for audience-participation shows as soon as they revealed their home town.

"I've talked to customers on the West Coast," says George Stone, head of the Independent Nail and Packing Company, "and they say, 'Oh, yeah? That's Marciano's home town.' There's one machine-tool manufacturer in Milan, Italy, who exports to this country, and do you know what he wanted? An autographed photo of Rocky."

"In Birmingham, Alabama, last year," says Dick Stevens, a salesman for Field and Flint, "I wasn't having much luck getting into one of the stores. There were some hard feelings, so I just dropped in and didn't talk business at all. We just talked Rocky. I never said a word about shoes, but now the orders are coming in."

As a matter of fact, the Brockton boy is also an instrument of shoe research. Each year the Doyle Shoe Company presents Marciano with ten pairs of black, vici kid road shoes, size 10½-EE. Even when he isn't in training for a fight, the champion does daily road work, and recently he returned one pair that, worn through on both soles, had carried him seven hundred miles.

Marciano's ring shoes, size 10-E, are made, two pairs for each fight, by the Howard and Foster Shoe Company, of black, yellow-back kangaroo uppers applied to a lightweight sole manufactured by the Potvin Shoe Company, also of Brockton. They are probably the lightest boxing shoes ever made.

Last year Charles R. Armey, vice-president of Howard and Foster, decided to put a lightweight street shoe on the market. The first lot went to a fashionable men's store on South Michigan Avenue in Chicago. Some time later the factory received a letter from the retailer stating that the first pair had been bought by Ezzard Charles, former heavyweight champion of the world, who is now challenging Marciano.

"It's a small world," says Armey, "but the important thing is that our employees feel as though they're helping Rocky in the ring. Just last week the women in the stitching room came out and asked if they could sign their names in Rocky's shoes. We decided they could sign one pair."

The economic influence of Marciano on Brockton industry is confused, of course, by many other factors governing business profit and loss. A clearer index is afforded by the effect of his success—forty-five wins, forty knockouts, and no losses—on the finances of various individuals.

"A lot of working people in this town are a lot better off because of Marciano," says one Brocktonian. "There are families that have suddenly moved into brand-new homes. The man is a factory worker, and everybody knows what he makes. They say, 'Where does he get the money to buy a house like that?' It's obvious. He's been betting on Rocky.

"And there are guys who have pyramided their cars. They

started out with old rattletraps when Rocky started fighting in Providence in 1948. They borrowed what they could on the cars. They won and bought better cars and borrowed again. Today they're driving high-priced automobiles that are paid for."

Before Marciano fought Rex Layne in Madison Square Garden on July 12, 1951, one old Italian woman pulled out of a kitchen coffee tin $500 she had saved in her lifetime without her husband's knowledge. Through a relative, she placed it with a local book-maker, and when Marciano knocked out Layne in the sixth round, she got back her $500 plus another $1,000.

"When Rocky was getting ready to fight Louis," says Ed Lalli, a Brockton auto dealer, "a guy I never saw before comes in here. He says he wants to sell his car to bet on Rocky. I say to him, 'Look, friend, don't do it. We all think Rocky is gonna win, but suppose something goes wrong? Be smart. Go to a finance company and borrow $200 on your car, and if anything happens to Rocky, you still got your car and twelve months to pay off the loan.'

"So he did it, and after the fight he comes back. You know what he says? He says, 'You make me lose a lot of money. Look at all the money I could have today if I don't listen to you.' "

It was two weeks before the Louis fight, the most important in Marciano's career up to that point and the second Marciano fight to be televised, that the avalanche struck Brockton's twenty-seven television dealers and twelve TV-service firms. By the day of the fight, it was impossible to buy a new receiver in Brockton or to get immediate repair service.

"People who never had trouble with their sets before," says Joe Nesti, of Corola, Inc., "wanted us to go and check them. They wanted us to guarantee they wouldn't have trouble during the fight. Who can guarantee a thing like that?"

A Marciano fight also exerts a marked influence on Brockton's social life. On such an occasion, it is *de rigeur* on the well-to-do West Side for Brockton's matrons to hold cocktail and supper parties in the stately white Colonials and imposing field-stone mansions where live the city's industrial magnates and more successful doctors and lawyers. Elsewhere in town, bars are crowded and so are Brockton's fifteen fraternal and social clubs that own television receivers.

In factories that employ night shifts, power is shut down between nine forty-five and eleven P. M. and employes gather before TV screens. Brockton's three motion-picture theatres are almost empty. On the evening of May fifteenth of last year, for example, when

Marciano fought Walcott the return bout that was televised from the Chicago Stadium, the Center Theater, with a 1,034-seat capacity, had sixteen adults and ten children in the house. At the other two theatres, the Brockton and the Colonial, business was equally bad.

"When Rocky fights on TV," says Bob Riordan, city editor of Brockton's *Enterprise-Times,* "the streets are deserted. You can look the length of Main Street and not see a soul. Then between rounds, you see a couple of people hurrying across the street. They're changing bars, looking for better reception or a better look at the screen. The moment the fight ends, everything busts right open."

Cars, their occupants and their horns sounding, tour Brockton streets, some until two A. M. Most of these finally descend upon Ward Two, where Marciano was born and grew up and where the Ward Two Memorial Club, of which Marciano is a charter member, is the nerve center of the celebration. The club, which started nineteen years ago in a garage on Winthrop Street, now owns, a hundred yards from Marciano's parental home, a single-story, brown-shingled clubhouse on which a $4,000 mortgage has been lifted, thanks to Marciano's fighting ability.

When Marciano's fights are neither telecast nor broadcast, crowds gather before the red-brick front of the Brockton *Enterprise-Times* at Sixty Main Street, where two loud-speakers are hung from window sills of the third-floor editorial rooms. For the first Walcott fight, anxious residents began collecting an hour and a half before fight time, and when the first succinct announcement was made—even round-end blow-by-blow reconstructions of the fight were banned by the International Boxing Club—there were ten thousand waiting before the windows.

"The first round was a bad one for Rocky," came the announcement, edited from the copy received by direct wire from ringside in Philadelphia. "He was down."

Considering that this was the first time Marciano had ever been knocked off his feet in a ring, it can be imagined with what trepidation the almost silent crowd received at three-minute intervals, the cryptic comments, which varied from that extreme to the occasional opinion that Marciano seemed to be doing a little better but still had a hard fight on his hands. Suddenly, at eleven thirty-four P. M., there came the word.

"The new heavyweight champion of the world," said the voice of staff man Ken Wheeler, "is Rocky Marciano!"

That started it. Four Marines were arrested for street fighting. Three additional police cruiser cars were dispatched to Ward Two, where young Rando was to lose part of his right hand and a man named Francis C. Reed, of Fifty-five Indian Head Street, Hanson, was to lose his wallet and $260.

At Police Headquarters, the members of the night shift assigned to house duty sat back satisfied. They had managed to pick up, on the short-wave radio, a blow-by-blow description from a Canadian station. When it had started to come over in French, they had moved the radio back to the cell block where a Bridgewater prisoner of French extraction had provided them with a translation. The next day in court, the bilingual benefactor was fined five dollars for drunkenness.

Marciano has, naturally, complicated the ordinary routine of the Brockton Police Department. Following his knockout of Louis, the department, the Brockton *Enterprise-Times,* and Rocky's mother, Mrs. Pasqualina Marchegiano, all got post cards threatening Marciano's life. The cards were traced to two teen-agers.

On the night of the first Walcott fight, all police leaves were canceled and twenty men were assigned posts on the block on Main Street from Green Street to Legion Parkway, which includes the newspaper's offices. When Marciano returned home after that fight to be paraded before a crowd of fifty thousand, all leaves were again canceled and sixty policemen were requisitioned from the near-by towns of Randolph, Abington, Whitman, Avon, Easton, and the three Bridgewaters. These, plus the hundred men on the Brockton force, were supplemented by a hundred civil-defense volunteers and six motorcycle men of the Massachusetts State Police.

Marciano, of course, could exert tremendous political influence on his city. So great was his appeal after he knocked out Louis on October 26, 1951, that he was exiled from his home town for three weeks during the close battle being waged for the mayoralty by the Republican incumbent, Melvin B. Clifford, and the present mayor, Democrat C. Gerald Lucey, who ultimately won by a margin of 343 votes out of 29,094.

"I was advised right after the Louis fight," says Marciano, "that if I wanted to stay clear of politics, I'd better wait until after the election before I went home. So Barbara and I went to all the shows on Broadway and lounged around for three weeks."

In 1952, during the Presidential campaign, Mayor Lucey discovered the heavyweight champion had more than local political significance. He received a request from Washington to arrange for Marciano to ride on the Adlai Stevenson campaign train between Providence and Boston. Although past heavyweight champions have received thousands of dollars for backing Presidential candidates, Rocky turned down the request in order to maintain outward political neutrality.

"Then last year," he says, "Paul Keith, who was running against Lucey, came to my house. He said, 'I just want to meet you because people ask me if I know Rocky Marciano and I want to tell the truth.' So we shook hands and talked a few minutes and then he left."

Brockton Republican leaders claim, of course, it was Mayor Lucey's many public appearances with Marciano that helped swing the last election for the Democrats. The latter, as naturally, assert it was the usual issues—streets, sewers, and schools.

Brockton has 272.36 miles of streets and roads, 123.78 miles of sewers, and twenty-seven schools. Where Marciano, as a manual laborer for the Brockton Gas Company and the Brockton Department of Public Works, once made a pick-and-shovel imprint on the first two, he now exerts another influence on the latter.

Before Marciano's first fight with Walcott, the pupils of the first three grades of the Belmont Elementary School sent him a scroll they had signed. In Brockton High School, where Marciano played one year of varsity football before leaving school to work, the champion is a constant subject of class discussion and a constant inspiration to the athletic teams.

Every coach in the school, according to Charley Holden, athletic director, has used the example of Marciano's climb at some time before or during an important game. Between halves of the Brockton-Quincy football game in 1952, with Brockton trailing 14 to 0, Marciano himself strode into the dressing room. He spoke to the team about Brockton's fine football tradition, about its fine coach, Frank Saba, and about the responsibility that rested with the players. Brockton won, 19 to 14.

Of all Brocktonians, however, those who have been the most deeply affected by the Marciano ascension are, besides the man himself, the members of his family, his childhood friends, and others who, in one way or another, played a part in his life. One of these is Dr. Josephat Phaneuf, who is now sixty-six years old and head of the red-brick, ninety-four-bed Phaneuf Hospital, at 688 North Main Street. At one A. M., on September 1, 1923, however, he was still a young, hard-working general practitioner who was to go on to deliver, in all, 7,235 babies in and around Brockton.

"I remember a delivery at that time at Eighty Brook Street," he says. "I recall it was fairly difficult because of the size of the baby."

The previous year Pasqualina Marchegiano had lost, in birth, a thirteen-pound boy. When Rocco, the first of six living children—three sons and three daughters—arrived, he weighed twelve and a half pounds.

"I say to the doctor," says Mrs. Marchegiano, "I ask him, 'How much this cost?' He say, 'Forty dollar.' I say, 'Well, Doctor, I give you cash.' He say, 'Well, thirty-five dollar.' "

"Strangely," Dr. Phaneuf says, "I have never seen him fight. A great many of my patients talk about him, though, and when they do I say, 'I was the first one ever to hit him.' "

In Brockton now, Red Gormley is a letter carrier. Less than ten years ago, however, he, like Marciano, was a good amateur baseball player, and they shared their dreams of making the big leagues together, Gormley as a shortstop and Marciano as a catcher. In the spring of 1947, they reported together in an old car to the Fayetteville, North Carolina, farm club of the Chicago Cubs.

"In April," Gormley says, "they released us. We went to Goldsboro, and they didn't want us, either. Our arms were gone. We couldn't throw. We were broke, and I guess we looked like a couple of bums, so we decided to come home."

Gormley's territory is in Ward Two. Standing in front of 168 Dover Street, his mail sack over his shoulder, he looks across at the five-and-a-half-acre James Edgar Playground, where he and Marciano, day after day, year after year, played ball.

"We were driving back in the old car," he says. "Finally Rocky said, 'The heck with it. I'm through with baseball. I'm gonna get some fights, and you're gonna handle me.' There I was, sitting right next to half the money in the world, and I didn't even know it."

He hitches his sack higher on his shoulder and starts up the steps to 168. It is the two-family, green-shingled house where Marciano lived from the time he was eleven years old until last year and where the Marchegianos still live. To this address, it has now become part of Gormley's job to deliver some of the mail that comes to the heavyweight champion from all over the world.

"So what's the sense of talking about it?" he says, turning back. "I've got a wife and three kids now."

The bulk of Marciano's mail is a burden on the backs of Norman

Fenn and Bill Riley, who deliver it to the cottage at Fifty-four Woodland Avenue, where live Mr. and Mrs. Arthur Bellao. Bellao, a short, intense, brown-eyed young man who sells cars for a living, is an old friend of the Marchegianos and owns a typewriter. When the mail began to submerge 168 Dover Street, he volunteered to answer it.

"It picks up just before and after a fight," he says. "When Rocky became champ, there were a hundred letters a day, some of them from Saudi Arabia and the British West Indies, asking for autographs or pictures or pieces of equipment to be used for raffles. My wife and I were working from six A. M. until eight-thirty A. M., and then from eight P. M. until one-thirty A. M. to handle it."

It is in the five immaculate rooms on the first floor of 168 Dover Street, of course, that Rocky's impact is strongest. For more than thirty years, Pierino Marchegiano, born sixty years ago in Abruzzi, Italy, and gassed and wounded fighting with the Second Marines on the Marne and in the Argonne, left at seven every workday morning with his lunch box under his arm to work as a No. 7 bed-laster in the shoe factories. The machine he ran forms toes and heels of shoes, and shoe workers say it takes more out of a man than any other machine in the shop. Two years ago he retired.

"Now I go back," he says, "and I see my old friends and everybody says, 'What a difference, Pete. Years ago you couldn't talk with the super, and now he take you around the shop.'"

Pasqualina Marchegiano, now fifty-two, was born near Benevento, Italy. She, too, worked in the shoeshops before the children came—Rocco, now thirty years old; Alice, twenty-eight; Connie, twenty-six; Elizabeth, twenty-two; Louis, twenty; and Peter, thirteen.

"I lose my first baby," she says. "The doctor say, 'You gonna have no more baby.' I cry. After a while I say, 'If God want me to have baby, I have baby, and if God give me children, I gonna do the best I can.'

"All I want is I keep my house clean, I keep my children clean, I make my supper. Always at breakfast I tell my children, 'Now try your best in the school.' I tell them the same like when they go to church.

"Now it's just sit in my heart. It's hard to say the beautiful thing that happen with Rocky. You feel happy, and you feel like crying when you think."

Pierino and Pasqualina do not move as freely in Brockton now as they once did. They are quiet people, and unexpected attention embarrasses them.

"I don't go downtown," Pierino says. "Too much talk."

"I don't go but one day a week," says his wife. "Last week I went to post office and there is a big line and I wait and a man I don't know says to me, 'How is our boy?' I say, 'Fine.' He say, 'You know, we're very proud of him down at the Cape.' Then he introduce his wife and his sister. Who is this man?

"I walk on the street and a woman come up to me. She say, 'God bless you, Mrs. Marchegiano. My son and my son-in-law they make a fortune on your boy. I tell no one, but I tell you because I want to thank you.' Who is this woman?

"I go in a store. In the store the man say, 'If you need credit, Mrs. Marchegiano, you get credit. Your son make me a lot of money for us.' I go to Rocky's house and I see there a letter from someone who wants his picture. I bring it home and I look at the letter and I say that God been so good to my son to give this beautiful luck, why can't I give to people who like my son? So I send these poor people the picture. Sometimes I cry."

In Goddard Junior High School, where the Marchegianos' youngest child, Peter, is a pupil, he, too, finds he is different. On the day of the second Walcott fight, John Zoino, the science teacher, announced a test.

"Then he asked me," says Peter, "if I thought I could take it. I said, 'I'm afraid I can't today.' Then he let me take it the next day."

When it was revealed in the Brockton *Enterprise-Times* last year that Marciano and his wife had bought a new home at Forty-six Harlan Drive, a neighbor counted five hundred cars that stopped there on the following weekend so the occupants could examine from the outside the as yet unfurnished, $35,000, nine-room, brick-field-stone-and-clapboard ranch house. Marciano, most of whose time is spent in training camps, on personal-appearance tours, or relaxing with his wife and their eighteen-month-old daughter, Mary Anne, at Grossinger's in the Catskill Mountains of New York State, has been home only a total of two months since he won the title, and then he found little privacy.

"When Rocky got home from that tour of the Pacific last December," says Al Colombo, his closest friend since childhood and the man who has helped train Marciano for all his fights, "he got into town late and nobody knew he was here. I went around to his house the next morning to walk with him before breakfast. While we were walking he said, 'You know, it was great to come back to my own home and to wake up and find my wife and the baby there and to have nobody else around.' We walked about five or six miles, and when we got back, there they were—five cars in front of the house."

Vic Dubois, Brockton *Enterprise-Times* sports editor, has appealed to his readers to allow Marciano some privacy. The champion and his wife, however, are reconciled to the inevitable attention focused on the heavyweight champion of the world. What disturbs them more is the change that has come over their old Brockton friends.

"They don't drop in like they used to," Marciano says. "When they do come around, they act different. They even talk different. I know what's bothering them. They think they're bothering me, and they're not and I can't convince them."

"It's the same with my old girlfriends," his wife says. "When I'm home alone it's fine, but the minute they come in and see Rocky, something comes over them. It's a shame."

As Brockton generally, however, basks in reflected glory, there is but one dark cloud on the horizon. That is the possibility of a Marciano defeat. Neither Brocktonians nor boxing experts envision that in the near future, but the hope is everywhere in Brockton that when their hero starts to slip, he will retire before succumbing to an opponent.

"God help this town if he ever gets licked," says one taxi driver. "There's one old Italian couple here I pick up before every fight and take up to a loan office. The last time they borrowed $3,000 on their house. Can you imagine what it will be like if he ever gets beat?"

MISTER BILLY

By Walter Stewart

From The Memphis Commercial-Appeal, November 12, 1954

Mr. Billy Haack, whose gallant heart ran out of momentum last Wednesday evening, was a sharply-hewn symbol—the symbol of knuckle-shaken nights and blood-lusts sharper than those we know today.

Mister Billy was a master of description in war-painted tones, and as he talked you could smell the stale sweat and the drift of powdered rosin and the knife-edged stench of horse liniment. You could hear the fierce shouts prowling squalid rafters like so many black leopards and the "splat" of wet gloves against wet faces and the whisper of leather on canvas. You would feel the spray of squeezed sponges and the violence of air stirred by towels flopping like the wings of frightened white herons.

For Mister Billy was a genius of pugilistic promotion in a time of roughneck purity. We don't mean that some feuds weren't fixed as neatly as antique china, for they were. But civilization hadn't gotten around to shaping hoodlums who own fight stables and control their properties with all the sentiment of a mechanical chess player moving pieces about the board.

And fighters weren't cynical young men crusading merely for cash and making up their pans for television. The big difference, most likely, was that the fighters of Mister Billy's era could fight, and did fight.

It was the difference between a plunge into some mountain stream and a bubble-bath scented with gardenia—the difference between an Alaskan sunset and the neon lights of Broadway.

An uncomfortably long time ago, our father took us to the Phoenix Athletic Club, where Pal Moore was going to punish a sparring partner. We had never seen a man pull on padded gloves, but instinctively realized that this was a place in which legalized mayhem was quite logical.

The modern fist-fight blunders to the surface in a hall which also frames dog shows, rodeos, ice spectacles, dance competitions, symphonies, agricultural demonstrations and stirring conflicts between

173

lumps of feminine nudity labeled "Miss Air Conditioning Week" or "Miss North Horsecollar, Neb., of 1954." In such surroundings, pugilism seems out of place as hip-boots at a formal wedding.

But you couldn't mistake the Phoenix for anything but a shrine of the unsymmetrical ear. The seats funneled down through the dimness to a ring spangled darkly with used blood. It smelled of mice and dust, and it was the most fascinating place we'd ever been in. Our mouth hung at halfmast while Moore, a spiteful imp in long gray drawers, jerked about the ring in the manner of a man seized by epilepsy—beat the face of his employe into a red mush.

And the Phoenix was part of Mister Billy as his right arm was a part of him. He built it and he breathed savage life into it until the gaunt hall wasn't just a place, but a personality. And it reached maturity in an age we like to think about—in a courtlier age of dressed deer and turkey swinging from the hooks of Front Street —of two-wheeled carts clattering cotton bales over the cobblestones—of steamers blowing for a landing. And no one had even heard about the atomic bomb.

The Phoenix was impregnated with a scrupulous honesty which would have been more than welcome in any bank you cared to name. For Abe Lincoln had no more probity than did Mr. Billy, a gentleman who had a short way with citizens of shabby morals.

If he convinced himself that a main event was a bag number, he'd heave both men through the ropes—put their purses on ice and announce that all admission fees would be refunded. And life was most unpleasant for dough-hearted characters intent upon taking a dive rather than soak up more punishment. For Mister Billy would sometimes string out the count so that the wretch would be saved by the bell.

And if the fellow wanted to make an issue of it, Mister Billy would take him into one of the dressing rooms, peel back his sleeves and issue a ringing challenge. Yet it is not recorded that he lost many decisions.

Mister Billy ran the show himself and was ever willing to accept the responsibility head-on. He was promoter, matchmaker and referee. And he was brilliant in every respect.

Concerning the making of matches, this requires genius of purest type. Two warriors with unflawed records and vast repute can bring fumigation crews into the arena because their styles don't match. And a pair of battered bums may be sensational simply because their offensives blend like Scotch and soda. Mister Billy just knew how to mix them.

In a way, Mister Billy lived so long he saw the epic violence he had loved so passionately degenerate into a nauseating mess which flips the stomach's lid.

But Mister Billy didn't leave emptiness behind him—not as long as men have memories which can fill space with a little man owning eyes like rapier points and pure laughter which rolled all the way up from his toes.

Hail, Mister Billy, and farewell.

HURRICANE ROCKY

By Jerry Nason

From The Boston Daily Globe, September 18, 1954

HURRICANE ROCKY hit here tonight.

The big breeze from Brockton, 48 hours and 30 minutes over-due, toppled Ezzard Charles like a towering jack pine in the forest . . . trunk rigid, limbs askew.

The crushing Marciano blow swept in upon challenger Charles at 11:34 o'clock, or at 2m 26s in the eighth of 15 scheduled rounds for the heavyweight championship.

Ten seconds later, or at 2m 36s of the round, Charles was counted O-U-T by the referee for the occasion, Al Berl.

Gusty Rocky, after two postponements since Wednesday, was still blowing them down as champion of the world.

The gust which devastated Charles, shaking him to the very tap roots and plummeting him violently to the canvas, was officially described as a one-two to the jaw, very lethal.

Actually it was merely the crowning blow of storms of Marciano punches which had buffeted the dusky challenger for two minutes and weakened him inexorably for the finish.

He fought bravely against the hurricane, did Ezzard. But he couldn't outlast the ferocity of it. When he finally yielded referee Berl could almost have shouted "tim-berrrr," because that's the way the challenger fell to the floor . . . like a stricken tree.

Those who witnessed it, an estimated 35,000 of them, agreed that Hurricane Edna of recent vintage was, after all, and by comparison, merely a zephyr.

September is the month for hurricanes, and Rocky was one again tonight—as he was at Philadelphia two years ago when that sturdy old oak, Joe Walcott, finally crashed under the velocity of Marciano's punch.

Tonight's fight was no carbon copy of their 15-round scorcher in June when neither man hit the floor. Tonight Charles tottered and fell three times—for a two count from a left-right combination to the head in the second round, for a three count under a long,

176

smashing right hand to the jaw at the top of the eighth, then for the full count after he arose and desperately attempted to withstand the swarming champion.

Ezzard actually swayed to his feet just as Berl's right arm dropped with the count of "10," but he was buckling at the knees and was glad in his heart that the storm was over for him.

There was no evidence that a hurricane had struck him beyond the rubbery knees and the weary arms that dangled at his side, for Charles, brutally punished to the head and body, showed no outward marks of the damage he suffered.

But Marciano, throw-back to the jungle fighters, was a vermillion landscape. The bulbous fleshy part of his nose had been split as if with a pen knife from a slashing left uppercut in the sixth round, and Charles' first winging punch in the eighth had ripped open that old wound just under the left eyebrow.

It was that punch, outlining Rocky's eye socket with a line of crimson, like an important date on the kitchen calendar, which seemed to bring the hurricane into a crescendo of fury.

There was Rocky, his nose spurting for two rounds like a punctured hydrant, and now his old eye wound agape and imperiling his championship.

He came storming into Charles like a berserk gale from the West Indies.

The punches started whistling past and into Charles' head. A short left hook, viciously thrown, bounded off his cheek bone. A right glove smashed him in the ribs. A bristling left grazed his jaw, a near miss.

And it was while he was in the act of escaping from this fistic fer de lance that Rocky unleashed a dynamic long right hand that spattered off the challenger's jaw and dropped him on his haunches.

The din in the ball park overwhelmed the cool, damp night.

But Charles had not come apart with that punch. He dragged himself upright at the count of three to face, once more, the fury of the gale.

And now the wind really whistled in the tree tops. Marciano, his face a flame of red, his torso pinkly adrip, exploded in a gust of punches. He drove them at the bending, swaying Charles as fast as you could count them. No, faster.

His head tossing from side to side, like the crest of a great pine in distress, his eyes glazed and his legs slowly giving away, Charles finally went down, under a chopping sort of right punch.

He went gently, at first, as do the great evergreens in the mighty storms . . . then crashed the canvas, his back poker stiff and his legs and arms asprawl.

And that's the way he was for, perhaps, four or five seconds when the voice of his conscience called to him and he attempted to rise again to face the storm.

He was all a tremble when he got upright again, a split too late on the stop watch, and this was good, because he was helpless to withstand more this night.

For me, the result was inevitably forecast half-way through the second round.

There, after Ezzard the challenger had won a wide first round, Marciano suddenly exploded a murderous right hook under Ezzard's heart.

From that punch on Charles was a beaten man. He started slowly coming apart. He was hurting inside from that moment forward. On my card, he didn't win another round—although the fifth and sixth were very close.

It was a roughhouse. There was a lot of grappling and tugging in close quarters. The bloodied champion claimed it was an elbow, not an uppercut which sliced the flesh of his nose. . . .

And a butt which broke open the old scar over his eye.

Three times in this fight, Marciano kept taking his swings after the bell had sounded—in the second, fifth and seventh.

On the second instance Charles, obviously irritated, countered with a smart punch to the champion's face.

In the sixth Berl, a busy little bee, warned Rocky to keep his punches up—for that was the round when the champion, who'd gone head hunting from the third round on, suddenly switched back to punching to the body.

The financial end of the affair made a late rally to hit estimated attendance and gross receipts of 34,330 and $350,000.

But the gustiest thing in the town tonight was Marciano.

He is a notorious slow starter. He has never been a round 1 man. He wasn't tonight, either. He was merely circling around, gathering momentum in the first three-minute session. Charles tied him up in a tangle of long, dark arms. Charles crisply snapped lefts and rights at his face and at the bell lodged a semiviolent right hook in Rocky's face.

It was a big round for Ezz, but the storm was just starting to brew.

Rocky started to churn once he barrelled in under the challenger's guard with that terrible right to the heart almost instantly in the second round. A moment later Charles was down under a right.

He chopped and clobbered Ezz in the third, bulling inside and throwing his short-range blows. They look like little from a distance, but they crack and smash and bruise.

Rocky moved his punches up to the head in the fourth, won the round big, and followed the same pattern in the fifth, although Charles seemed to have revived both physically and spiritually.

It was that way well into the sixth, when suddenly Marciano came stumbling out of a melee with his nose spurting from Charles' flashing uppercut.

That's the way it moved toward the end—the twin knockdowns in the eighth round—Marciano's grimacing face and hairy chest crimson with his own gore.

Then the tempest roared to its crest, and Ezzard Charles went down at last after facing the fists of boxing's most brutal puncher for 23 rounds.

Golf

DIZZY DEAN OF THE LINKS

By David Eisenberg

From The New York Journal-American, April 15, 1954

THE MASTERS was history and the veteran reporters, their stories finished, were relaxing at the bar of the Bon Air Hotel in Augusta, Ga. Like the closely-knit group they are, the writers from all sections—Chicago, Dayton, Pittsburgh, Cleveland and New York—had gravitated toward each other.

Sports was the general subject of their conversation, with the emphasis on the Masters golf in which Sam Snead beat Ben Hogan only six hours before. But the two great veterans were barely mentioned. It was Billy Joe Patton, the 31-year-old amateur, who had captivated the sports writers just as he had the crowd. Billy Joe had more fun and was more relaxed, than anyone else in the tournament.

"Wouldn't it be something if he were in baseball," said John Carmichael, the Chicago columnist. "What copy he'd make."

That he would, magnificent copy as the most colorful athlete since Dizzy Dean. This is a Dizzy Dean with a college-trained accent. What made Patton the sensation of the Masters, more than the fact that he was the first amateur to lead this event to the half-way point, was the genius with which he phrased the right words at exactly the right time.

You could fill a column just listing what he said, starting with his prediction of an 80 after he and Dutch Harrison had tied with 70s at the end of the first day.

His have been classic quotes. When he still led at the end of the second round, he said:

"You won't believe me but my friends back home are sore about me playing here because they take me every weekend. My being here is costing them money they would be winning from me."

There was the Saturday round when he was lining up a shot to the 10th green. Just as he was about to swing, a galleryite called out:

"Play it safe, Billy Joe, play it safe."

Billy Joe stopped, turned to the galleryite, and said:

"You didn't pay $5 (the Saturday ticket price) to see me play it safe."

When Billy Joe quit the Wednesday driving contest after his first shot won it with 338 yards, he later explained why he didn't take the other two shots allowed him:

"I'd never hit a ball that far in my life before. I knew I couldn't come even close. Why try?"

Several years ago, Patton was in the North and South finals with Hobart Manly, the long-hitting Georgia amateur. A question of the rules came up on the eighth hole, in which Patton got the wrong information. Thinking he had the hole won, he putted safely. A later ruling resulted in the hole being halved. When the two players stepped to the next tee, Patton said:

"I didn't come here to win with the rule book." Then pointing to the nearby soft drink stand, he added to Manly: "You buy the drinks and we'll call it square."

Patton had always been a wild golfer who took a terrific cut at the ball. Study the pictures of the finish of his swing, and it looks just like a baseball player's.

When he returned from service he determined to become a steady golfer. He tried to control his swing. Now let's listen to Billy Joe:

"I tried hitting easy. I got nothing but 82s and 84s. So I went back to the full cut and got the fun of shooting a 68 one day and an 82 the next."

If you think he is kidding about that, just look at the golf he played in the Open at Pittsburgh last year. He shot an 84 in the first qualifying round at the Pittsburgh Field Club. But a 71 at Oakmont the next day kept him in competition. Then he shot an 80 as the regular part of the U. S. Open began. But a 73 on the second day made him the last man to qualify for continuing in the final 36 holes.

"I got in with my last shot and became the only amateur in all golf who played the final 36 holes of both the 1952 and the 1953 U. S. Open championships," said Billy Joe.

When this reporter suddenly heard a terrific uproar from the gallery surrounding the sixth green, an uproar which came just as Hogan was preparing to tee off on the fourth hole Sunday, he knew instinctively that Billy Joe had scored a hole-in-one. Things happen when Patton is around.

When he flounced to the seven on the 13th hole which kept him from becoming the first amateur winner in the history of the Masters, Patton was the only person who could still smile. Jimmy Demaret, playing with him, kept murmuring:

"If he'd only played for the middle of the green."

Patton had the answer to that one, just as he had the answer to everything that happened in what was for him and all golf, a historic four days. He said:

"I don't feel bad about the six on the 15th. I don't feel bad about the seven on the 13th. I don't want all you folks to feel bad about it. I want to explain it.

"I made up my mind I was going to go for that pin 72 times if I got the chance. And that's how I played it. That bold play brought me a lot of birdies. And it brought me the six, and the seven."

But the quote Patton prompted which possibly was his greatest tribute, came from Hogan. Patton made the man who only last year was called the greatest golfer of all time worry about him. After Hogan shot the six on the 11th hole which dropped him to a tie with Snead, he said:

"I was thinking of Patton. I had to go for the pin because I didn't know that he had gotten a seven on the 13th."

When a weekend golfer makes a Hogan worry about him he has achieved a very great measure of fame.

WINNING THE OPEN CHANGED MY LIFE

By Ed Furgol and Will Grimsley

From The Saturday Evening Post, September 4, 1954

I LOOKED across the table, and there was Helen bawling as if she had been slapped across the face. I was dumbfounded. I didn't know what to make of it. We were on the winter golf tour in 1946—a pretty lean tour for us, I might add. We were having lunch at the City Park Club course, in New Orleans.

"Hey, honey," I asked, "what gives?"

"What's the matter with us?" my wife sobbed. "Nobody wants to sit with us."

I glanced around us. At all the other tables I noticed gay little groups of players and club members having a wonderful time. Here we were, sitting alone, and I could see Helen was hurt.

"Honey," I said, trying to console her, "you've got to get used to this. Old Ed's not doing so good this year."

I could tell she didn't understand. She is a friendly girl who always had and always liked friends. We finished our meal in silence and I went out to play golf. I never saw Helen cry like that again, althought the situation was repeated countless times during the next seven years, in which I never won a championship.

I couldn't help remembering this recently when I was in New York after winning the National Open golf championship at Baltusrol, in New Jersey. Our telephone jangled every few minutes. We were showered with invitations—lunch at Shor's, dinner at the Waldorf, a theater. It was wonderful.

A few weeks ago I was just a broken-down old golf pro with a crooked left arm. Most people wouldn't give me the time of day. Today I'm on top of the world and riding a merry-go-round. I'm in demand for television appearances and golf exhibitions—take your pick—at $1000 a throw. Everybody's my pal.

Until I won at Baltusrol, I never had a "monkey suit" in my life. Now I've got two. I've got a white dinner jacket and a midnight-blue one. I've had to go on the banquet circuit and do my first public speaking. And, of course, I'm getting plenty of advice on how I should spend my money and keep Uncle Sam from taking

183

too big a bite. This irritates me. If I'm able to get into the $80,000 bracket, Uncle Sam can have his cut and no gripes from me.

They say the National Open championship can be worth $100,-000 the first year to the winner, if he's smart. Of course, Lloyd Mangrum, who won it in 1946, calls such talk so much malarkey. Lloyd says the Open is highly overrated and not any different from any other tournament. He says the pros would rather win the Tam O'Shanter because of the big purse—$50,000 cash this year, with $50,000 more guaranteed in exhibitions. Personally, I think Mangrum is all wet on this point. The Open is the "big one." Certainly it's the one I wanted more than any other. And it turned my world upside down.

It hasn't been an immediate bonanza. The cash prize was $6000. The company I represent—Dunlop Rubber Company, whose golf balls I use—matched this with another $6000. I guess television and exhibitions raised the early total to nearly $20,000.

In the past I have given exhibitions for as little as $100. My price now as Open champion is $500 on weekdays, $1000 on weekends. Other things are on the fire, including a world tour this fall with Peter Thomson, of Australia, the new British Open champion, and Bobby Locke. I intend to get it while I can. Next year I may be a broken-down old pro again.

But it's not the money which has brought me the greatest satisfaction. It's the feeling that I'm no longer a nobody. I belong. It may sound silly, but this has been gnawing away at my insides ever since I was a kid. It has been a driving force behind me.

People seem amazed that with a withered left arm like mine, an arm ten inches shorter than my right, I could win the toughest of all golf championships. I feel that I didn't win despite my handicap, but because of it—just as Ben Hogan came back from that automobile accident in 1949 to win his greatest championships, and Babe Zaharias came back from a cancer operation more than a year ago.

This driving force in my own life dates back to the time when I was a wild kid of eleven and busted my left elbow in a fool stunt on some playground bars. The arm never was set properly. I always felt that because I was a poor immigrant's son I never got the attention I needed.

I became embittered. The bitterness wasn't eased when all the boys started calling me "Crooked Arm" and made fun of my efforts to take part in sports like anybody else. I had to fight my way out of many situations. Later came those years of repeated failures on the golf circuit. By this time I was hardened to my handicap and thought nothing of it when the old pros nicknamed me "Wingy." The thing I couldn't get hardened to was my growing feeling of insignificance.

I was never more depressed than just before the Open at Baltusrol. Helen had to stay back home to keep the pro shop for me at the Westwood Golf Club outside St. Louis. It was the first time in nine straight Opens that she had not been with me.

There was a St. Louis newspaperman aboard my plane coming east, but he was going to cover the Rocky Marciano-Ezzard Charles heavyweight fight. St. Louis papers didn't think enough of me to send a man out for the golf tournament.

Riding in a cab from the Newark airport to my hotel in Elizabeth I suddenly got a feeling of emptiness. It didn't seem to make any difference whether I was here or not. I mention this because I think all these things played a part in my winning the Open.

At the hotel I found that the company, Dunlop, had provided an automobile for Bobby Locke, who is also on its payroll, to make the trip to and from the course. I was given to understand I could ride along with Bobby when convenient. This wasn't often. I'm an early riser, while Locke likes to lounge around until noon. Besides, we had different starting times. So I rode a cab to the course. It cost six bucks each time.

The leading golfers are teamed with players of proportionate rank. I was bracketed with two outsiders, MacGregor Hunter, of Pacific Palisades, California, and Bill Ogden, of Chicago. We had an undesirable starting time for the first round, 2:08 p.m.

Top players also get the best caddies. I was very much let down when I found that the caddie assigned me wasn't a regular caddie at the course. Not only did he know nothing about the course, he had very little knowledge of golf. At no time during the entire three days and seventy-two holes of golf did I ask him for one bit of advice. On two or three occasions I pleaded with him to keep my iron clubs clean—he would leave the grooves and face of the clubs dirty.

I paid him fifty dollars for the week, and then I gave him what must have been one of the biggest tips a caddie ever got. I wrote him a check for $1000. I understood he was married and had a number of children.

I think the first inkling I had that this might be my year came in the Colonial Invitation at Fort Worth over the Memorial Day weekend. This was a rather long, difficult golf course, and I played well there. Although my putting was spotty, I finished only four strokes out of first place. Johnny Palmer won it, but I definitely was encouraged.

I figured that if I was to win the Open I would have to have complete self-control for the full seventy-two holes. I knew I would have to have greater self-control than Ben Hogan, whom I regarded as the man to beat. However, once the tournament started, I never thought of Hogan during the entire three days. Somebody asked me afterward if I played Hogan. "No, I played myself," I replied. I knew I had no control at all over what Hogan did. I could only control myself.

Hogan is a man of limited physical ability. Yet he had the determination and intestinal fortitude to drive himself to the point where he mastered self-control and the mechanics of the golf swing. It's his amazing self-control which has made him the champion he is. He is really a defensive player. He never extends himself to the point of gambling.

Sam Snead, on the other hand, physically is the greatest golf machine we have ever had. But emotional control is lacking. Snead says Open championships are lost, not won. In his case, that's true. Snead is negative. He has never been able to shake off the memory of Philadelphia in 1939, when he lost an Open by taking an eight on the final hole. But in actuality, Opens definitely are won.

Cary Middlecoff is the jittery, fidgety type who would be greater if he had more self-discipline. He probably has picked up in more tournaments than any other top-liner. Locke has wonderful poise. Mangrum is one of the most aggressive and confident players on the circuit, but he has allowed himself to play Hogan instead of playing his own game.

If I was going to finish ahead of Hogan, I knew my determination would have to be as great as his, if not greater. Tactically, I decided to use what has become known as Hogan strategy. I knew Baltusrol was a long, rugged course. One slip could be costly. I decided I would be neither spectacular nor bold. I would play the course. I would shoot for the greens and not the pins.

Just before the start of the tournament, I became gripped by the strangest sort of feeling. I was convinced that destiny was with me. For years I had dreamed of winning the Open—I had told Helen many times back in our leaner years that someday I would do it. Somehow, I knew that my time had come.

I wasn't at all dissatisfied when I shot a seventy-one, one over par, for the opening round. That placed me in a tie with Hogan and Al Mengert, two strokes back of amateur Billy Joe Patton, who led with sixty-nine. Gene Littler, Bob Toski and Ted Kroll were in between with seventy. Nobody paid me any attention then or the next day, either, when I shot an even seventy to tie Hogan for second place at 141. Littler, who cut a shot off par, was the halfway leader at 139.

I went back to my hotel and called Helen at St. Louis. I told her I thought I was playing very well and had a good chance to win it. Of course, she didn't dare hope. "Good luck, Ed," she said as we signed off, "and keep your head." It was her favorite expression.

Then the strangest thing happened. I am disinclined to mention it because it sounds so fantastic. But it's the truth. This was the Friday night before the final thirty-six holes. I went to sleep and woke up, in what seemed to be the middle of the night, with the sudden realization I was about to be Open champion. Say it was a dream. I don't know what it was. I only know that my whole body shook with the emotion of it, and I began to cry.

I can't remember when I shed tears before. But I cried this time —it seemed I cried the rest of the night. The weirdest part was that this experience, instead of leaving me tired and weak, gave me added strength. I felt stronger than ever before for the final thirty-six holes.

But I did not relax. I couldn't relax. For example, on Friday night my younger brother, Ted, had called me from Utica, New York, and said he was coming over to see me win the Open. I knew he would have to drive all night and then run into parking problems and fight a big crowd. But I didn't discourage him. We hadn't seen each other in a long time and we had always been very close. When he showed up Saturday morning, though, I just shook hands with him. I didn't say a word to him during the last two rounds of play. I felt that any distraction might have thrown the whole thing out of gear. It wasn't until afterward that I could sit down and talk to my brother.

Everybody knows me as a congenial, talkative type of fellow, even on the golf course. This was one time when I'd just shoot and get out of the way. I rarely said a word to my caddie or my partners, so wrapped up was I in my concentration.

People began noticing me for the first time, I think, after I shot a seventy-one in the morning round Saturday to take the three-quarters-point lead with 212, a stroke better than young Dick Mayer. Littler fell off in the morning and so did Hogan, who, along with Snead, was five strokes back. I knew I was the leader because the press questioned me for the first time. I didn't ask about anybody else. I didn't want to know.

I continued to play safe and shoot for the greens. On the last round, I hit sixteen of eighteen greens. My only comment during the final round was one made to my caddie after I had three-putted the seventh and eighth holes. I didn't feel I was losing control. My confidence wasn't shaken.

There's been a lot of talk about the final hole, where I hooked into the woods and played a side-door shot from an adjoining fairway. This is what actually happened.

I was going great, I thought, until I came to that final hole and found that there was a log jam at the tee. Doc Middlecoff and I had a fifteen-minute wait while watching the preceding twosome tee off. It relaxed me to the point of becoming too loose. So I missed my tee shot, which veered into the woods at the left. I had a sick feeling, but took heart when I went into the woods and saw that the ball was playable.

I saw an opening to the eighteenth fairway of Baltusrol's upper course which would give me a shot at the green. We were playing the lower course. Some reporters write that I asked a United States Golf Association official for permission to play onto the adjoining fairway. That's not true. I am familiar with white lines and stake boundaries. Seeing none, I knew the fairway was on club property. I simply surveyed the situation and made the safest shot.

My third shot to the green was crisp, and after I hit it the crowd let out a roar. When I walked to the green, though, I found the ball short. I still had a tough par five to make. I chipped to the glass-slick, downhill surface, and the ball skidded six feet past.

But I struck the ball into the hole for my five. I knew I was home. I was in the television booth with Craig Wood when Littler came to the final hole with a chance to win or tie. When he lined up an unsuccessful eight-foot putt which would have given him a tie with me at 284, I never lost faith. I knew this was the fulfillment of the dreams I'd had when I was a poor boy in upstate New York.

I was born March 22, 1917. My father and mother both were Polish immigrants who came to America in the late 1880's and settled in New York Mills, New York, a cotton-mill town just outside Utica. Furgol is my father's family name. There was no "-ski" on it and it wasn't Americanized. My mother's name was Catherine Prymas. They were two simple names for Poles.

We were a family of five children—two girls and three boys. Both my sisters were older than I and died before I was born. My older brother, Henry, is three years older than I am. He is a golf pro at the Utica Valley View Golf Club. He had much more natural ability and could have been the best golfer in the family if he had chosen to apply himself. Ted, the youngest, is a carpenter in Utica.

Our early life was a real struggle. My father and mother worked in a mill, operating two spinning machines sixty feet long. Their pay was small, just enough to keep the family going. My mother was heartbroken over the death of her little girls. For two years she would work ten or twelve hours in the mill, come home and fix supper for the family, then walk two and a half miles to the cemetery to visit my sisters' graves. My older brother and I caddied at the Utica Golf Club. At first, I did odd jobs around the course. I started at twenty-five cents an hour. I got fifty cents for caddying eighteen holes, and I was lucky to get one bag a day—there were so many youngsters around trying to bring something home to their families.

From 1930 on, things got tougher. My father was laid off at the mill. We had a small plot of ground, about half an acre, on which we raised vegetables for our food. I used to work on the farm plot with a hand hoe. Now, as I look back, I think how many times I visualized myself swinging a golf club instead of a hoe. Even then I loved golf.

I was a pretty reckless kid, no different from the rest. One day when I was eleven years old I went to the playground, and I noticed a fellow six or eight years older than I swinging on some crossbars. From a three-foot elevation, he would leap to the six- or seven-foot bars and swing by his arms like mad. "This is for me," I said.

Foolhardily, I tried it. It was a hot, sticky day and my hands were wet with perspiration. I made a big lunge, and slipped. I fell with a thud to the asphalt-and-cinder base below. I must have tried to cushion my fall with my elbow. The bone popped out like a boiled blister, and there was an ugly gash in the flesh. The pain was almost unbearable.

I grabbed my injured arm with my right hand and started walking toward home, about a mile away. I had on a sleeveless shirt. A man passing in a car saw my trouble and took me to the hospital.

There was one operation, then another. I had to lie flat on my back in a cast for five weeks with my arm extended in the air.

Every time I had X rays taken, they would make my arm bleed. I knew the doctor who took the X rays. I had caddied for him on the golf course. He seemed to have very little sympathy for me, and I resented it. I thought nobody was concerned about me because I was just a poor immigrant's son.

The doctor who set my arm went on a vacation. No specialist was called in. The nurses were wonderful, but I thought the doctors could have treated me a little better. Once, on an elevator, I heard a nurse upbraid a doctor for treating me so rough.

When the cast was removed, I could lower my arm from the shoulder but it was limp. They tried to bend it at the elbow. The pain was excruciating. They pumped me full of ether and gas to kill the pain.

I went home and was sick for about two years. My system was full of those anesthetics and I couldn't absorb them. Then three or four years later I began to mature. My system was weakened and I blew up like a balloon. My mother wanted to get a doctor. I refused. I just lay in bed and suffered it out. It was like ivy poisoning. My face was so swollen I couldn't see. I had a high fever. One day it finally broke. I got well. That particular winter I must have grown three inches. I was sixteen.

My left arm was still virtually useless. It was withered from the elbow to the shoulder, no bigger than a mashie shaft. I determined I wasn't going to be an invalid. I did everything possible to rebuild the strength of my left arm. I would carry sponge-rubber balls and coins in my hands at all times, so I could squeeze them. I began going to a gymnasium, where I punched a bag, skipped rope and worked with elastic pulls.

When the other kids called me "Crooked Arm," I vowed I'd show them. I took up boxing. I won two bouts as an amateur. I had a lot of power in my left shoulder. I couldn't jab much, but I had a mean hook. A friend of mine, Joe Tedesco, wanted me to turn pro. He applied for a New York State boxing license for me, but I was turned down because of my deformity.

Then I knew I had to make my place in golf. Nobody helped me with my game. Everything I did was on my own. My swing was awkward, like a one-armed swing, but down through the years my hand got stronger and my swing became more compact.

How do I manage with that crooked left arm? Well, my backswing is much shorter than the average player's, but I wind up my body a lot more. I have accurate body movements to co-ordinate with my hand speed. By coiling and uncoiling my body to synchronize with my hands in the hitting area, I can get good distance and accuracy.

Much of my power generates from my feet. I have to have all my heels built one inch higher on the outside to give better balance, because I shift my weight so much. I seem to stand closer to the ball than most golfers, and appear to be chopping at it because I come down so viciously with my right hand.

At the age of seventeen I had to quit high school and get a job as a metal polisher, but I kept on working at my golf. I was twenty-one years old when I played in my first tournament. It was the city amateur at Utica. I surprised everybody by beating the defending champion and gaining the semifinals. Only two guys had confidence in me. One was my older brother, the other was a fellow named Walter Paprock. It was Walter who beat me in the semifinals.

This tournament made me realize I could be a good golfer. So I intensified my work at the game. The next big tournament for me was the National Public Links at Cleveland in 1938. I led qualifying the first day at Cleveland, but lost in the opening round. I played in two more Public Links meets—at Baltimore in 1939, where I also lost out early, and at Detroit in 1940.

The last one I almost didn't make. That year, 1940, our association was unable to raise the money to send a team to the tournament. I was sitting on the porch at the Utica Golf Club on this particular day when a local businessman, Art McMann, came up and asked why I was brooding. I told him. "See if this will help you," he said, and handed me thirty dollars.

I had about fifteen dollars of my own, giving me forty-five dollars. I hitched a ride with a Catholic priest going to Detroit. I set a National Public Links qualifying record with a thirty-six-hole score of 138, sharing it with Worth Stimits, Jr. Then in the match-play eliminations I went to the semifinals.

I remained in Detroit to work in the transportation department of the Ford Motor Company. I got room and board at the River Bank Golf Club in Birmingham, Michigan. It was at this semi-public course that I first met Helen.

An elderly lady at the club, a friend of mine, said one day, "I'm going to bring over a very nice girl for you to play golf with—she's just your type."

She brought over Helen Bucsko, a pretty, green-eyed brunette of Hungarian descent. She lived in Royal Oak, Michigan. This was June, 1941. We hit it off together from the first, but she was from a well-to-do family—at least in comparison with mine—and I felt I wasn't in a position to give her the things she was accustomed to. So we didn't get married until October, 1945.

Meanwhile, I had become a pretty fair amateur golfer. I saved the money I got from the Ford plant and bought a car. All the time I was thinking about the rich prizes waiting on the pro circuit. Helen and I discussed this at great length before we were married. I told her I would never be happy until I took a fling at tournament golf. She was understanding and encouraging.

Nevertheless, after getting Helen's O.K., I decided to try the circuit as an amateur first, just to see if I could make the grade. This was 1944, and I played in four tournaments. I finished twelfth in the North and South Open at Pinehurst, North Carolina. I finished in the top ten at Charlotte and Durham, North Carolina, and at Knoxville, Tennessee.

This convinced me. After winning the 1944 amateur title in the All-America at Tam O'Shanter, and then beating Frank Stranahan for the North and South amateur championship in April, 1945, I turned pro in the Victory Tournament at Chicago in June. I collected my first purse—$225. Then I went to the St. Paul Open, where I finished fifth and collected $550.

This was too good to be true. With my pockets bulging, I left the tour and married Helen in October. Then we set out together as a team. At the end of the year an accounting showed I had won $8394.58 to rank as the eleventh leading money-winner—and I had been a pro for only half the campaign.

My elation at this early success was soon chilled by some hard facts of life. The pro tour is fickle. After the successful 1945 season, we hit the winter tour. Our full earnings on this tour amounted to $312.50.

The entire 1946 year was a bad one for us. All together, I won only about $5000. It takes a minimum of $8000 to make the full tour, and that's cutting it pretty fine. With Helen along, it took about $12,000 minimum for both of us to get by. When we went under that, it meant dipping into our hard-earned savings.

This was just after the war, and good equipment was scarce. I was playing with a set of clubs I had won as amateur prizes. I had to use reprocessed golf balls. It's been said that some of the top-notch players felt sorry for me and occasionally slipped me prewar balls. This would have been nice, but it wasn't so. When I played with prewar balls, you can bet I paid dearly for them.

For seven years after turning pro, I played in every tournament possible, sometimes two a week. According to a count somebody has made, there were 208 in all. I craved recognition. I drove myself unmercifully. I got down to 148 pounds. I was much too thin, and as a result my game lost its sharpness.

In those seven barnstorming years, I played more than 1000 rounds and averaged 71.4. That was the frustrating feature of it. I could score well, I could make money, but I couldn't win a tournament. I never qualified for the Ryder Cup team. When I had a chance in 1947—I won more than $14,000 that year and tied for first in the Bing Crosby tournament—I wasn't eligible, not having been in the PGA the necessary five years.

Those years on the tour weren't always pleasant. It was a dog-eat-dog competition, with constant travel and no regular home. Then, too, golfers are clannish, like anybody else, and they have their petty jealousies and differences. Incidentally, there never was a more considerate man on the circuit than Ben Hogan. He got the reputation of being cold and aloof. On the contrary, I have found him one of the most warmhearted and friendly of persons— not just to me, but to any struggling golfer.

The tour began to make its mark on Helen and myself. In 1950 we took stock of ourselves. I could feel the grind catching up with me. I began to realize I was slipping. I hated to admit it, even to myself, but my eagerness was gone and my scores weren't getting any better.

Helen and I talked it over again. I was winning $10,000 and up in purses each year. We were living well, and I was doing what I wanted to do. But when we took an inventory of our finances, we found we were just getting by. "Is this the life we want?" we asked ourselves. The answer this time was "No."

So when I got a chance to become permanent home professional at the Westwood Golf Club in Clayton, Missouri, just outside St. Louis, I was happy to take it. I was recommended for the job by a gentleman named Harry Tennenbaum, who introduced me to Sidney Salomon, an influential member of the club.

Salomon thought at first that my bad arm might disqualify me as a teaching pro, but changed his mind after playing with me a few times.

In January, 1952, he and the Westwood board hired me. Since then I have been giving 600 to 1000 lessons a year.

Under my contract, I was permitted to play in four tournaments a year—the two Tam O'Shanter events, the PGA and the Open. This year I got permission to play in an extra tournament. After

I won the Open, the club members gave me a big reception and a leave of absence for a year, so I could capitalize on the victory.

The Open was my first important victory. I don't think it's my last, even though I am now thirty-seven, and some good young hot-shots are coming on. Everybody is high on Gene Littler. He's young, has a fine golf game and terrific hands. But I don't think he's going to be an all-time great. Of the younger crop, I personally see a greater future for Frank (Bud) Holscher, of Santa Monica, California. He is as young as Littler, but he's had it tougher. He's hungrier. I also think Gardner Dickinson, Hogan's protege, and Bob Toski, a fine mechanical swinger, will win some Opens before they're through.

As for me, I sincerely believe I can go on to bigger things. If a man wants something long and hard enough, and if he puts every ounce of his ability and self-control behind that wish, he can attain it. I think my Open victory proves it.

Tennis

VICTOR'S FIRST

By Allison Danzig

From The New York Times, September 7, 1954

VICTOR SEIXAS and Doris Hart were rewarded yesterday for their years of striving to gain the pinnacle of American tennis. They were crowned as the new champions of the United States in the Forest Hills Stadium.

The 31-year-old Seixas, competing in the tournament for the fourteenth time and in his third final, stopped the onrush of Rex Hartwig, conqueror of the defending champion, Tony Trabert, and Kenneth Rosewall.

With the crowd of 11,000 giving whole-hearted support, the fast-moving, clean-cut Philadelphian rallied to win at 3-6, 6-2, 6-4, 6-4 as the favored 25-year-old Australian went into a decline after a brilliant opening assault.

Miss Hart, runner-up for the title five times without having won a set, stood on the precipice of a sixth failure before she achieved her first national singles title on grass. Three times only a point stood between her and defeat as she overcame Louise Brough of Beverly Hills, Calif., 6-8, 6-1, 8-6.

The victories of Miss Hart and Seixas both were much to the satisfaction of the gathering, after their years of effort in the championships. Each had won the British crown at Wimbledon and numerous other titles and international laurels, but their own championships meant far more to them.

The spectators sensed that this might be the last big opportunity for both, particularly for Miss Hart, with Maureen Connolly expected back in 1955. The little Californian was unable to defend the title she had won the past three years because of an injury she received while horseback riding.

Miss Hart's brother, Richard, sat in a box in the marquee to witness her long-awaited triumph. And there, too, Seixas' wife, father and mother watched. In her remarks after receiving the championship cup, Miss Hart mentioned that her brother had flown to New York six times from Chicago to see her in the final and expressed her satisfaction that his loyalty at last had been rewarded.

The Australian Ambassador to the United States, Sir Percy Spender, witnessed the finals. He was called on by Col. James H. Bishop, president of the United States Lawn Tennis Association, to address the crowd during the presentation of the men's cup. Sir Percy paid tribute to Seixas for his sportsmanship and the quality of his tennis and spoke of the high regard in which Vic is held in Australia.

In the final event of the day, the mixed doubles championship, Miss Hart and Seixas joined to win the mixed doubles championship. They defeated Mrs. Margaret Osborne du Pont of Wilmington, Del., and Rosewall, 4-6, 6-1, 6-1.

So Miss Hart and Seixas each made a sweep of the national grass court championships. Seixas had won the men's doubles with Trabert, and Miss Hart and Shirley Fry had taken the women's doubles for the fourth successive year.

Seixas' victory is a tribute to the Philadelphian's splendid match play qualities. He was not thought to have much chance of winning the tournament at the outset, when Trabert and Lewis Hoad were the prime favorites.

Seixas was indeed thought to be nearing the end of his years as a player of the top flight. His failure to win either of his matches in the Davis Cup challenge round last December was followed by defeats by Arthur Larsen in the French championship, by Budge Patty at Wimbledon, by Bernard Bartzen in the clay court championship and by Jack Frost at Newport.

Now, with his victories over Hartwig and Hamilton Richardson, who put out Hoad, Seixas is squarely in the Davis Cup singles picture again. Trabert, despite his disappointing showing against Hartwig, will be back in the thick of the fight for a berth, and Richardson has to be considered.

All of them are certain to be named on the team to go to Australia, should the United States defeat Mexico, and the two who are playing the best tennis at the time of the matches will get the call. That is all that any one can say with any assurance at this time.

Seixas' form in the championship was his best all season. He was at the peak of his game both physically and in his stroke production, and he deserves the fullest credit for his victory, even though Hartwig did not play the tennis he had flashed against Trabert and Rosewall.

The Philadelphian made the most of his equipment and he never lagged in carrying the attack to his opponent. His speed and quickness, the effectiveness of his service, his strong return of service and his stanch volleying all contributed to the victory. Too, he found a vulnerable point in his opponent's game and exploited it by directing his twist service to Hartwig's backhand.

The Australian's inability to deal with Seixas' kicking service to his under hit backhand had much to do with the result. In the first set, though, he was so strong from every quarter that there did not seem much hope for an American victory.

Hartwig was serving like a streak and punching his volleys to the far corners. His ground strokes, particularly his backhand, were so good that Seixas was having trouble gaining the volleying position and was missing his volley and half volley. In the first set, Hartwig scored 14 earned points to 3 for Seixas.

Twice Hartwig broke through service in the first set, but in the second the wiry Australian suffered one of those lapses that had characterized his play in the past. His service suddenly cracked and two double-faults cost him the third game.

From that time, Hartwig was never the same player again except when he recovered to go from 0-2 to 4-2 in the fourth set. He had lost much of the sting of his strokes, particularly from the backhand, and his errors mounted.

Seixas maintained command in the third set, in which he won two love games on service and broke through in the ninth as Hartwig's volleying slumped. In the final set Hartwig attacked and was stopped by looping passing shots to fall behind at 0-2. Then he rallied so brilliantly that it seemed a fifth set was in order as he won four games in succession.

At 2-4, Seixas' backhand came to his rescue while Hartwig's backhand buckled. Brilliant with the volley, Seixas had the ground strokes to stop the Australian at the net, and he ran out the next four games to win the match.

The women's final was not up to the best standard of either player. Miss Hart was a long time in finding herself. She did not hit with confidence nor her usual power off the ground in the first set, nor did she serve at her best. Her volleying was off most of all.

Miss Brough was not at her best either, missing particularly on her overhead, but by mixing her spin on her forehand and getting fine length on her backhand she provoked Miss Hart into errors or opened the way for the finishing volley. In the second set Miss Brough, finalist at Wimbledon this year, began to miss more and more and lost five games in a row.

The best tennis was played in the final set. Both were hitting more cleanly. Miss Hart was getting more pace and length off the ground and going to the net more. They fought on even terms to 4-all and then Miss Brough stood at match point in the tenth game.

The California girl hit the ball into the net then and Miss Hart was saved. Twice more in the twelfth game Miss Brough had match point, and each time her backhand return of service found the net. Thus saved three times, Miss Hart broke through in the thirteenth game as her opponent tired and failed on her backhand.

Miss Hart then served at her strongest in the fourteenth game and Miss Brough was helpless to return the ball safely.

Racing

BIG LITTLE HORSE

By Ed Danforth

From The Atlanta Journal, May 2, 1954

Louisville, Ky.—

DETERMINE, a grey ghost on a motor scooter, slipped through a plunging pack of big horses and put on his own California gold rush in reverse Saturday to win the eightieth Kentucky Derby in a stunning finish by a length and a half.

This time it was a rematch of the Derby Trial that was run last Tuesday in which Hasty Road led the wee speed demon to the wire by a nodding head. This time Hasty Road again sped away as if the others were cans tied to his tail, but Determine had the speed and heart to overhaul him a sixteenth of a mile from the wire.

Popping out of the tiring pack in the dust of the last quarter mile came Hasseyampa, stamped by the crowd as an outsider, to finish well in front of Eddie Arcaro on Goyamo, the second choice.

And farther back came Correlation, the handsome favorite, with Willie Shoemaker vainly trying to make up too much ground lost on the last turn where these long gallops are decided so often.

It was a popular victory for the throng of 100,000 had sent the dark grey youngster away at 4 to 1 odds, and as he came bouncing back to be collared with the stole of roses, jockey Ray York waved his cap as the crowd gave him a mighty roar of acclaim.

The trim little colt was met at the winner's enclosure by trainer Willie Molter, owner Andy Crevolin and what seemed to be a family gathering.

It was a notable pickup Determine made when he added $102,050 to his bank balance, already a tidy sum from his six stake victories this season.

And now the Californians will let it be known that Determine never really left home. When they flew him over the mountain they brought along 20 five-gallon bottles of home town water and a load of home grown hay.

Determine's sire was Alibhai, which sired two other Derby horses—On Trust, which finished fourth in 1947, and Your Host, ninth in 1950. The dam was Koubis, which had not produced a starter in the Derby until this year.

Evidently quite a few of those who saw the low-slung job chase Hasty Road so gamely to a track record in the Derby Trial invested in his chances for he returned a mutuel payoff of $10.60, $5.80 and $4.80. With so many well played horses in the field it might have been different.

Hasty Road's fine effort paid off $6.60 and $5.60 and Hasseyampa, a genuine long shot, was $12.00 to show.

What seemed like a crowd of normal size, perhaps larger, poured $1,543,097 through the mutuels, larger than last year's but not quite up to the record in 1952.

After Determine, Hasty Road and Hasseyampa finished off by themselves in a swiftly moving procession, here came the others in this order: Goyamo, Admiral Porter, Correlation, Fisherman, James Session, Allied, Gov. Browning, Super Devil, Red Hannigan, Black Metal, Sea O'Erin, Timely Tip, King Phalanx and last of all Mel Leavitt.

It was the first time a California horse had won a Derby since Morvich did it away back yonder and the first grey horse, too. And for Ray York it was his first Derby victory after two other starts.

This Derby may go into history as the roughest scramble ever put on for the Roses. It's a wonder that three or four of the horses were not knocked down. They were bouncing off each other like pool balls on the break.

It was a sticky humid day instead of the chilly rainy afternoon that had been forecast when the red-coated outrider led the field of 17 out of the paddock gate.

Most of the horses were escorted by stable ponies and grooms, but Determine bounced along unattended. He was not much bigger than the lead ponies anyhow, but he was polished like a gun barrel. Most impressive in the parade was the husky Correlation who towered over his lead pony.

They were in the gate but a short time and the starter got them off before many breaths had been missed.

The little men in bright silk jackets came out yipping and yelling like Indians and it was rough going for a time. Determine was bumped as he took off when Hasty Road and Timely Tip gave each other a shoulder.

Correlation slammed into Goyamo as they came out of adjoining stalls and both colts lost ground as Shoemaker and Arcaro set them down to running near the end of the parade.

All this time, Hasty Road was being sent into a lead near the middle of the track, a bit faster than Johnny Adams would have liked no doubt, but as he barreled into the first turn it was Hasty Road, Timely Tip and that little Determine almost unnoticed in safe quarters with Admiral Porter and Black Metal nearby.

Puffs of dust like bursting hand grenades marked the progress of the eager cavalry as they strung out behind Hasty Road like toys he was pulling along. Goyamo and Arcaro were eating dust alongside Correlation and Shoemaker and bless you they had only one horse beaten after going three quarters.

As they swung into the last turn Correlation and Goyamo started their move and began picking up horses as if they intended to go right on to the leaders, but Hasty Road and Determine were just too good. They were out there along with Timely Tip all finished and limp as a sackcloth and it was the two speed horses in mortal combat again.

Johnny Adams so far had been letting Hasty Road run his own race and as they turned for home Adams batted the colt once. Now Hasty Road was supposed to object to whacks from the bat so he gave out nothing. Maybe he just did not have it. At any rate, York touched up his little grey and they picked up Hasty Road about the sixteenth pole.

It was a stirring finish, but Determine was even sharper than he was in the trial and he pulled away to a length and a half running easily as if he could go on and on back to the barn.

Hasseyampa was the only one of the badly beaten bunch who could hit good licks in the stretch and he moved within two and one half lengths of Hasty Road. The same distance back of him Arcaro had worked Goyamo loose and was finishing well for fourth to beat Admiral Porter.

Correlation was blocked on the last turn but came on willingly enough. The others just did not figure beyond building up the biggest pot of gold they ever opened at the Downs.

Most of the riders told their stories of rough going and bodily contact at various stages of the heat except Willie Shoemaker, who had little or nothing to say. What happened to his horse was obvious. Just as Ben Jones had predicted, the race was decided largely by riding skill and the breaks.

Ray York brought Determine out of a bad jostling and finished strong. Shoemaker did not do so well with Correlation and was screened off at the last turn beyond recovery. Arcaro had a turbulent passage on Goyamo and lost too much ground to make up on a fast moving pair like Determine and Hasty Road.

The time of 2:03 was good but not sensational. The horses had to buck a head wind through the last quarter and they were all glad when the race was over. Not a one of them wanted to go another furlong, or even another 10 yards.

So Determine smashed the jinx that rode with California horses and grey horses, too. Now if he keeps his health he could go on to become another Equipoise, who was a big little horse just like Determine seems to be.

DERBY DAY DEBUT

By Ben Byrd

From The Knoxville Journal, May 2, 1954

Louisville—

THIS WAS MY first Kentucky Derby. I know I shall always remember it better than others which will follow, for a first Derby is an event in a man's life. Like his first job, or first kiss, or first drink.

Until today Kentucky Derby to me had been—at various stages —huge black streamers across the sports pages, the rasping sound of Clem McCarthy's voice on the radio, the clamor of office telephones as a thousand subscribers called to ask who won, and how much he paid.

But today the panorama of Churchill Downs on Derby Day was unfolded before me, and it was a wonder to behold . . . the lush green infield big enough for a dozen football fields, the sweep of the sprawling stands, the thousands of sportsclad spectators swarming like technicolored ants on the infield grass. New not only to me, but always new and fresh and wonderful to older eyes who have seen it thirty times or more.

There is the long, interminable wait from late morning until Derby post time at 4:30 p.m., made endurable and even enjoyable by six preliminary races run off roughly at half hour intervals. You can win, or lose just as much on a six-furlong stakes race as on the Run for the Roses. Lots of people do.

There was the thrilling moment when the band, to our right on the infield, struck up My Old Kentucky Home for the first time. They repeated it several times as the sun slowly moved behind the clouds and the electric clock on the scoreboard relinquished each minute like a miser handing out his gold. Through it all the tension builds and thickens until you can slice it with a knife.

Then the Derby itself. Just a little over two minutes, really, but the hopes and dreams and traditions of 80 years are crammed into those two minutes. Here today, with 17 strong steeds going, little Determine—smallest of the lot—had what it took when it counted.

203

That moment when the winner passes the green and white finish pole is an apex in sports thrills.

Then the aftermath. Jockey Ray York, grinning like a weasel coming out of a chicken coop, alternately waving to the crowd and leaning over to kiss his plucky little mount and that dramatic moment as the horseshoe of roses goes around the winner's neck. The crowd ponderously filing from the huge oval as the recorded voice of Bing Crosby drones over the loud speaker: "When You Come To The End Of A Perfect Day."

There will be other Derbies, but this was my first, and I will remember it. I know I will. I had Determine, two dollars, straight across the board.

ALL THE QUEEN'S HORSE

By Lou O'Neill

From The Long Island Star-Journal, November 2, 1954

Laurel, Md.—

FREUD'S THE WOID down here, just 24 hours before the field goes to the post in the third Washington International horse race, a 1½-mile grind on the turf . . .

Yep, this big event, which pits two of America's best horses against five from abroad, features, for the first time, a nag that has been under psychiatric care, with results that have been truly startling. The horse in question is Landau, owned by Queen Elizabeth II . . . Incidentally, this is the first time in the history of the "tight little Isle" that a horse owned by an English monarch has raced in the United States . . .

The story behind Landau's treatment is a simple one, with none of the overtones one would associate with such an unconventional method of getting a horse to win a race . . .

Landau was always fast, but last year, under pressure, he had an inclination to throw his head high in the air and stop . . .

Everything the Queen's trainer, Captain Cecil Boyd-Rochfort, did was to no avail and the good Captain finally reported to Her Majesty that he was about ready to give up on the rangy colt . . .

But Queen Elizabeth would have none of that talk. Her Majesty, who owned her first horse, a pony, when she was four years old, knew there was nothing physically wrong with Landau that caused him to put on his "head-in-the-air" act, so she decided to go beyond the realm of treatment usually given to race horses.

Into the picture at Her Majesty's request came one of London's most famous neurologists, Charles Brook, for a command look-see at what was what with Landau.

Brook was as patient as a 10-horse parlay player. He watched and he waited and finally he decided that the horse was a fit subject for the Brook technique, "one that substitutes, for existing impulses in the nervous system, impulses that dictate the conduct or condition desired." As the doctor explains it simply, "It is a non-physical treatment of the nervous system."

The Brook treatment seemed to work on Landau like Arcaro on Native Dancer. While the racing fans of perfidious Albion waited with bated breath, Brook spent day after day in Landau's stall. Placing one hand on the horse's withers and the other on the girth muscles, Brook lulled Landau to sleep and the fact that the horse's head rested on the good doctor's shoulder during these siestas seemed to indicate that the Queen's nag knew and appreciated what was going on.

And what is more Landau demonstrated in the most important way a horse can, that he was grateful for the most extraordinary care he was receiving: he won his next three races in a row. Truth insists, however, that we print the information that on Sept. 28, in the Old Rowley Stakes, his final race before tomorrow's Big One, he finished last in a field of four, causing the English press to question the wisdom of having him represent the Queen in America. Especially since he went back to his old trick of lifting his head in the air . . .

But in America he is, Her Majesty deciding to send him regardless of that bad race . . .

Try as we might, we have been unable to ascertain down here whether or not Charles Brook is with the horse and, if he is, whether he intends to give the Queen's representative the old soporific before call to post . . .

The Queen, as you must know, is in England and will be represented here by the Queen Mother . . . You should realize, too, that you cawn't even approach the Queen Mother to say hello, no less ask her about a horse . . .

As for the race itself, this is one in which American prestige and American stock is on the spot . . .

The international race was started by James Butler of the late and unlamented Empire City Racing Association, but was abandoned, because the foreigners made such poor showings.

'Tis not so now, however. England's Wilwyn won Laurel's first International in 1952 and last year France's Worden II took the top prize.

This year, Landau and his fellow Englander, King of The Tudors, France's Norman and Banassa and Ireland's Northern Gleam will comprise the representation from over the sea.

America's hopes ride with C. V. Whitney's tough little Fisherman and Stanley C. Mikell's Brush Burn, a veteran turf course runner. Eddie Arcaro, who was to have ridden King Ranch's High Gun tomorrow, will be aboard Fisherman, which should command considerable financial attention for the Whitney steed.

But for us, the big lure of the race is to see just how Landau makes out.

Can't you picture what will happen if the Queen's 'orse, with a big assist from Charles Brook, pounds down in front? Psychiatry will replace workouts in getting a horse ready for a race.

And if this thing gets out of hand and spreads to America, it doesn't take much to conjure up a picture of the tip-sheet card vendors in front of Belmont Park bellowing: "Aw right, aw right, get your winners here. WE GOT THESE RIGHT FROM THE COUCH."

Basketball

TOWN OF CHAMPIONS

By Edith Roberts

From Coronet

Copyright, 1954, Coronet Magazine
Reprinted by permission of copyright owner

THE DAY the Milan High School basketball team played in the state championship finals, the little Indiana whistle-stop became a ghost town. Every man, woman and child in Milan (pop. 1,200) who was fit to travel had made the pilgrimage to Indianapolis to cheer the boys on to victory.

The extraordinary support and enthusiasm of the townsfolk, which had carried an obscure high school squad to the final round of the championship in a conference of 751 schools, stood solidly behind the Milan Indians on that memorable Saturday.

By noon there was no one left in town but a few dogs, the postmaster and barber Russel (Rabbit) Hunter, who explained his odd behavior by stating he didn't deserve a ticket because he hadn't attended all of the school's games during the season. But to show his heart was with the boys, a sign in his window read: "Clip 'Em Close, Indians!"

To help out while Milan was deserted, neighbor communities stood by valiantly. Batesville sent over a fire-truck and crew so that the Milan Volunteer Fire Department might enjoy the game without worry. Madison lent part of its police force in order that town marshal Roy LaFollette could root for the Indians without fear that burglars might be busy back home.

Indianapolis, where the big basketball final was being played, had become accustomed to the delirious descent of the Milan motorcade. "Seems like they hardly go home but they're back again," commented Indianapolis motor patrolman Pat Stark. But he said it good-naturedly, for Milan was the popular choice to win.

He vowed that if its Miracle Men won the championship, he'd escort them against traffic around the city's famous Circle. And when they won the 1954 championship by beating the Central High School of Muncie, 32-30, he carried out his promise.

What Milan did in support of its Indians before the game was mild compared to what it did afterwards. Anyone seeing the 500 cars full of cheering fans escorting them home from Indianapolis would certainly have recognized it as a triumphal procession. But then, Milan's feat in reaching the finals was in itself something of a miracle. The escort was 13 miles long, and an estimated 40,000 people managed to cram themselves into a town normally holding 1,200.

"Menus?" cried restaurant-owner Frank Arkenberg incredulously. "Say, when our team wins, you're lucky if you get anything to *eat* here, let alone a menu!"

"Is this *heaven?*" Pete Nocks at the filling-station kept shouting after the victory, spilling half the gas he was pumping.

Some practical soul calculated that the cost of attending the tournament, plus the loss due to closing of business, had cost Milan at least $50,000 each Saturday it closed up. But someone immediately countered with: "Who cares? We won, didn't we?"

Win or lose (and it has been mostly win), Milan has been setting basketball records the like of which no community of equal size has ever matched in this basketball-crazy state.

The Milan High School has an enrollment of only 83 girls and 84 boys, which is infinitesimal compared to the hundreds of larger schools in Indiana. Yet in two successive years, this virtually unknown team reached the final tourney, winning the championship in 1954 with a victory that Hoosiers will talk about for years.

By the time the second triumph came round, Milan had proved beyond doubt that its brilliance was no fluke, but the result of a team's skill, a coach's inspiration, and a whole town's faith and enthusiasm. And all those qualities were needed to turn the kids from an obscure tank town into state champions.

Milan, now a familiar name to every Indiana basketball fan, is no more than a dot on the map. The tiny town straddles the Baltimore & Ohio Railroad, its stores and houses bunched round the main street.

Every storekeeper and householder in Milan works or roots for the Indians in some way. Drop into Frank Arkenberg's restaurant, or Emmett Lawless' drugstore, or Louis Kirschner's dry-goods emporium, and the chances are they will be discussing the basketball squad.

The same holds good for Bob Peak's law office or Red Smith's insurance agency or Chris Volz's garage. It was Volz who sent the team to the regional games in Pontiacs, to the semi-finals in Buicks, and to the state championship finals in Cadillacs.

Over on a side street lives Mrs. Anna Cross, who traditionally washes the Indians' uniforms and prays for the boys as she hangs up their jerseys. Out yonder is the Milan Furniture Company, the town's modest industry, whose general manager, Bill Thompson, had enough "LET'S GO, INDIANS!" placards printed to deck out everything on wheels in Ripley County. Up on a shady hillside stands the yellow-brick schoolhouse, no different from thousands of others all over America.

This is Milan, Indiana, the home of the champions, and it looks very much like any other country town its size. What made Milan great in the sporting sense is something you can't see. But it's there just the same, and you can find out what it is if you stay around and get acquainted.

Everyone is friendly and eager to talk, especially if it's about basketball and how the Indians got to be Champs. The townsfolk will tell you it was the kids and the coach. The coach will assure you it was the team and the town. The boys will declare it was the coach and fans. It was all of these, fired by an abiding faith and mutual confidence.

It all started two years ago with the new coach who came to Milan, one of the most remarkable figures in basketball today. No one believed young Marvin Wood was remarkable then, except perhaps in a derogatory sense—for he had taken a decided step down when he left well-known French Lick to coach unknown Milan.

"Woody" himself admits it was a kind of self-imposed demotion; but he says that when he came to Milan to look over the "material" he'd have to work with and found it averaging a good six feet, clear-eyed, wonderfully nourished and healthy, with a history of playing "barn-door" basketball all its young life, he had such a strong hunch that this could be turned into a victorious team that he couldn't resist playing that hunch.

Marv Wood, who is only 26 years old, had been trained under the veteran Tony Hinkle, coach at Butler University and now president of the American Basketball Coaches Association; and was wise enough about basketball to know that it required more than faith to make a winner. So, with characteristic thoroughness, he set about developing what sports writers have now made famous as "Woody's cat-and-mouse technique."

Disgruntled losers have been known to call it a "stall," but it is really a highly controlled slow-motion game. To see Milan's fine physical specimens carry this mental exercise in restraint and judgment to its utmost possibilities is a revelation in will power and nerve.

"We don't freeze the ball," explains Coach Wood. "We take our time and work it in for good shots. This type of game gives the boys a chance to *think,* and thinking enables them to take advantage of the breaks. It's as simple as that. But it pays off."

With this last, both his friends and his opponents agree. They'll be telling in Indiana for years to come how during the final quarter of the 1954 championship game, with Muncie Central High School leading by two points, Milan actually retained the ball for 4 minutes and 14 seconds without even attempting to shoot. Later, with only 18 seconds left to play, the crowd in pandemonium and the score tied, Milan calmly called time!

Two years of patient, incessant, endless drilling on the part of Coach Wood to be deliberate, to think, to look for the break, and then—and only then—to act, were about to pay off. With three seconds left to go, Bobby Plump of Milan, as coolly as if he were practice-shooting in his own backyard, took aim and dropped in the winning basket.

"Marv's technique," says Willard Green, Milan Superintendent of Schools, "certainly turns out some fine basketball players. And we think it contains all the elements for turning out fine men as well."

A few minutes after his dramatic final shot, Bobby Plump was singled out for the tourney's greatest individual honor—the Arthur H. Trester Award—given each year by the Indiana High School Athletic Association to the player with "the best scholastic record and mental attitude." It was the first time that this trophy had ever gone to a player on the championship team.

Bobby won it, but it might with equal justice have been awarded to the team as a whole, for the majority of the Indians are leaders and honor students. As for the team's "mental attitude," attorney Bob Peak says, "Throughout the season I noticed that a boy would forsake a chance to shine, and pass the ball to a player in a little better position. That's teamwork!"

When Wood came to Milan with his "hunch," nobody else in the town shared it. The local citizens warmly supported their boys, of course, as they had always done; but they felt their team, which had done no more in 40 years than win an occasional section game, had as much chance of flying to the moon as of winning the championship.

But Marv Wood began urging "heads-up" ball and firmly inculcating the conviction that defeat is never inevitable. Practice and drill were incessant, while the townsfolk watched and cheered.

A month before his first 1953 sectional tourney, the coach startled the team by drawing up a program showing how Milan could go all the way to the finals. Everyone thought he was crazy. When subsequent events proved him right, team and town got behind him.

In 1954 they knew they could win—which is one reason why they did. The solid backing of Milan's citizenry was behind the team, and every player knew it.

When the season ended, the coach folded away his lucky green necktie till next year. People began to speak again of secondary things, like politics and the weather. The boys themselves settled down to books, home life and chores.

Back to Pierceville, a stone's throw from Milan, where there are 100 inhabitants and 100 fans, trouped three of the Champs—Gene White, Plump, and Rog Schroder. Nor were they above joining in the games at the home-made basketball court behind the Schroder residence.

"We've got lights," explained Rog proudly, "and we play every night. Our dads play, too, and our mothers are real fans. The little kids use the court afternoons."

A visiting reporter who had come to Milan to see what it had taken to make a championship team, reached this conclusion: "It all adds up to a few sweating, panting boys in the driveway, the backyard or a vacant lot somewhere in Indiana. That's where champions start—and that's where they plan to stay."

THE LANDING OF THE CATS

By Jim Obert

From The Peoria Star, November 8, 1954

THIS IS HOW it was:

It was 4:40 Sunday afternoon and you stood in the crowd and watched the TWA Constellation make the usual three-point landing.

When the spectators shifted you shifted with them. You had to. The movement was insistent, for among them were those who were lonely, only they wouldn't be for long.

And then, out of the tail of that big bird, strode the passengers and suddenly this was the moment and the people surged forward and carried you with them.

Now the surge has pinned you against the fence, but it really doesn't matter, for around you the families of the Caterpillar Cats are locking their heroes in embraces and it's the time when sports writers leave their pencils in the pocket.

You watch the players and you think at the moment just how far away basketball is now and how unimportant the World Championship they won last Friday at Rio de Janeiro, Brazil, must be with this greeting.

You also try to speculate on how huge the greeting might have been had not the team arrived now instead of the Monday morning as previously announced.

You see Frank McCabe coming off the plane and it almost floors you, for you know Frank is retired and never made the trip. And then you find out that pure luck placed Frank, completing a business trip out west, on the same homeward flight with his former teammates.

You follow the crowd into the lobby and still you can't get out the notebook and pencil for these guys aren't in the mood to talk. They're glad to be home and that's okay because they've got it coming.

Underneath that elation they look tired and pretty soon you find out why. They slashed Brazil in the finals Friday night and got back to the hotel at 1 in the morning. Four hours later they were at

213

the Rio airport and on their way home and they've been traveling
ever since. Some of them haven't slept.

You look around and you don't see B. H. Born, or Don Penwell
or Publicist Jack Wilson or Bill Johnson. Then someone tells you
that the passage back home was really fouled up and the four missing
passengers are due in at 11 that night.

Later on you find out that the squad drew lots to determine who
would leave Rio last and when Trainer Pat Doyle was one of the
losers, Penwell gave Doyle his ticket, for the tournament had taken
a lot out of Doyle and he was at the point where he was about to
swim back if need be.

You see Ron Bontemps and his wife in the lobby and Coach
Warren Womble shakes Ron's hand and quips, "We could have
used you on the baseline, Ron," and Bontemps makes some remark
about who won the tournament, Caterpillar or Brazil?

After a while the lobby starts thinning out. You tell the coach
you'll see him later and then you drive Joe Stratton and Allen
Kelley back to town and on the way you talk to them.

They tell you that it was a rough tournament and probably the
toughest team they played was not Brazil at all but Uruguay. There
seems to be truth in that for Caterpillar only beat Uruguay 64-59.

Stratton tells you that the food wasn't the greatest and that he
ate ham almost every meal. You ask him about breakfast and he
says that they don't have breakfast in Brazil and about all you can
get is coffee and rolls.

Later in the evening, when you're talking to Womble, he, too,
brings up the subject of coffee and tells a story about the time he
and Wilson were in the stands scouting Uruguay. Wilson orders
coffee from a vendor and when he takes a sip his hair stands on
end. Womble tells you that the way to drink coffee is to order one
part coffee and then fill the cup to the top with cream.

In the car, Stratton and Kelley talk about officiating and Stratton
says it was rough on the defensive man because the guy with the
ball would run over you and you'd be called for a foul.

Stratton recalls the final game with Brazil and he talks about
policemen on horses holding the spectators in check. He says that
there was no trouble to speak of, though in the first game of the
tournament two rocks were tossed at the Cat bench.

You ask about the play of individual players and Stratton says
that Kirby Minter was outstanding, but no sooner than Stratton
gets the words out of his mouth than Kelley cuts in and says, "Joe
was plenty tough in there too."

At that time nobody in the car knew that the Brazillian press voted Stratton the Most Valuable Player of the tournament with Minter second and a player from Brazil third.

And then you find yourself at Womble's house and Mrs. Womble almost runs over you, for Warren has brought her a ring and a vase and probably a lot of other things because Hazel has got her eyes on the suitcases in the corner and only because she's so darn polite keeps her from tearing them apart.

You sink into a big chair and you accept the "soda pop" that Womble puts in your hand and you sit back and listen for Womble has got things to say.

He tells you about the Copacabana, the hotel where the team stayed, and says that he could have tossed a rock into the Atlantic ocean from his window.

He talks about the food and said that the team missed "variety" but it was still satisfactory. He said at one time or another each player had dysentery and that during the stay seven or eight different types of medicine were taken.

The phone rings like crazy and Hazel keeps answering it but Womble keeps the interview going. Pretty soon the talk gets around to that plane ride over the wilds of Bolivia during which motor trouble developed.

A furrow of concern cuts across the coach's brow as he tells about one motor going out and the pilots cutting another one off to create a balance or something.

And then there was the emergency landing at a joint called La Paz on a gravel runway. Pretty soon another plane comes along and this one springs an oil leak in an engine and when you eventually get into the air a terrible storm hits the plane and Womble says it was "the worst experience" he's ever had in six years of flying. He says "we were tossed around like a banana and we had some pretty sick boys."

And the coach touches on other subjects, too, like language and tours and prices of souvenirs and the tournament itself.

He tells about the time in the hotel when he called a practice for 2 in the afternoon and tells Doyle to get on the house phone and alert the players. So Doyle picks up the Ameche and tells the operator in his best Irish tongue that he wants room 1002.

Well, the operator can't speak English and pretty soon he and Doyle are going round and round. Doyle finally averts a national crisis by hanging up the phone and going to each room in person.

The conversation switches to the Cat team, a squad sprinkled with rookies who came through in veteran fashion to add what may be the peak of basketball at Caterpillar. For who does not know by now that the past four years have produced an Olympic title, three National AAU crowns, a share of the NIBL and now this?

You ask the coach if he thinks that he might have a dynamite-laden team under his wing, one that might prove to be the greatest ever if that were possible. And when he hesitates to answer you slide to the edge of your seat for maybe you've taken the words right out of his mouth.

He thinks for a moment and then tells you, "Let's put it this way. We have an exceptional opportunity to have a wonderful ball club. We might have a real good season."

You look at him and you get the idea that he'd like to elaborate on the point a little, but then you realize that he's always been a master of conservatism and isn't about to say something unless he's certain it can actually happen.

You take down his words on individual play:

"During the early stages Minter and Stratton carried the load. . . . Then (Bill) Johnson had a real good game. . . The latter part of the tournament (Kendall) Sheets and (Eddie) Solomon played very well. Kendall was very effective against a zone which we met in six of the nine games. (Dick) Retherford and Minter consistently provided the board power and (B. H.) Born scored well against a zone."

Pretty soon you're walking out the door. The interview is over and all's right with the world.

Then you remember and you stick your head back inside:

"When are you going to practice?"

"Thursday," says Womble.

DAYTON'S DAY

By *Si Burick*

From The Dayton News, March 7, 1954

Copyright, 1954, Dayton News
Reprinted by permission of copyright owner

New York—

THIS WAS University of Dayton's day in the big town, the big garden and the big National Invitation Tournament. For Dayton's loyal following, this was the start, it was hoped, of a glorious adventure that would go on and on through tonight's tussle to and through the finals next Saturday night.

What kind of day was it for the hopeful Flyers before their game with Manhattan? Manhattan, incidentally, is a tournament representative that many believed was in on a raincheck because local representation was demanded, along with tiny St. Francis of Brooklyn, which was playing in the evening's first contest against Louisville.

A relaxed Tom Blackburn had his men in bed by midnight last night with "reveille" at 9:15 a.m. at the Flyers' hotel hideaway, just beyond the Times Square area. The orders to the telephone operators are explicit. At no time, day or night, is a call to go through to any player's room. All calls—but positively all—were to clear through Blackburn. If the coach did not happen to be around, neither heaven nor earth nor lightning nor thunder could move the operator to clear a call. This included outside calls and inside calls; they were all taboo.

Breakfast at 9:45 a.m. was leisurely with no restrictions on the kind or amount of food the boys could eat. Within reason, of course. The trainer, Hank Ferraza, advised there would be no formal noon meal. There never is on game days. If a boy felt like having a sandwich at noon, he could do. Dinner promptly at four in the hotel dining room. And everybody ate alike. A large tomato juice, medium size steak, baked potato, fruit salad and hot tea.

Then each man to his room—all were paired—until time to leave for Madison Square Garden at 6:15 p.m.

Promptly at 6:30, the Flyers arrive at the Garden. They come into the vast arena as the buzzer sounds ending the first half of the opening game between St. Francis, the 300-student-body Brooklyn school, and heavily favored Louisville. The locals leave the floor with a two-point advantage at 27-25. This one is not running true to form.

The Flyers, as a group, watch the third period as things continue to go badly for Louisville. Then Blackburn sends them to the dressing room. The boys consider it a good omen that they are assigned the white uniforms, which usually represents the home team. Manhattan is in green.

When only two minutes of the first game remain, Blackburn goes into the dressing room, reporter behind him. It is a quiet scene, no excitement, no sign of hysteria, some talking, some smiling, no loud laughter. Sallee is having his legs and his back worked on by the trainer. Blackburn begins to talk.

"If you get on the floor first, start your practice shooting at the basket away from our bench. I'll want you on my side in the second half, if possible. It isn't important, but try. Donoher, you are the acting captain. Bill," he says to Uhl, "do you remember the number of the man you'll be guarding?" Uhl mentions the number. Blackburn checks the assignments of each starter. They had been given those assignments before arrival at the Garden.

To Donoher, "Don't waste any times-out early. You may need them later."

To the group, "Let's not stumble or fumble. Let's make it a good showing. Don't relax on their out-of-bounds plays." To Donoher, "Study your man's habits—especially his shifts. He's faster than you but you can stop him."

To Uhl, there were specific instructions on tipoffs, the coach taking it for granted that the Greenfield giant would get his tips.

Chris Harris said, "It's been a long season; we've come a long way; let's go out there tonight!"

"Let's really hustle, men," said Sallee. Quiet invaded the room for a moment.

Blackburn broke the silence. "The biggest mistake you can make out there is to be outhustled. Make me proud of you no matter what happens. You fellows on the bench, we may need any one of you at any time. Be ready. Things always happen. Watch the ball game. Know what you will have to do."

Outside, the buzzer sounded, signaling the end of the first game.

The boys gathered around for an enthusiastic cheer and ran out on the court, hopefully, to get the basket Blackburn wanted and to learn that Louisville had been eliminated, 60-55. That was a prime upset. Was it a forerunner of things to come?

Now the whistle sounds for the tipoff. Uhl gets it to Donoher, who dribbles casually down the floor and passes to Long John Horan, who misses. Harris gets the rebound; he misses. Uhl is fouled. He makes it. Dayton is out in front, 1-0.

The score begins to see-saw. First one team, then the other takes the lead. Manhattan takes it again at 8-7, and what is this beginning to develop?

Dayton is missing. Manhattan is hitting.

When the first quarter ends, it is 24-16, Manhattan. More dangerous than the score, it appeared to a Dayton rooter, was the foul-count on Uhl. He had scored three baskets. He also had three personals on him.

Within two minutes of the second quarter, there is a fourth personal called on him, and Gordon Dodane becomes the first substitution for the Flyers. Uhl is on the bench.

Manhatttan continues hot; Dayton continues colder than usual. Much colder. Could this be the team that embarrassed great Duquesne only a week ago?

Manhattan's margin goes to 10 points. Then 11, 12 and 13. Those subs Blackburn talked about are going in now. Here's Bob Fiely and there's Larry Pedicord. Fiely gets two baskets. At half time, it is 34-44. This is bad.

You check the statistics—and they are amazing! For the half, Manhattan has taken 32 shots; the Jaspers have made 17. That's a remarkable 52 per cent. And what of Dayton? The Flyers have taken 35 shots, made good on 12 for a measly 34 per cent.

Can Manhattan stay that hot?

Let's look at the individual Manhattans. Jim Lake, a speedy Negro, four out of six shots good; Jack Paschal, five for six; Ed O'Connor, five for 11; Gerry Cahill, two for six; Willard Doran, one for two.

And on the Dayton side, Horan, one for six; Donoher, nothing for four; Uhl, four for 11, Sallee, three for six, which is respectable; Harris, two for five; and the late-arriving Fiely, two for two.

Can one team stay that hot; can another stay that cold for an evening? There is a second half to come.

And now a remarkable thing begins to develop. The Flyers, the Thrombosis fieldhouse kids, start a spirited comeback. This is John Horan taking charge. And Capt. Donoher. And the others complimenting. Uhl is in there for as long as he can stay. This is Horan the magnificent. Down goes Manhattan's margin to nine, to seven, to six, to five points.

You wonder if the game does not have a turning point when Cahill of Manhattan drives in for a basket and knocks Harris down in the effort. The officials rule no basket and charge Cahill with a charging foul. Harris makes it and it is four points now. Just as quickly it goes back to eight and then Uhl fouls out with six-and-a-half minutes gone in the period. The two fouls that are made on his fifth personal bring the Manhattan edge back to 54-46.

And now the real challenge to Dayton. Fiely goes in for Uhl and Long John—the magnificent Horan—takes the pivot. Horan is everywhere. His long arms and legs are all over the court. Manhattan is missing where it was hitting before and Dayton is getting the rebounds. The ball is bouncing the Flyers' way at last.

With 40 seconds left in the period, Dayton grabs the lead. Horan—who else?—does it with a hook shot at the buzzer. Manhattan regains it at 58-57. That's where the fourth quarter begins.

It is no contest from this point. Dayton is in complete control. It is like the Cincinnati game of several weeks ago. The Flyers are hitting and making no errors. They are nearly perfect.

With four minutes left, Horan fouls out. The Garden, with 16,259 in the stands, gives him a rising ovation. These are not Dayton fans; these are sincerely appreciative fans from all over the country. Horan goes out too late for Manhattan's good. Dodane takes over for him and the big sophomore follows suit. When Dodane hits two free throws after the final buzzer, it is Dayton by 90-79. This, by a team underdog by 13!

Hunting and Fishing

NEW HIGH IN SAILS

By Don Ollis

From Outdoor Life

FOR HOURS WE had trolled the deep-blue waters around Cocos Island, a tiny bit of tropical paradise in the Pacific some 300 miles southwest of Costa Rica. I sat hunched on the blistering cabin of Woody Krieger's 22-foot fishing launch, clamping my legs around the signal horn for support and shielding my cameras from the blazing December sun.

Woody was trolling for Pacific sailfish, one of the fightingest aerial acrobats of the sea. But so far he had attracted nothing but a flock of black-and-white frigate birds. They circled soundlessly overhead, eyeing the two flying-fish baits that skittered nervously, one on each side of the wake, some 40 feet astern. Repeatedly they dived down and grabbed at the choice baits, apparently trying their darndest to get hooked.

We yelled and cursed. Finally, in complete exasperation, we hurled all our empty pop bottles at the flock.

Suddenly a sailfish braved the commotion on the surface and whacked the bait soundly with its bill. The boatman never had a chance to cut the motors and let the bail play dead. A brazen frigate bird swooped past the fish and snatched the bait 10 feet into the air. The rest of the flock closed in, fighting for a share of the prize. The sailfish disappeared.

At this point, we quite accurately agreed that light-tackle big-game fishing was strictly for the birds.

It was late afternoon before an approaching tropical squall sent the frigate birds winging back to Cocos Island. Meanwhile we rolled persistently at about seven knots. Woody Krieger and the mate, Eddie Naponelli, stood in the sweltering cockpit below, resolutely tending the lightweight tackle.

Our fish guide, John Holden, hung out the open hatch of the cabin, his eyes constantly scanning the water. Suddenly, right

221

behind my left ear, he let out a yell that nearly split my head open.

"Right rigger! Sailfish on the right rigger!"

A dim shadow hung behind the skipping bait. Tensely, all eyes shifted to the outrigger pole. Suddenly the line snapped free from the clothespin and floated down, then slipped beneath the surface.

Holden threw the motor into neutral. The launch slowed to a standstill, the motor coughing quietly.

The sailfish had struck the bait solidly with its needlelike bill and was no doubt expecting it to sink slowly, naturally. The slack in the line played out. With infinite patience, Krieger held the rod motionless. Then his line began to free-spool out.

Cautiously, Krieger touched his thumb to the line on the reel. "The bait's going down," he said, as if speaking to the fish. Gradually he increased the pressure on the line. "Don't spit it out," he coaxed. Then there was a light but steady pull on his line. Krieger flipped the star drag on the reel. "Now!" He yanked the glass rod nearly double. With three quick successive jerks of the rod he set the hook firmly into the fish.

Instantly line peeled from the reel. Crew, ocean, and launch exploded into action. Eddie, the first mate, yanked the other rod out of its socket in the gunwale and reeled in the baited line. Hand over hand he pulled in the brightly painted wooden teaser plug that presumably had attracted the fish.

The field was now clear for Krieger's line. He needed it. He was tied fast to a mighty big and fighting-mad Pacific sailfish.

Suddenly the ocean boiled far to the left. The motor roared and the launch leaned hard in pursuit. The horizon flipped perpendicular in my view-finder and I clawed the air trying to regain my balance. Krieger howled as his knees struck the gunwale. Fifty yards of line sang off his reel in the sweet sound of battle.

Straight out of the sea leaped a breath-taking flash of silver and purple lightning. That's what the first appearance of a jumping sailfish is like. Water poured from the fish's sides, revealing the rapier bill and the wide-spread pectoral fins. On and on it shot from the depths until even its tail, clearing the surface by several feet, was outlined against the sky. Air-borne, with its pointed jaws agape, the great fish shook its head back and forth wildly trying to throw the hook. The force of the leap waned and the fish crashed heavily back into the sea.

Krieger braced himself for the next leap. A few tentative turns of the reel gained him no line.

"Here he comes," yelled Holden. The sail was rushing toward

the stern. One, two, three times it stitched the water. The launch surged ahead. Krieger rocked back and forth, pumping line back onto the reel.

Since taking the bait, the sailfish had spent almost as much time in the air as in the water. It was a spectacular display of energy, but it took a heavy toll on the fish. Gradually the extravagant leaps subsided into short, head-shaking runs. Eddie took the wheel while Holden pulled on his gloves to boat the fish. Krieger worked the fish in closer and closer. Finally the doubled section of the line reached the tip of the pole. In a surge of white water the sailfish shot away from the launch, taking yards of hard-earned line.

Again Krieger cranked furiously, working in the line. This time he got the double line down through the rod guides and a couple of turns around the reel itself. Now he could apply some pressure. A moment later the wire leader and swivel rose from the water.

Holden reached far out and grabbed the metal leader. Eddie crowded forward with the persuader, a sawed-off baseball bat with a thick lead core. Holden heaved on the wire leader. "Got him!" he yelled as his free hand closed around the bill of the fish. "He's worth weighing."

The fish struggled to get free, churning suds into the cockpit. "Hit him, Eddie, hit him!" Holden's hand was being clobbered against the side of the boat, but he hung on. Though he has mangled and broken his hand billing a fish in this manner, Holden never uses a gaff on sailfish. Even the weight of the blood lost by gaffing may mean the difference between a record and just another big fish. Eddie clubbed the fish until it stopped struggling.

"I think you've got a record," gasped Holden as they maneuvered a line around its tail.

"You think so?" said Krieger hopefully. "Oh, it looks pretty small to me," he added with the patient resignation of a life-long angler whose *wife* holds all the records in the family.

It was dark by the time our launch pulled alongside the brilliantly lighted Observer, the 97-foot converted harbor mine sweeper from which we operated. When his sailfish was measured and weighed on officially tested scales, Woodrow G. Krieger had his first world record: a 184-pound Pacific sailfish, 10 feet 4 inches long, on 30-pound-test line. Fighting time: 40 minutes.

Woody grinned happily, shaking hands and laughing off congratulations. He was still grinning like a kid when I finally got him posed for the traditional big-fish photograph.

Only a month before I had sat in Woodrow G. Krieger's office in Paramount, California, discussing this trip. He had the enthusiastic air of a desk-ridden executive just itching to hang up a Gone Fishing sign, and this looked like a real opportunity. Krieger is head of a West Coast oil company that was looking into tidelands oil off the coast of Peru. He could use his big boat as a base for business as well as for fishing. A group of scientists from the College of Medical Evangelists at Loma Linda, Calif., would also be aboard, collecting fish and other marine specimens of that area for an Office of Naval Research project. So the Observer would be fitted for a nine-month cruise. Krieger's wife, Thelma, and their two young sons, Dennis and Stephen, would also go along. I was invited to photograph the scientific work. Like the Kriegers, I would be able to fly back to California when business and sport were concluded. The Observer would stay in southern waters the full nine months.

"It would be nice," Krieger mused, "if you could also get some sport-fishing pictures. You see, we're going through areas where the big fish hangout. My wife and I have been big-game fishing for about 10 years now. She already has four world records."

He leaned back, cupped his hands behind his head, and looked at the softly lighted aquarium near the window. "Me? I haven't any. I'd rather like to get one this trip."

"Well, you catch the fish and I'll take the pictures," I promised.

A month later we dropped anchor at Cocos Island and Krieger's mildly expressed wish for a record was fulfilled beyond his dreams. And I photographed one of the greatest sprees of record breaking in big-game-fishing history.

The Kriegers hadn't intended to stay more than a day at Cocos before proceeding south to the Galapagos Islands. But Woody's magnificent sailfish swinging from the davit changed that. After dinner, Thelma hauled out the tackle and happily began assembling her rods and reels.

The next morning a small task force of boats and fishermen cast off from the yacht. The scientists loaded one launch with their paraphernalia and went collecting close to the shores of the island. Dennis and Stevie Krieger stowed their light rods and feather lures aboard their little ouboard boat and fished close to the Observer.

Thelma Krieger joined our boat, bringing along a hamper of sandwiches. We headed eastward for the area where Woody had scored the day before.

When Holden slowed the launch to trolling speed, Woody and

Thelma dropped their baits out. The outrigger poles held their lines far out on each side of the wake. Eddie dropped the teaser plug over the stern where it wobbled merrily after us.

Surprisingly enough, no frigate birds appeared. We learned later that they had chosen to harass the scientists that day.

Once more I climbed on top of the canopy, knotted my legs around the horn, and prepared for action. It was a long time coming but when it did, it was fast and furious.

On her 20-pound-test line, Thelma hooked a 137-pound sailfish that put on a breathtaking surface fight. In fact, it got too thrilling for comfort. Thelma had the sailfish within 40 feet of the launch when it suddenly lashed itself into a frenzied series of leaps and greyhounded straight for the boat. I counted five leaps and snapped a picture just as the great fish crashed into the water less than six feet from the stern. One more leap would bring it right into the cockpit.

"Hang on!" Holden shouted. He spun the wheel and gunned the motor. The stern skidded sideways for an instant before shooting ahead. The sailfish charged on, smashing into the water where the boat had been seconds before.

When the fish did not reappear, Holden slowed the launch, watching anxiously to see what this fighting fish would do next. But its fury was spent.

Thelma reeled in carefully, getting only token resistance. By the time she had the leader out of the water, the fish rolled on its side and coasted quietly into Holden's hands. With the fighting heart of a thoroughbred, it had actually jumped itself to death.

It was midafternoon when we brought the sailfish into the Observer and checked the International Game Fish Association records. Mrs. Krieger had a world-record sailfish for 20-pound-test line in the women's division.

On the third day, Cocos Island waters were at their unbelievable best. In the morning Thelma broke one of her own established records.

She was trolling with 12-pound-test line when the sailfish struck. Thelma set the hook with the merest flick of the rod—anything more strenuous would have parted it. The sailfish streaked away underwater until the sheer weight of the extended line itself was almost enough to break it. When the fish reappeared it was no more than a speck on the horizon, performing in the distance like a circus aerialist.

Holden sent the launch in pursuit. With such fragile lines, boatman and angler must operate as a perfectly coordinated team. Any sudden strain or twist or backlash, and the line would snap in an instant. Too much reeling in and running out quickly wears out a thin line. Thus the trick is just to stay tied onto the sailfish while it exhausts itself trying to throw the hook right back at you.

Thelma reeled in cautiously, the dainty 4-ounce rod tip fluttering at the strain. She was muttering, "Maybe I'll make it. Maybe I'll make it."

"It takes a feminine touch," Woody admitted. "I get excited and snap those little lines every time!"

The fight lasted only about 20 minutes. Fish and guide tangled briefly at the side of the launch, then Holden and Woody heaved the brilliant-blue sailfish into the cockpit.

It weighed 134 pounds, the largest ever caught by either man or woman on 12-pound-test line. Thelma had beat her previous world record by 29 pounds.

For sheer thrill of sports fishing, this was an unforgettable day. Woody and Thelma hooked and played innumerable smaller sailfish, releasing them at the side of the launch. Sportsmen seldom boat a sail unless they are trying for a record.

Once, from my vantage point on the canopy, I saw a sharp fin cutting the water behind the bait. "Fin!" I yelled. "Maybe it's a striped marlin."

I braced against the horn, expecting Holden to cut the motors. Holden's sharp eye appraised the fin for an instant: "Hammerhead shark!" he shouted, and the launch shot forward. Totally unprepared for that move, I somersaulted down into the cockpit. Still clasping my reflex camera to my stomach, I luckily landed on my feet on top of the motor housing.

"What you guys will do for a new angle," chided Holden as he swerved the launch to cut the baits away from the shark. Gingerly I remounted the canopy.

"Strike!" shouted Woody as the line snapped free from the left outrigger. Holden squinted at the water. The launch jolted dead in its wake.

"It's a sailfish," Holden decided.

"I thought you said it was a shark fin!" objected Woody.

"It was. Now you've got a sail after the bait. Let it go down."

Woody wasn't fully convinced, but he held the rod motionless letting the bait sink gently in the water.

Suddenly he felt the now-familiar steady pull on the line. Instantly he set the hook. A sail charged out of the water like an angry bulldog. Shaking its head belligerently, it leaped free of the water again and again. We could see a large remora, or suckfish, clinging to its belly.

"Shark fin again!" yelled Holden. "Work fast. Bring it in green." The shark, attracted by the struggle in the water, was slowly circling the hooked sail. It was now a battle against time, for if the shark took even a nip out of the sailfish it would be disqualified for record consideration.

Woody strained his 20-pound-test line within a twitch of breaking. The fish fought valiantly. It was still fighting fresh even when Woody reeled the wire leader out of the water. On the second try, Holden grabbed the wire. Foam churned into the cockpit as Eddie clubbed the thrashing fish.

When it relaxed, we saw the remora calmly detach itself and swim away.

Holden threw a hitch around the mill. "Haven't got time for a tail rope. Get it in."

They pulled the sailfish up on the bow just as the shark, like some dark stalking submarine, cruised under the boat.

It was night and raining lightly by the time we returned to the yacht. Hurriedly, we hung the sailfish on the scales—Woody had his second world record, a 154-pounder caught on 20-pound-test line.

That night two great shimmering sailfish hung from the davits. Never before, to our knowledge, had two different world records been established from the same boat on the same day.

The next day was Saturday and the Kriegers, being Seventh Day Adventists, did not go fishing. Stevie, Dennis, and I took the outboard and landed in the heavy surf at Chatham Bay. Cocos Island was deserted at the moment. But everywhere was evidence of those adventurous souls who, with map in hand and implicit faith in rumors of pirate gold, had dug up the island looking for the ancient Loot of Lima.

Unofficially, Costa Rican authorities scoff at the idea of pirate treasure on the island. Officially, however, they take a very practical view of matters. Hundreds of treasure hunters have paid a $1,000 fee for the privilege of a month's digging on Cocos. For a treasure that is still buried, the government turns a tidy profit on the Loot of Lima.

Because of the heavy surf and impassable cliffs, we were unable to land at the little cove where Dennis, Stevie, and the steward the day before had discovered a sailfish carved in weathered stone.

Whether it had been carved there by ancient whaler, pirate, or modern practical joker, somebody had admired the sailfish of Cocos Island enough to spend hours chipping its image in stone.

The last day we took the fishing launch out, we were again plagued with frigate birds. Holden had spent hours preparing an ample supply of frozen Cataline flying fish for baits. He had sewn the mouths shut, fastened the hook in front of the jaws, and run a line tightly over the eyes so that the continuous trolling wouldn't tear them to pieces. They were works of art. He was furious when the frigate birds demolished them.

We trolled all morning and rebaited half a dozen times before a sailfish dared the birds' commotion and tapped the bait with its bill. Without waiting for the sinking reaction of a stunned fish, it swallowed Thelma's bait.

Her rod swished twice and the sailfish flashed into the air.

After the first wild attempt to throw the hook, this fish didn't jump again. It just pulled steadily and powerfully away from the launch.

With her 30-pound-test line, there was no possibility of Thelma checking those bulldozing runs. Time and again Holden sent the launch bearing down on the fish. Thelma retrieved line, only to have it peel off again as the fish charged off in another direction.

By the time she had worked the fish up to the launch, Thelma was shaking with fatigue. Again there was the flurry of fish and foam as Holden held the wire leader and Eddie used the persuader. Everyone was soaked by the time they pulled it into the cockpit. Its sail was an iridescent, incredibly deep blue. This coloration, typical of sailfish, fades almost immediately after death. By the time we had the fish strung up on the Observer, it had dulled and darkened to a steely blue-black. Both sides of the fish were deeply scored with line burns—marks of those tremendously powerful runs. It tipped the beam scale at 146 pounds and earned for Thelma the Kriegers' fifth and last world record of the trip.

The Observer continued south, cruising the big-fish waters of Panama, Ecuador, and Peru for almost nine months, but found nothing to equal the fast and furious fishing at Cocos Island.

Woody and Thelma talk about returning some day. By then, of course, the islands may be alive with fishermen, because the Kriegers' records are now an open book to big-game fishermen the world over. The official I.G.F.A. report lists the five new records, and competitors will be able to translate the data into fabulous fishing at a glance, for record dates come in rapid-fire order—the first on Dec. 24, 1952; another on the 25th; two on the 26th, and the last on the 28th. And they're grouped at Cocos Island.

But the Kriegers aren't worried by the competition they may find on another trip. After all, if the fishing waters get crowded, they can always pay their treasure-hunting fee and go dig into Cocos Island.

M-DAY

By Grant Matthews

From The San Francisco Chronicle, April 18, 1954

THE WAY I got it figured I am living on borrowed time from here on out.

The reason is that, for me, this was M-Day, Marlin Day. Today I caught my first marlin and anything else that happens to me now will be anti-climactic.

It might not be the biggest marlin ever caught and it might not be the fastest or the fightingest but I caught it and I love it like a brother. And it turns out to be the first marlin caught in the waters around here this year.

I have read quite a few articles and books by guys like Senor Ernest Hemingway and Senor Philip Wylie on big-game fishing and, quite frankly, I couldn't see what they were getting so excited about. Now I know.

A couple of the Mexican boatmen reported yesterday that they had seen marlin out in the deep water. Actually it is a little early for marlin this far north. The boys have been creaming them down around La Paz but it was generally believed that Senor Marlin had not worked his way up here as yet. But he has. He's here.

And when my fishing companion Don Wolden and I heard they had been seen in this area we forgot all about the good yellowtail, garropa, Sierra, cabrilla and bonito fishing in these parts. We cornered our friend Ken "Tio" Cowl, who superintends the fishing parties here at the Flying Sportsman Lodge, and put it up to him. With no strain we persuaded him to take us out for marlin.

And here we are.

Just as in any other kind of fishing, you have to have bait before you fish. Therefore, on your way out to the marlin grounds, you fish for Sierra mackerel which will be the marlin bait. Tio says that flying fish or mullet are better but we don't have any of them around.

Anyhow, the three of you catch a sufficient number of Sierra and head for the deeps. On the way out Eduardo prepares the bait.

First he cuts the backbone out of the Sierra. This, Tio explains, is so that when the marlin clubs the bait with its bill, the Sierra will appear dead to him.

After the backbone has been removed and the tail cut off, Eduardo sews up the back of the Sierra and he also sews closed the gills and the mouth. He then ties a small loop just forward of the bait's nose and attaches the hook. (In other words, the hook is just forward of the nose.) The hook is secured to about nine feet of steel leader which is looped into the 500 yards of 72-pound test line.

There are two rods and they are put into rod holders on either side of the boat's stern. Eduardo lets out only about 20 feet of line on each side and the bait is trolled on the surface of the water. The boat speed is about four knots. You are now ready for Senor Marlin.

Eduardo tells you, by pointing to his eye and then pointing out to the bait, to keep watching same. He then goes up topside to scout for marlin.

"Sometimes marlin will come sashaying in from out of no-where," Tio explains. "Sometimes they don't even show a fin before they hit."

So you and Tio and Don stand in the cockpit of the boat and they are scanning the horizon and you are policing the bait and you wish you knew what you were looking for. You cruise along for about half an hour.

"Tio?"

"Si, Eduardo?"

"Marleen!" Eduardo points off to the right, and Tio nods his head.

"So, Eduardo . . . marlin," he answers.

But you can't see a marlin. You wouldn't know one if he came up and shook hands. Tio points and you say yes, you see the mar-lin—but you don't.

"Better get into the harness," Tio tells you.

The harness is a kind of leather vest with straps that can be clamped on to the reel. It helps you play the fish with your back and shoulders instead of your arms, Tio tells you.

You find you are having trouble getting into the harness. Not because it is difficult, but because your hands are shaking and your stomach feels like a cue ball. You finally get the harness on and sit down in the "fighting chair." You still don't see the marlin.

Then you DO see him!

He is a fin on top of the water and Rudy has maneuvered the

boat so the bait will be trolled in front of him and he can look it over. It is very quiet on the boat.

"Esgranday marlin," Eduardo whispers to you.

"You mean esbeeg?"

"Si, esgranday," Eduardo nods.

It is very quiet again.

"He sees it," Tio whispers eagerly. "Now's the time. Will he take it or won't he?"

And you see the fin slithering in towards the bait and the bottom drops out of your stomach and you know you will be too weak to play him if he does take it. You wish Senor Wolden was sitting in the "fighting chair." You wish Tio was. You wish Eduardo was. You wish you were home in bed but you wouldn't be any other place in the world. This is like just before the kick-off, or your first kamikaze.

"He's following it!" Tio whispers into your ear and startles you so that you almost fall.

And he is following it. He works his way over to the starboard bait and cases it, then he looks over the portside bait, then he winds over to starboard again. And all this is happening only about 20 feet aft of the boat's stern.

"He'll take that one there," Tio says and nods toward the starboard side. "He likes that one."

He does, but not enough. He follows it for a while, but he's suspicious. He makes a graceful turn and disappears under the surface. He has sounded.

You look at Senor Wolden and Senor Wolden, who is first time out for marlin, too, looks at you. Neither one of you says anything; you both look at Tio who is grinning from ear to ear.

"What'd I tell you?" he says.

You say three words, you and Senor Wolden. The same three words. Simultaneously.

Twenty minutes later you see another marlin but he won't go either. He'll almost buy, but he takes it on the Arthur Duffy.

"Third time's the charm," Tio comments as we start looking again. The third one goes. As a matter of fact he doesn't play hard to get at all. He moves in, he likes what he sees and whoosh.

But he doesn't do things the way he is supposed to. Tio has already briefed you. He tells you that a proper marlin, after sizing up the bait and deciding yes will come up to the bait and belt it with his bill. This is supposed to kill it. He backs off to be sure it is dead and, after taking a bearing, winds up and bites. He takes it from 150 to 200 yards out and stops. All this time you are in free spool; if you try to hold him he catches the act and spits out the bait. That's what Tio tells you.

He also tells you not to do anything after this initial run by Senor Marlin.

"After he stops," Tio tells you, "count to 30, and then count to 30 again."

This, Tio explains, is to give the marlin time to swallow the bait. After he has swallowed it and it is down in his stomach is the time to set the hook, Tio says.

But this one doesn't act that way. He is very unorthodox. He is the most unorthodox marlin in the Gulf of California and you are stuck with him.

He does not hit the bait with his bill. He hits it with everything he has and takes off like a jet job. All is confusion in the cockpit of your boat. Senor is going one way, the boat is going another way, Eduardo is grabbing the rod, Tio is taking it in stride, but Senor Wolden has taken off forward and right over the windshield above the cabin.

"I don't know," Senor Wolden tells you later. "All of a sudden I found myself on top of the cabin. I guess I just wanted to get out of the way."

Meanwhile your marlin has streaked out a good 200 yards and, instead of stopping, is leaping like a startled deer and tail-walking all over the horizon. You never even get a chance to count up to two, let alone 30—and then 30 again—unless you do it by tens.

You are too busy, you and Eduardo, trying to get the rod into the rod holder on the "fighting chair." You finally get the rod set up, the drag set, and your harness hooked up to the reel. By that time your fish has sounded; he has gone down through a hole in the bottom of the ocean. He finally stops but you can't gain any line on him. You work for 10 minutes and gain two inches and then he breaks your heart by taking eight feet out on you. This goes on, and on.

It goes for one hour and 50 minutes to be exact and there are times when you wonder. You wonder shouldn't you be in San Francisco, where the fog makes it nice and cool, instead of this furnace with a tiger by the tail.

Eduardo comes over with a can of beer in his hand and pours a couple of gulps down your throat. You love Eduardo. Eduardo es your amigo.

"Esgranday marleen," he tells you.

"Gracias, Eduardo."

Finally Senor Marlin begins to give a little. Inch by inch you gain on him and Eduardo tightens the drag . . . just a little. You don't want Senor to break the line and take off after all this battle.

You begin to gain in bigger hunks . . . foot by foot, yard by yard. You're winning at last.

Finally you can see the leader, and Eduardo and Rudy get your marlin to the side of the boat. It's all over and you get the first look at fish. He only weighs 143 pounds but to you he is granday.

All hands shake hands and there is much congratulating and graciasing.

Tio raises the marlin flag on the boat and you're off for the Lodge.

When you get there, the guests have spotted the flag on the boat through the binoculars and are all down at the beach to greet you.

You are tired and very happy—and so is everybody else.

I'm telling you, Senors, if you want some real great fishing, try the Flying Sportsmen Lodge at Loreto.

"Esgranday."

Marathon

"WE CONQUER," HE CRIED, AND FELL DEAD

By Edward Linn

From True

APRIL 19 IN Boston is Patriots' Day, a legal holiday celebrated in honor of the Minutemen who defended Lexington and Concord from the British, thereby kicking off the Revolutionary War. April 19 is also the day the storied, 57-year-old Boston marathon is kicked off, when upward of half a million people line the streets to watch a swirling mob of runners compete in a foot race originally conceived by the ancient Greeks over 2,000 years ago.

All the valiant athletes have to do for the privilege of romping the 26 miles and 285 yards is pass a physical examination and put up $1 apiece. What do they get for their money? Why, the winner gets a laurel crown flown over from Greece at the expense of an enterprising hotel owner named George Demeter. The rest of the runners—for their dollar—get a post-bellum bowl of beef stew and a plate of ice cream. The aches and pains they pick up en route come free of charge.

There is a general delusion that marathoners are knobby-kneed old gentlemen who pad sedately over the course at something less than a jog. Let's get one thing straight right away: The average winning time of two hours and thirty minutes breaks down to just under six minutes per mile. Since a finely trained college miler—and we're excepting the standouts—is happy to do it in four and a half minutes, we can assume that the average American, in the prime of life athletically speaking, would be hard put to run one mile as fast as a marathoner runs each of his 26.

And you could bet the family jewels that only a very good middle-distance man could stay with a marathoner for two miles.

These, then, are superbly conditioned athletes blessed with running ability as well as durability. An untrained entry has about the same chance as a flat-chested cover girl.

But, make no mistake about it, no matter how faithfully these men train, the pace begins to gnaw at them. They have to fight off side-stitches and run off muscle cramps and learn to live with the stale, cotton-dry taste of blood in their mouths and the hot chug-chug of rivets in their brains. And their feet begin to heat up and swell and maybe blister. And if the blister breaks and the feet begin to bleed, the coagulating blood cements the shoe to the foot.

Joie Ray, the great little miler of the early 1920's, tried the Boston marathon in 1928 in a last-ditch attempt to make the Olympic squad. The aging Ray finished third on feet so raw and bloody that his shoes literally had to be cut off. (Joie, as gritty as they came, finally made the team three months later by winning the Olympic tryout at Long Beach. He was the first American to finish at Amsterdam.)

Since Joie Rays are not universal even in as tough a sport as marathoning, a Red Cross ambulance stalks the field like a white-coated jackal, scooping up the wounded and exhausted, and administering footpads, spirits of ammonia or sympathy as the situation warrants.

An added hazard of recent years has been the appearance in force of yapping, snapping dogs and—even more deadly—of small boys set loose upon society atop bicycles. One prudent marathoner, 62-year-old Clovis Bourdelais, sports a walking-stick at his side to discourage any assault upon his thin shanks by boy, beast or bicycle. Bourdelais will be competing in his 37th consecutive Boston A.A. marathon this year, a record of faithful attendance which has won him permanent possession of the number 13. He has won little else.

The ambulance picks up a couple of dozen slightly frayed passengers in the course of a busy afternoon, but these, for the most part, are the undertrained and the overmatched. The dedicated marathoners almost always manage to stagger onward, if only on heart and pride.

Two years ago, Norman Tanamaka, a 45-year-old Hawaiian, finished sixth only because he willed himself on after his strength had been spent. Husbanding one last wisp of energy for a final lunge across the finish line, he collapsed into the arms of Boston's mayor, John P. Hynes. He was carried to the locker room where he remained paralyzed from the waist down for eight hours.

And this feat of immolation does not even begin to challenge, in either intensity or virtuosity, the all-time suffering-championship won by a young brakeman named Fred McGlone. McGlone's initial brush with fame was coincident upon the fact that the marathon course cut through Natick, his home town. In addition to the felicitations of his friends and neighbors, McGlone could look forward to an annual greeting from his sister, an athletic girl who would accompany him, stride for stride, through the town, imparting refreshing head-baths and sisterly advice. (And, incidentally, providing photographers with a moving family portrait.)

Aided by such unstinting family devotion McGlone improved steadily, became "sprint" (20-mile tune-up) champion of New England and entered the 1941 race as a solid favorite. He led the pack for 20 miles, clambered up the rugged hills of Newton in the best of health but—as is not infrequently the case—came tumbling down a total wreck. Yet he lurched and reeled six more miles, collapsed with the finish in sight, and started to *crawl* the final 200 yards down Exeter Street.

A policeman, overflowing with the compassion of his calling, rushed out to help him, but McGlone fought him off, sank back to the pavement, and continued doggedly on to the finish on hands and knees.

As a tribute to his courage, Fred McGlone was disqualified.

McGlone had fought off the policeman not in any excess of pride, but in the knowledge that the rules specifically prohibited any kind of physical aid. The disqualification left him so shaken that he suffered a stroke of sanity and announced his retirement. Fortunately, he recovered in time to finish third the following year. Satisfied that he had finally achieved the immortality—if that's the word for it—of the record book, McGlone then quit for good, dragging his sister into undeserved anonymity beside him.

A somewhat similar situation cropped up in 1899, two years after the Boston Marathon had been devilishly conceived by the B.A.A. Larry Brignoli, the village blacksmith of Cambridge, rambled down the then unpaved thoroughfare of Commonwealth Avenue, miles ahead of the pack. While he was modestly accepting the plaudits of the crowd, Brignoli stumbled into one of the sportsworld's most embarrassing situations. He tripped over a stray rock and knocked himself out.

The police of that era, their simple minds uncluttered by any nonsense about which vehicle has the right of way at an intersection, knew better than to lay unclean hands upon him. Instead, they formed a cordon around the body—to protect it, presumably, from runaway horses and circling buzzards—and watched with idle curiosity for signs of life. After ten minutes Brignoli began to stir. He rubbed his head. Got to his feet. Ran. Won.

The turn of the century may seem like a long day's digging, but it almost seems as though we have to go down that deep for an American winner. The national amateur associations of other lands have been flooding Boston with their marathon champions and if the situation continues to deteriorate, the homegrown product will have to lobby for tariff protection. The last American to lead the pack home was little Johnny "the bridegroom" Kelley (two firsts, seven seconds) who won in 1945.

In 1946 a Greek meter reader, Stylianos Kyriakides, crowned the BAA's Golden Anniversary with a surprising, but most fitting victory, and then was himself crowned with the laurel wreath he had personally carried to Demeter from the mayor of Athens. In 1947, the winner was the little Korean record-breaker, Yun Bok Suh; and since then, Gerard Cote, a Canadian cop; Karl Leandersson, a Swedish landscape gardener; Ham Kee Yong, another Korean (the Koreans finished 1-2-3 that year) ; Shigeki Tanaka, a Japanese survivor of the Hiroshima A-Bombing, and Doroteo Flores, a Guatemalan cotton weaver.

Last year's winner was Keizo Yamada, a 5-2, 97-pound Japanese mining engineer who got picked up in a heavy tail wind and kited across the course in 2:18:51, the fastest marathon ever run by anyone, any place, any time. To indicate that the wind might have been some help, the next two finishers, a Finn and a Swede, turned in the next two fastest times ever run.

Each of these winners became national heroes and recipients of state patronage. But an American winner—back there when Americans won—could look forward to little more than 24 hours worth of renown around the Greater Boston Metropolitan area and, if unemployed, a number of job offers. Yet the relative decline of the American marathoner is due not so much to a lack of incentive as to the mechanical mode of American travel. For marathoning is not so much a hobby, in the sense of coin-collecting or even golf; it is, to use a badly strained phrase, a way of life. And an exceedingly jealous one.

A marathoner runs to work. He runs home. He eats only the simple, solid foods. He pickles his feet in a rock-salt solution every night to toughen them for the never-ending battle against blisters. While his neighbors are going to the movies or to night clubs or even sitting at home watching television, he is out on the road rounding out his daily dozen miles.

The social life of a marathoner's wife can, as you may have guessed, become something less than riotous. About ten years ago the wife of one of the leading marathoners handed him a flat three-word ultimatum: "Me or marathoning."

He's still running, though. Got himself a new wife.

The product of this spartan regime is a spectacularly rugged breed of men. Dr. Lawrence Morehouse, who has studied and trained marathoners as part of his work at both the University of Southern California's physical education department and the Harvard Fatigue Laboratory, has found that "through habitual dosage, they have acquired an immunity to fatigue. That is, their bloodstreams automatically dispose of most of the waste material which should, normally, lead to exhaustion.

"In addition, their pulse rates are abnormally slow both when they're running and when they're at ease. This gives their heart an unusually long period of rest between every beat."

Flores, the 1952 winner, finished with a pulse rate of only 92, scarcely above normal. Yamada, last year, needed only three minutes to drop his pulse back to normal. Consider, now, how your own pulse pounds after a short dash for the bus.

And yet Dr. Morehouse's research has failed to indicate that either the stamina or pulse rate is innate. On the contrary, it has convinced him that marathoning is well within the capacity of any normal heart, so long as that tolerance to fatigue is first built up through long hours of faithful training.

Mike Ryan, probably the greatest coach of long-distance running we've ever had, is willing to go a lot further than that. Mike won the 1912 BAA race in the mud and snow, ran or coached in every Olympics between 1912-1924, then went to make tiny University of Idaho the cross-country power of the giant Pacific Coast conference. The Republic of Guatemala finally enlarged Mike's horizons by appointing him athletic director of the entire country, and he trained Flores.

Mike proceeds on the rather startling theory that running is the natural metier of man. A baby crawls, he pointed out, then walks and finally runs. Thus, if the human race could be dissuaded from frustrating nature practically at the fond, man would be running with the same ease with which he now walks. And, conversely, walking would become as uncomfortable to the fully flowered adult as crawling.

Mike used to exhort his Idaho students to literally get out of bed running. Run to the toothbrush. Run to meals. Run to classes. He has not, of this date, found any other anthropologists to indorse this theory of the stages of man's mobility and, indeed, his

Idaho students seemed inclined toward a somewhat similar skepticism.

Except for this willingness to spend all their spare time testing the limits of their endurance—and a marathoner would be the last to deny that long-distance running is a form of self-torture—there is little to distinguish marathoners from saner folk. Of the best American runners, Vic Dyrgall is a New Jersey accountant; Tom Jones is a history professor at Lincoln University in Oxford, Pennsylvania; Johnny Lafferty, a naval petty officer; and Jesse Van Zant, a Boston postoffice worker out of California. Old Clarence DeMar, the seven-time winner, who ran his 32nd marathon last year at the age of 65, is a compositor.

The incomparable DeMar's victories bridged the years 1911 and 1930, but his greatest hour did not come until 1938 when, at the usually sedentary age of 50, he took a rousing seventh.

There is one physical constant, though. Marathoners come in small sizes. The only difference between them and jockeys is that a jockey's weight sits on the back of his horse, whereas the marathoner's sits upon himself.

"Marathoners," Dr. Morehouse has found, "are completely fatless, a condition most difficult to attain because extra food, the body's usual reward for extra work, must be denied. Why? Because ounces of food become tons of work when a man is running uphill."

The average marathoner stands 5-4 and weighs about 140 pounds. Yamada was the smallest. At 97 pounds, he was almost too small to be a jockey. The biggest is James H. Montague, a 220-pounder who comes up from Washington, D. C., every year. Montague is a cousin of the Duchess of Windsor, thereby lending tone as well as weight to the festivities. However, the king-sized socialite has added little to the competitive luster of the event. A man that big simply cannot lug his carcass over the course.

The heaviest winner was Plain Joe Smith, a Medford, Massachusetts, milkman, who stood 6 feet tall and weighed 170 pounds when he led the boys home in 1942. That's hitting the scales awfully hard for a marathoner.

Despite the suffering that goes on, the BAA is considered a speed course in comparison to, say, Yonkers, which is an endurance course. This is because the BAA starts 220 feet above sea level and works its way down. There are occasional rises along the way but there is no grueling uphill challenge until the "Heartbreak Hills" of Newton. At Boston College Heights, with 20 miles of travail put behind, the runner is back where he started, 220 feet above sea level. But the race is practically over because the run for home—the old BAA clubhouse—is predominantly downhill.

What strategy there is—and how much can there be?—is perpetrated upon those hills. Unhappily, the two most popular stratagems collide head-on. Some runners try to build up a long lead so that they can loaf over the hills, others prefer to "level them off" by hitting them in high.

As a matter of fact, the only race ever won by sheer brute strategy was stolen long before anybody got to Newton.

In 1907, the runners were startled to see Tom Longboat, a marathoner of no little experience, erupt into a scorching sprint only a few miles from the start. Too late they saw the reason. Longboat, anticipating four score and seven movie thrillers, was racing a train to a crossing.

Longboat won.

He then romped merrily along while the rest of the field piled up behind one of the longest, most leisurely freights in the annals of American railroading.

Things like that happened back in those days—and on into the forties—because the BAA flourished in a frankly carnival atmosphere. It used to be a dull day that didn't bring out a couple of cigar-puffers, a smattering of Gay-Nineties bathing suits and a representative collection of the mustachioed, the bearded and the tattooed. Restraint was so inconspicuous that even good runners would plunge into the pond beyond Natick, paddle around for a few minutes, then resume their carefree, waterlogged journey.

In more recent times, unhappily, the BAA has become solemn with tradition and swollen with dignity. Exhibitionists have been ruled off the track. Two years ago, a young man from Michigan named Joe Supanich came to the starting line armed with a serene optimism and a pair of sprinter's starting blocks—innocent enough weapons both. Mr. Supanich immediately found himself under siege from a task force of grim and frowning officials. There was little he could do but surrender his blocks—thus losing, perhaps, as much as one-tenth of a second.

Last year a Mexican named Pedro Jiminez precipitated another minor crisis by insisting that in Mexico it was permissible to run in stockinged feet. In Mexico, they must build their mountains softer. Pedro was with the leaders for 15 miles, but then his stockings wore out. Two barefoot miles and the skin wore out.

Pedro decided he'd better leave before he found himself running on the stumps of his ankles. This year, to the relief of the officials, he has promised to bring shoes.

The old BAA mare ain't what it used to be in other respects, too. Once the track and field center of the country and the headquarters of the sporting bloods of New England, the Boston Athletic Association is now little but a name and a memory perpetuated by the Boston Garden's president, Walter Brown, as a monument to his father, George V. Brown, one of its earliest leaders. It rises from the ashes only to conduct an indoor track meet in the winter and the marathon in the spring. The profits from the track meet eat up the marathon's deficit.

The origin of the marathon takes us back, of course, to 490 B.C. when the Greek courier, Pheidippides, raced from the battlefield of Marathon to the city of Athens to inform the populace that the Persians had been routed. "Rejoice," gasped Pheidippides, according to contemporary press agentry. "We conquer!" And so saying, died.

The Boston edition was not laid out haphazardly. The BAA surveyed all roads out of Boston in 1898 and discovered that the shag end of Route 1, the historic old Post Road, was an almost exact topographic replica of Pheidippides' original course. It could tell because the Greek course had been recharted for the revival of the Olympiad in Athens two years earlier.

The BAA chose Patriots' Day—a peculiarly Bostonian holiday —only because its mid-April weather seemed most suitable for the runners. The overlapping of Greek and American history was a happy accident.

The humpbacked marathon distance conjures up visions of historians crawling through the mountain passes of Greece with tape measures, but the prosaic fact is that the original Olympic distance was set arbitrarily at an even 25 miles (translated from a just-as-even 40,000 meters).

The added mile and 385 yards marks the marathon's curtsy to royalty. During the 1908 Olympiad in London, the Games Committee decided it would be nice to have 11-year-old Princess Mary, daughter of the Prince of Wales, act as official starter. Since there was an unwritten law against the young Princess performing such strenuous duties beyond the palace grounds, the committee, with characteristic generosity, carried the starting line back to Windsor Castle.

Rather than befoul the record books with that one year's odd distance the committee then decreed that all future marathons be adjusted to conform to this purely accidental new distance. There is no record that any marathoner was ever consulted about it— hardly surprising since all amateur committees automatically assume that marathoners have abandoned indignation along with reason.

The BAA—predominantly Irish as it was—had no intention of surrendering that easily to anything smacking of royal prerogative. It was, in fact, thirty years before it capitulated.

And then, on a cold blustery day in 1926, a Nova Scotian named Johnny Miles (and there is a name for a marathoner) blazed over the lengthened course in such incredible time—2:25:40.4s.—that it was obvious to everyone that it must have been laid out short. And everyone was right. It was short. All of 176 yards. Miles could have run that in about 30 seconds with the chairman of the Rules Committee on his back, but since he had not covered the full distance, his record-shattering time was not accepted.

On the record or off, though, Miles' run stood as the BAA's greatest until the 115-pound Korean schoolboy, Yun Bok Suh, ran the full distance 1 2/5 seconds faster. Yun Bok might have done a mite better at that if he hadn't been upended by a dog, knocked down by a bicycle and tripped up by his own loose shoelaces. Considering the hostile attitudes of man, machine, animal and God (it was a still, hot day), most students of the run still claim it was superior to Yamada's.

Bok, who had done all his previous running over the roller-coaster topography of Korea, portended what was to come when he returned from his first trial run over the course. "Where," he asked innocently, "are all those hills everybody's been telling me about?"

And even the redoubtable Yun Bok had his troubles—not of condition, obviously, but of tradition. The coach of that Korean team, the first ever sent to this country, was Kee Shung Sohn, the Korean who had won the 1936 Olympics under the enforced *nom-de-Jap* of Kitei Son. Sohn, who was also supposed to run, didn't discover until the eve of the race that Yun Bok had decided it would be an unforgivable show of disrespect to run ahead of such a great national hero in a foreign land. Unable to disabuse his charge of that rather touching deference to both himself and Oriental tradition, Sohn solved both their dilemmas by withdrawing from the race.

Better than anything else, Bok's attitude illustrates the wide difference in the social standing and prestige of foreign and American marathoners. Far from being regarded with awe, the American is abused and ridiculed by both the curbstone critic and the sports writer. He is looked upon as a freak or, at best, a harmless eccentric.

What, then, makes Sammy run . . . and run . . . and run?

Johnny Semple, the Glasgow-born marathoner who coaches the BAA's own team—he is the BAA's sole employe—is convinced in his heart that every jeer is a tribute in disguise. "They see 40 and 50-year-old men running along," Semple says (and we're brushing the heavy growth of Scottish burr from his voice), "and they feel sort of ashamed for letting themselves go soft and flabby. What are they really saying when they call us freaks? They're saying, 'I could do this too if I were crazy enough.' "

Johnny, who's been running thirty-three years, thinks he and his breed are regarded with a sort of brusque affection.

"Sometimes when I'm in a race I hear a father tell his boy, 'That's Johnny Semple. I can remember him running when I was a boy.' I like that. Or when I'm running along in practice some guy will stick his head out his car window and yell, 'Hi, Johnny.' I don't know, that makes me feel good."

Actually the boys seem to be held to the road by a closer camaraderie than exists in any other sport. They are a superior breed of men, these marathoners; they know it and they glory in it. There are three qualifications for this tight, exclusive fraternity: ability, condition and courage. And the greatest of these is courage.

It is the men of courage who are trotted out when marathoners get together to rerun the old races. Men like Smiling Jimmy Hennigan, who labored under the enormous handicap of leg muscles which stiffened when he ran uphill. Jimmy used to carry a branch-switch and when he'd feel the muscles begin to tighten he'd "massage" himself on the run. It took him seventeen years before he finished a race, but just three years later, in 1931, he found a day hot enough to keep his muscles well-oiled and won the most popular victory in BAA history.

And there was Tarzan Brown, a full-blooded Narragansett Indian, who literally ran himself blind in 1936, yet won by following the beam of his coach's voice down Commonwealth Avenue and into Exeter Street.

And there were Ham Kee Yong, Kil Yoon Song and Yun Chil Choi—not the Blue Plate special on a Chinese menu—but the three Koreans who swept the 1950 race. As Choi was turning into

Exeter Street that day, he suddenly collapsed to one knee, his features screwed in pain.

Johnny Lafferty, who had been only a few yards behind, ran on by him, but here the Korean coach leaped beside Choi screaming that Choi could give Korea the sweep by catching Lafferty. So Choi, spurred perhaps by the knowledge that the Voice of America was broadcasting the race to his countrymen, pulled himself to his feet, galloped past the astonished Lafferty and hurled himself across the line—all this, with his left thigh bound by a baseball-sized cramp which would have kept an ordinary human being flat on his back.

Condition and ability? Sure, says Semple. But also courage of an extraordinary degree.

When you come down to it, Semple asks, what's so wacky about kids keeping themselves in shape, eating good food and using their legs as God intended them to be used?

"That's all it amounts to," he says. "Look at me. I'm 50 years old. Do I look over 40?" (He doesn't. If his hairline were not receding he'd look no more than 35.)

"The first thing I tell any new kid," he says, "is that I want him to quit as soon as it becomes an ordeal.

"Nobody quits, though. We run because we love it." And Johnny Semple shakes his head and smiles a little ruefully. "Anybody would *have* to be crazy to do this for any other reason."

Hockey

THE FORGOTTEN RED WING

By Stan Saplin

From Sport, March, 1954

Copyright, 1954, Macfadden Publications
Reprinted by permission of copyright owner

HAVE YOU HEARD of Marty Pavelich? He's a hockey player, a left wing who came up to the majors with the Detroit Red Wings six years ago and has been with them ever since.

We conducted a survey in the Madison Square Garden lobby recently to discover what hockey patrons knew about this young man.

A lady fan who has been attending every home game of the New York Rangers for, "Oh, about six years," never heard of him. An equally-ardent male customer knew him—"very well." He said: "He's with the Black Hawks."

Two veteran New York sportswriters strolled in. One covers eight to ten games each year and sees another five or six as a spectator. "What is this, a gag?" he demanded. "Of course I know who Pavelich is." His first name? "Pete." His team? "Montreal." The other writer was more to the point. "I dunno," he answered.

Twenty people were asked to identify Pavelich. Seven placed him with the Red Wings but two of these thought he was a defenseman, rather than a forward. Only one of the seven was accurate all the way down the line—position, first name, etc. Five couldn't identify Pavelich at all. Three assigned him to the Chicago Black Hawks. Then there was the Montreal reply. Four others were "sure" they had seen him in action but couldn't recall the team he was with.

None of these was a casual visitor to hockey games. They were not necessarily fans who see every contest, but before any interview was permitted to pick up steam, it was established that the subject knew the difference between the crease and the blueline.

Prompt and correct replies to another set of questions verified this. Each was asked to identify three other Detroit players—Ted

Lindsay, Gordie Howe and Len (Red) Kelly. These are the stars
of the Red Wings, the skaters generally credited with being the
reason Detroit holds an unprecedented string of five National
League regular season championships. They'll receive additional
acclaim if the Wings make it six this season. Everybody we asked
knew Lindsay, Howe and Kelly and most people were able to tell
us something about each of them.

Lindsay has been the League's all-star left wing for four years,
and was the NHL scoring champion in 1949-50. Howe has won
the Hart Trophy as hockey's most valuable player for the past two
seasons and has been all-league right wing for three. He took the
scoring crown away from Lindsay three years ago and hasn't
relinquished it. Kelly, top-scoring defenseman in the league, has
been on the all-stars three years and twice has won the Lady Byng
Trophy, which is awarded for sportsmanship plus effectiveness.

Only four men in the lineup this year have been members of
every one of Detroit's five pennant-winning teams. Kelly, Howe
and Lindsay are three of them. Marty Pavelich, the man nobody
seems to know, is the fourth.

Pavelich has never been up close in the scoring race. He's never
been a contender for a league trophy. He's never figured in the
voting for all-league selection. Why do they keep him? What has
he got?

Jack Adams, general manager of the Detroit club, has often
said, "I'm not married to any of my hockey players." In other
words, he never hesitates to get rid of a player he doesn't want.

Since the Wings moved out front to become the Yankees of the
ice world, he has disposed of plenty of top-drawer talent. Those
sold or traded include Jack Stewart, Sid Abel and Bill Quacken-
bush, each an all-league performer, Harry Lumley, an excellent
goalkeeper, and Leo Reise, a sound and outstanding defenseman.

Pavelich, who averages 11 goals a year in a league in which a
player who scores 20 per season no longer creates excitement,
doesn't appear to be on a disposal list. Disposal? "Pavelich is one
of the key men around whom we build our hockey club," says
Adams.

Marty shares the fate of the blocking back in football, who's
essential to the success of a team but who watches the headlines
go to the fellow who scores the touchdowns. This comparison is
intended to convey only the anonymity of the job, not its function.
Pavelich's role as a wing, by title, calls for him to score the goals,
not to clear the way for others.

But as the figures show, he doesn't score them. However, Marty has two qualities which make him something of an indispensable man in the eyes of his bosses, even if those who cast ballots each year for awards and honors fail to recognize or reward him for these attributes.

His primary asset is his ability as a defensive or "checking" forward and there is no one in the sport today who can match him in this department. Marty draws the assignment of checking the league's great right wings. He's the man who covers Maurice (The Rocket) Richard, hockey's all-time record goal-scorer, when Detroit meets the Montreal Canadiens. He's "on" Wally Hergesheimer when they play the Rangers. Against the Black Hawks, Willie Mosienko is his man.

Detroit attained a peak of achievement in 1952 by winning eight straight playoff games. It was much more than coincidence that the forward line headed by Pavelich and containing Tony Leswick and Glen Skov did not permit a single goal to be scored against it throughout the playoffs. In the final round of four games with Montreal—the Toronto Maple Leafs were disposed of in the preliminary round—Marty completely tamed the dangerous Richard, not permitting him so much as an assist, much less a goal.

This left wing's secondary value to his club suggests a story-book touch, for it is wrapped around the old rah-rah theme, a rare item these days, at least in professional sports. It is a fact, though, that Pavelich is like a tonic to his teammates. Spirit is an intangible commodity but Marty clearly bubbles over with it, spreads it among his mates. How many games have been won by the Red Wings as a result of Marty's morale-boosting, hustle and defensive work cannot be estimated but the figure must be considerable.

It was spirited labors of this youngster that earned him his big-league chance, shortly after he turned 20, in December of 1947. Marty—his teammates call him Sabu because his black hair and flashing white teeth make him look something like the little Hindu boy in the movies—had turned pro only two months before with Indianapolis of the American League, a Detroit farm. A need developed to plug some holes in the Detroit lineup and Tommy Ivan, the dapper and quiet little fellow who coaches the champions, took advantage of an open date one night to watch the farmhands in a game.

Next morning back in Detroit, in Adams' office at Olympia

Stadium, the general manager asked, "Is there anybody down there who can help us?"

"That Pavelich kid won't get us many goals," Ivan replied, "but how the boy works! He'll never stop trying." A day later Marty was summoned to the parent club.

Working, in the case of Sabu, means never letting up. A Wing should sail down the ice when his team is on the offense. But when a play is broken up and the opposition takes the puck and swings quickly to the attack, far too many forwards let their men get away. They rely on their defensemen to prevent a goal. Pavelich torments the man he's covering. He makes passing difficult, shots almost impossible and as often as not he steals the puck. The mere presence of this 170-pounder on ice, players from other teams will tell you, makes it tough to get a goal.

When a Red Wing is sentenced to the penalty box and the team faces the hazardous job of playing five men against six for two minutes, Sabu's defensive skills pay off by preventing enemy scores and saving games.

"Why, it's a job to keep him off the ice even when he's injured," Adams says. "We practically have to put handcuffs on him to hold him down."

Hockey fans in Detroit and the Ontario cities of Sault Ste. Marie and Galt will probably react to our findings in the Pavelich survey with consternation and indignation. A native of Sault Ste. Marie and a performer in junior amateur ranks at Galt, Marty is extremely popular and very much a sports hero in both communities.

For the small kids playing shinny to the all-league stars on his team, Pavelich (you pronounce it Pavelitch) has a smile, a word of encouragement and a pat on the back. On the bench or on the ice during a game, he is the Wings' holler guy. On train trips when the club is on the road, Marty plops into a vacant seat next to a player who has been in a slump and offers encouragement.

On the latter point, Red Kelly, Marty's roommate, explains, "Sab's had so much bad luck on scoring goals that a fellow with a little slump going gets to thinking: 'Marty's missed so many goals himself and he isn't down in the mouth. What right have I got to be that way.' At least, it goes something like that—and it works miracles."

Kelly recalled that he was having some trouble in mid-season last year. "I couldn't get my shots away fast enough. My timing or my judgment was bad and I was beginning to walk around with a long face. First thing I knew, Sab had started in on me. He heard my complaints and suggested that we work on my shooting after practice.

"That's what we did. Just the two of us in the rink. He'd stand there with a hatful of pucks and pass them to me . . . to my right, to my left, off the boards and so on. I shook the slump in no time. Imagine the guy, giving up his own time, getting no benefit out of it himself. Just helping me."

Ivan, too, offered an illustration of the value of the Pavelich spirit to the club. "I don't know how many times we've gone into the dressing room between the second and third periods a goal or two behind . . . and before I can open my mouth to say a word to the fellows, Marty starts in. Before he's through, he's got them all fired up, and as often as not we'll pull out of the game with a win," the coach said.

Pavelich did just that early this season. The Wings had played three ties in a row, and for the champs that's not good hockey. Their next game was with the Rangers and they were trailing 1-0, going into the last period. Marty not only got results from others with a fight talk but he set up plays that resulted in a pair of goals to put the team out in front to stay.

Probably the first hockey pep talk ever delivered by Marty Pavelich was to his mother when he was six years old. He went through some soft ice in Sault Ste. Marie when he was indulging in shinny and almost drowned. A minister walking by rushed to his aid and took him home. When his mother got over the initial shock of the near tragedy, she ruled, "You'll never play hockey again!"

"I loved the game so much, even then," Marty recalls, "I talked her out of it, eventually."

After playing in midget hockey ranks, he moved up to the juvenile classification at Sault Technical School where he got his first formal coaching from a coach who had never skated in his life. His name was Ben Littner and Marty still remembers his teaching—endless chalk talks, shooting against mats over and over, penalty killing, passing. "I really got my grounding in the fundamentals under Mr. Littner," Pavelich says. "Joe Klukay, who's with the Boston Bruins, was one of his players, too. Tech won the city title about six times."

When Sabu was 15, a Red Wing scout, Fred Cox, saw him and

offered him a berth with the Galt Red Wings, then a Detroit-sponsored junior team. He played three seasons there, two under Al Murray and one under Normie Himes, both former National Leaguers. One of his opponents in league games there was Red Kelly.

Detroit brought Marty in from Galt at the end of the 1946-47 season and the following fall sent him to Indianapolis. He played only 26 games before joining the Red Wings.

His NHL debut was marked by two unique developments. In his first game, Pavelich likely played a shorter time than any man before him. In the second, he undoubtedly got the fastest goal ever scored.

In his first appearance in the league, against Toronto, Marty was on the bench when Ivan suddenly called for a change of lines, while play was on, and signaled for the rookie to go in. Pavelich climbed over the boards to replace a skater coming off and as he hit the ice, a linesman detected a player offside and blew his whistle to stop play. During the pause, Ivan decided to send out a different line and Marty returned to the bench, where he remained for the rest of the game. He estimates he "played" a half-second that evening.

The next game was against Chicago three nights later. In the first period, Ivan sent him out, again on the fly, to replace Ted Lindsay. The action was heading for the Chicago net and Pavelich skated furiously in that direction. He reached his destination just as goalie Emile Francis was brushing aside a shot by Gordie Howe. The rookie got his stick on the puck instantly and poked it into the net before Francis could wheel around to defend against the rebound. Not more than five seconds had elapsed from the moment he left the bench until he scored his first major-league goal.

Pavelich, who is of Croatian descent, might have made his way in baseball had he not preferred hockey. A catcher and a hard-hitting left-handed batter, he played in both junior and senior company at Galt. In the summer of 1946, Dick Fisher, a scout for the Brooklyn Dodgers, invited him to Olean, New York, for a tryout. On the strength of his showing there, the Dodgers offered him a contract and wanted to send him to their club at Zanesville, Ohio. He declined, however.

In 1947, he accepted an invitation to a St. Louis Cardinals tryout camp at Hamilton, Ontario, and again was offered a contract. This was just before he entered pro hockey and he refused once again. In '49, while he was in Boston with the Red Wings, Jeff Jones, a scout for the Braves, attempted to interest Marty in a baseball career but again he elected to stay with hockey.

Marty's baseball activities these days are confined to summer ball in his hometown, where as playing coach of the Lock City Beverages nine, he has led his team to the city senior title five years running.

Since last summer he has been an off-season sales representative for the Carling's brewery in the Soo. He did well in his first year at the job and he expects to stick with it, and perhaps make it a 12-month job after he is through with hockey. The Red Wings, however, don't plan to release this underrated hockey player to full-time beer selling for some time yet.

Track and Field

DUEL OF THE FOUR-MINUTE MEN
By Paul O'Neil

From Sports Illustrated, August 16, 1954

THE ART OF running the mile consists, in essence, of reaching the threshold of unconsciousness at the instant of breasting the tape. It is not an easy process, even in a setpiece race against time, for the body rebels against such agonizing usage and must be disciplined by the spirit and the mind. It is infinitely more difficult in the amphitheater of competition, for then the runner must remain alert and cunning despite the fogs of fatigue and pain; his instinctive calculation of pace must encompass maneuver for position, and he must harbor strength to answer the moves of other men before expending his last reserves in the war of the home stretch.

Few events in sport offer so ultimate a test of human courage and human will and human ability to dare and endure for the simple sake of struggle—classically run, it is a heart-stirring, throat-tightening spectacle. But the world of track has never seen anything quite to equal the "Mile of the Century" which England's Dr. Roger Gilbert Bannister—the tall, pale-skinned explorer of human exhaustion who first crashed the four-minute barrier—won here last Saturday from Australia's world-record holder, John Michael Landy. It will probably not see the like again for a long, long time.

The duel of history's first four-minute milers, high point of the quadrennial British Empire & Commonwealth Games, was the most widely heralded and universally contemplated match footrace of all time. Thirty-two thousand people jostled and screamed while it was run in Vancouver's new Empire Stadium, millions followed it avidly by television. It was also the most ferociously contested of all mile events. Despite the necessity of jockeying on the early turns and of moving up in a field of six other good men, Bannister ran a blazing 3:58.8 and Landy 3:59.6. Thus for the first time two men broke four minutes in the same race. (Though far back in the ruck, five other runners finished under 4:08—

253

Canada's Rich Ferguson in 4:04.6, Northern Ireland's Victor Milligan in 4:05, and both New Zealand's Murray Halberg and England's Ian Boyd in 4:07.2.)

Landy's world record of 3:58, set seven weeks ago in cool, still Nordic twilight at Turku, Finland, still stood when the tape was broken. But runners are truly tested only in races with their peers. When the four-minute mile was taken out of the laboratory and tried on the battlefield, Landy was beaten, man to man, and Roger Bannister reigned again as the giant of modern track.

Seldom has one event so completely overshadowed such a big and colorful sports carnival as this year's Empire Games. The Empire's miniature Olympics, for which Vancouver built its $2,-000,000 stadium, a bicycle velodrome and a magnificent swimming pool, would have been notable if only for the rugged, sea-girt, mountain-hung beauty amidst which they were held. They were further enlivened by the sight of Vancouver's kilted, scarlet-coated Seaforth Highland Regiment on parade, by the presence of Britain's Field Marshal Earl Alexander of Tunis, and—more exciting yet—of Queen Elizabeth's tall, handsome husband, Philip, Duke of Edinburgh.

During seven days of competition 20 of 27 games records were cracked in track and field events alone, and England, by virtue of her peerless distance runners, walked off with the lion's share of glory (scoring by unofficial points: England 514½, Australia 363¾, Canada 339, South Africa 260¾) and served notice on the world of tremendous new strength. Canadians and U. S. tourists alike were startled at the Elizabethan rudeness with which the Englishmen (Oxonians almost to a man, and thus held to be effete) ran their opposition into the ground in races demanding stamina and bottom. They placed one, two, three in the six mile (won by Peter Driver), one, two, three in the three mile (won by amiable, beer-quaffing Chris Chataway, who paced Bannister in the Oxford mile), and one, two, three in the half mile (won by Derek James Neville Johnson).

There were also alarums and sensations. Australia's bicycle team protested English tactics, were rebuffed, withdrew from competition in a scandalous huff, cooled off, and duly re-entered the lists. Vancouver's world champion weightlifter, Doug Hepburn—who stands 5'8", weighs 299 pounds, measures 22 inches around the biceps and wears the look of a Terrible Turk—lifted an aggregate of 1,040 pounds with contemptuous ease while his fellow citizens watched with unsurpassed pride and glee.

Canada's big, beautiful, blond woman shotputter, the Toronto schoolteacher Jackie MacDonald, was barred from competition in mid-meet for publicly endorsing Orange Crush. And the big closing-day crowd in the stadium was treated to one of the most gruesome scenes in sports history after England's marathon champion, Jim Peters, entered the track a mile ahead of his field but almost completely unconscious from strain and weariness. Peters fell as he came in sight of the crowd, rose drunkenly, staggered a few steps and fell again, until he was lifted to a stretcher and thus disqualified short of victory.

But for all this, nothing in the games remotely approached the tension and drama inherent in the mile. The race developed, in fact, amid an atmosphere much more reminiscent of a heavyweight championship fight than a contest of amateurs on the track. This was not unjustified; it was obvious from the beginning that Bannister and Landy would be engaged in a sort of gladiatorial combat, a duel of endurance in which no two other men who ever lived could even have engaged.

At first glance they seemed like an odd pair of gladiators. Like most distance men both look frail and thin in street clothes. Landy has a mop of dark, curly hair, the startled brown eyes of a deer, a soft voice with little trace of the Australian snarl, and a curious habit of bending forward and clasping his hands before his chest when making a conversational point. As a student at Australia's Geelong Grammar School ("A Church of England school," says his father with satisfaction, "where the prefects whack the boys, y'know") John developed a passion for the collection of butterflies and moths and an ambition to become an entomologist (which his father cured by sending him to Melbourne University to study agricultural science).

Roger Bannister is taller (6'3/4" to Landy's 5'11 1/4"), slightly heavier (156 pounds to Landy's 150) and slightly older (25 to Landy's 24) but he too would be the last man in the world to be singled out of a crowd as an athlete. He is stooped and negligent in carriage; he has lank blond hair, a high-cheeked, peaked face, and a polite and noncommittal upper-class British voice. The face is expressive and can flash with instant animation and warmth. He can use words with precision and humor, and at times, even with a sort of conversational eloquence. But scholarly is the word for Dr. Bannister. It is apt—he is a scholar and a brilliant one. Perhaps five per cent of London medical students go through their courses without failing one exam and Bannister was among that small fraction when he received his degree at London's St. Mary's Hospital this year.

But men are seldom what they seem; Bannister, a complex and many-sided person, is both repelled and fascinated by the hurly-burly of big time sport, but for seven years, he has driven himself, stoically as an Indian brave or a man climbing Everest, toward the four-minute mile. So during the last five years has John Michael Landy. Both men have engaged in endless and grueling effort to explore and push back the furthest boundaries of their own endurance.

Neither has ever been coached—in the casual British club system of competition, unlike the more regimented U. S. college team system, runners are presumed to be able to train themselves. Separately, half a world apart, both Bannister and Landy arrived at curiously identical conclusions; both decided that overtraining and staleness were simply myths and that the more the body endures the more it will endure. Both drove themselves to extremes of exertion (training sessions of 10 to 14 58-second quarter miles with one lap walked between) which would have staggered the average U. S. athlete.

Bannister carried his preoccupation with the mysteries of exhaustion into the world of science when he was a medical student at Oxford in 1951. He ran to the point of total collapse on a treadmill almost daily, with hollow needles thrust into his fingers to measure lactic acid and with an oxygen mask clapped over his face to give him extra fuel. Meanwhile at Oxford, and all through his three years at St. Mary's (where he ducked out to Paddington Recreation Ground and paid three pence to use the cinder paths), he went on with his massive burden of running.

The two four-minute milers developed into unique beings—men whose hearts have enormous capacity and power and whose bodies can utilize oxygen with fantastic economy and resist the inroads of fatigue with fantastic success. Bannister's pulse rate, which was a normal 65 when he was 17, is now 45. Landy's is 50. But there their similarities end. In Vancouver, as the remorseless pressure of the world's excitement pressed down on them, and race day neared, their differences of temperament became obvious. Landy seemed assured, relaxed, cocky. Bannister became quiet, remote, and fled daily to a golf course to train.

But Bannister's teammates were not misled. "Roger hates the idea of having to beat Landy—of having thousands of people expecting him to do it," said one. "But he'll do it. Nobody gets in such an emotional pitch before a race as he does. He's got a cold now, you know. I suspect it is psychosomatic and I suspect he suspects it—he had one just like it before the Oxford mile. Roger may tell you he has slept before a race, but he hasn't. When he goes out to run he looks like a man going to the electric chair. There are times the night before a race when he actually makes involuntary sounds, like a man being tortured. But Roger is a hard man to comfort—if you try he'll give you a look that goes right through you."

Whatever their preliminary travail, both runners seemed equally intent and equally oblivious of the rumble and roar of applause as they warmed up on the infield grass in the moments before race time. Bright sunlight bathed the jampacked stadium. The temperature stood at a pleasant 72, the relative humidity at a pleasant 48. Only the faintest of breezes moved on the track, as the field of milers was called to the mark. Landy, in the green of Australia, stepped quietly into the pole position. Bannister, in the red-barred white of England, had lane 5—he drew one deep, shuddering breath and then leaned forward for a standing start.

The gun puffed and popped and New Zealand's darkhorse Murray Halberg burst into the lead with his teammate William David Baillie at his heels. Landy let them go—he wanted speed, but he wanted top cover if he could get it—and settled into a docile fourth on the turn. He stayed there for less than the lap. The pacesetters showed, almost imperceptibly, and Landy moved instantly and decisively into the lead. His strategy was simple and savage—to run the first seven furlongs at so blazing a pace that Bannister would be robbed of his famous kick.

As Landy moved, Bannister moved too. They ran Landy first, Bannister second at the end of the stretch and the duel had begun. "Time for the first lap," the loudspeakers grated as they entered the turn, "fifty-eight seconds." Then bedlam began too. It increased as Landy moved away—five yards, ten yards, fifteen yards—in the backstretch of the second lap, and Bannister let him go. "It was a frightening thing to do," said the Englishman later, "but I believed he was running too fast. I had to save for my final burst and hope I could catch him in time."

Landy's time was 1:58 at the half. The groundwork for a four-minute mile had been laid. The field had faded far to the rear. The duelists ran alone in front with Landy still making the pace. But now, yard by yard, easily, almost imperceptibly Bannister was regaining ground. He was within striking distance as they fled into the last, decisive quarter amid a hysterical uproar of applause. He stayed there on the turn.

Two hundred yards from home, Landy made his bid for decision and victory. But Bannister refused to be shaken, and with 90 yards to go he lengthened his plunging stride. He came up shoulder to shoulder, fought for momentum, pulled away to a four-yard lead and ran steadily and stylishly through a deafening clamor to the tape. He fell, arms flapping, legs buckling, into the arms of the English team manager a split second after the race was done.

"I tried to pull away from him in the backstretch of the last lap," said Landy after he ceased to gasp for breath. "I had hoped that the pace would be so fast that he would crack at that point. He didn't. When you get a man in that sort of a situation and he doesn't crack, you do. From then on I knew it was only a question of time. I looked over my left shoulder to see where he was on the turn, and when I looked back he was ahead of me." He paused, grinned, shook his head and added: "I've had it."

Dogs

CANINE KING

By John Rendel

From The New York Times, February 10, 1954

A BUFF-COLORED cocker spaniel that was all sweet-flowing gaiety in motion gave the answer to the main question in Madison Square Garden last night. The question was, "Which one would win?" The answer was Ch. Carmor's Rise and Shine from High Point, N. C.

He was the one that became best in show from the competitive stresses of the Westminster Kennel Club event. He was the one that was projected from obscurity to national prominence and bore his owner, Mrs. Carl E. Morgan, to prominence, too. He was the one that became a new ruler of dogdom, the winner of the highest honor the American bench can offer.

There were 2,571 other aspirants. All had fallen along the way during two days of the great elimination. Only Rise and Shine remained to gather the purple and gold ribbon and the polished silverware that stood for supremacy.

This was a passive sort of sports event. There was no swirling action, only the swirling of the fine feathers of the long-haired finalists when they were gaited. There was no physical contact except the judge's hands on the dogs when he tested them, no quick turns of fortune except when the judge wheeled and pointed to the spaniel as the winner.

When it was over the spaniel stood on a block-long expanse of green matting. A yellow wooden sign next to him read in red letters, "Best Dog In Show." There were 10,000 spectators in the surrounding seats. Flash-bulb lights glinted from the trophies and from Rise and Shine's golden flanks. There was applause, comment on the merits of the decision, then a seeping away of the crowd. The seventy-eighth Westminster was over.

Behind the 2-year-old was a long line of careful breeding, with Ch. Carolina Cotton Picker-Carmor's Honey Dew the immediate forebears. One man's opinion made Rise and Shine supreme. The judge was Virgil D. Johnson of Savannah, Ga., mail order house executive.

"There were six great dogs in the ring," the judge said afterward. "I couldn't have gone far wrong on any of them. He (the cocker spaniel) was as smooth as he could be. He moved excellently and was in beautiful coat. He is one of the best buff cockers I have ever seen."

The tribute was to a polished show dog in rich, beautiful coat who moved as impassively as though he never had performed before any but large metropolitan crowds. That wasn't altogether so, for Rise and Shine had been shown only six months. He had been only moderately successful, having won four breed awards in specialties and two previous groups in all-breed events before taking Westminster's big one.

When it was all over, Rise and Shine rose and shone, for Ted Young Jr., the handler, flung the dog high in his arms in joy. The victory restored Westminster's highest accolades to a member of the sporting breeds for the first time since another cocker spaniel, the greatest of all, Ch. My Own Brucie, won in 1941.

That year Brucie turned in the second of his two Westminster bests. As momentous as was the Southern dog's triumph, only the rashest in the Garden would dared have likened the latest winner to that famous black dog.

Rise and Shine's victory struck a high note of popularity with the gallery. The spectators warmed to him slowly, but when he was gaited the final time it was apparent from the applause that the spaniel had won many supporters.

There were admirers, too, for an imported bulldog up from the classes, Kippax Fearnaught, who moved with the deliberate rolling gait of a portly old sea captain, as casual as could be.

There were others who fastened upon a clean-limbed fawn and white boxer, Larry Downey's Ch. Spark Plug. The boxer was loaded with quality in his finely formed frame, but he showed he was still new to the ring by wanting to romp when he was gaited

There were others who doted upon a stalwart kerry blue terrier Mrs. M. Eileen McEachren's Ch. Miss Showoff of Cognewaugh an American-bred from Todmorden, Canada, or upon a beautiful blond-colored Afghan, belonging to Kay Finch of Del Mar, Calif. Ch. Taejon of Crown Crest.

Others like a Yorkshire terrier, Mrs. L. S. Gordon Jr.'s and Janet Bennett's Ch. Star Twilight of Clu-Mor. The toy had a silky blue and tan coat trailing to the ground and a lavender topknot festooned gaily on his head. But the judge liked the cocker spaniel, and that was that.

It has been years since the dog-wise at a Garden Show have buzzed about a dog as enthusiastically as they did about the bulldog. Kippax Fearnaught, a house pet owned by Dr. J. A. Saylor of Long Beach, Calif., was said by some experts of long standing to be the best they ever had seen, by others the best in many years.

The bulldog qualified at the matinee and so did the Afghan Taejon and the Yorkshire terrier.

The hound and the toy were dogs of rare sustances, but expressions of praise for them were whispers compared to the comment on the "sour-mugg" that was in this country from England only two months.

Edward H. Goodwin put the 15-month-old dog up in the variety group and the decision was uniformly approved. Dr. Saylor himself refrained from superlatives but quoted a British judge, Roger Bolton, on the dog when Fearnaught was in England.

"He doesn't have a great front," said Bolton, "but all points put together tend to form a perfect whole as near the standard as possible."

The dog is predominantly red. The face and chest are white and so are the feet on forelegs that are strong and bowed. The chest is deep and wide, the muzzle flat, the head massive. He moves with the rolling gait that is desired in the breed. There is an indication of power under restraint.

Dr. Saylor had admired the dog's sire, Ch. Koper Kernal, for a long while and bought the son after seeing two photographs. "Jock," as the young general practitioner calls him, was an immediate sensation in California. He was entered in three Coast shows, won best at two of them.

The owner was persuaded to come East to Westminster for his first visit and wasn't sorry. In addition to the other honors, Fearnaught finished his championship in this, his fourth ring appearance. Dr. Saylor has turned down an offer of $10,000 for the dog. He doesn't intend to show much, but will concentrate on breeding in a hope of improving bulldogs in America.

Besides projecting the bulldog into national prominence and sending the Afghan and the Yorkshire terrier into the final, the matinee removed two defending variety group winners of last year from the contention.

Tom and Pearl Sheahan's bloodhound, Ch. Fancy Bombardier,

best of the hounds in last winter's Westminster, placed second behind Taejon this time. That was a reversal of the 1953 order, when the Afghan was the runner-up. The defending toy, Ch. Pugville's Mighty Jim, placed third in the group behind the Yorkie and Mrs. Peter Frelinghuysen's toy poodle, Ch. Smilestone's Fancy Free.

The Yorkie, like the bulldog, was an importation. Taejon is an American-bred. The toy, "Tuffy" to his friends, was brought from Ireland two years ago and has fared spectacularly well. Among his honors are six all-breed bests. He's a four-pound 4-year-old with a beautiful, trailing blue and tan coat.

The Afghan, winner of last Sunday's specialty show, is a 3-year-old blond dog with a fine black mask. He's a nicely balanced dog called "Johnny," with an imposing record that includes fifteen bests in all-breed circles and three specialties.

General

BASEBALL EYE

By John Lardner

From Newsweek, May 31, 1954

Case 1

I'M JACK LARKIN, a private eye. You name it, I'll do it. Right now, I'm on a trick in Philly, tailing ballplayers.

You think I'm a lucky guy? Well, I've got to admit it looks that way. I'm 6.2. I'm hard as nails. I'm beautiful. Dames follow me, and I follow ballplayers. If they don't get home by midnight (or 2 a.m. after night games), they're dead. I've sent many a left-handed hitter to the hot squat. That doesn't bother me. I see it this way: If a ballplayer gets in at 12:01 (or 2:01, after night games), he's not fit to live. He's a mad dog. In this game, society calls the shots.

But the assignment is not all steak and eggs. It's mean. It's murder. You probably read in the papers the other day where a private op, name of Charles Leland, was picked up by the cops while tailing Hamner, the Phillie infielder. What happened? This Hamner pulled a hidden-ball gimmick on him. He spotted the tail and phoned police headquarters.

Before the shamus knew what had happened, he was in the can, under $500 bail. He had to pretend he'd got Hamner mixed up with a divorce case, driving the same make and color heap.

Bob Carpenter, the Phillie president, finally took him off the hook. He said that all ball clubs put tails on their players. He said it's for the good of the game. Suppose Hamner got in at 2:02 some night? Suppose he took a beer? What do we want here, Russia?

Well, Mr. Carpenter was right. But that didn't do the dick any good. For him, it was tough. It was embarrassing. These ballplayers are mean as foxes.

263

I had a trick the same night. The Old Man said: "They want you to tail Robin Roberts. If you lose him, don't come back." I looked right at him. I figured I could do one of three things: Punch him, borrow $10, or do what he said. So I sneered, "OK," and drove to Philly.

I took a plant at the ball park. Pretty soon, out came Roberts, looking innocent. He climbed into his boiler, and drove away. I followed, keeping two blocks between us all the way. Don't ask me which two blocks. Probably Walnut and Chestnut.

Suddenly, at the corner of Third and Peanut, crash! Bam! Another bucket, a blue-gray sedan, hit me from the side. The driver came out with his gun in his hand. I came out the same way.

But it was only Charlie Schultz, another op from our office. I recognized him before we'd exchanged more than half a dozen shots. I said: "What's the matter with you?" He said: "I'm tailing Richie Ashburn. He can fly." I told him to get lost, and we went back to work.

For a few blocks, I still thought I had Roberts in front of me. But then he scratched his nose with his left hand, and I knew it was Simmons. Well, I thought, what's the difference? These pitchers are all alike. One of them is just as liable to get drunk, or sell our secrets to Hawaii, as the next one. And just then, sure enough, he parked his car across a sidewalk at Fifth and Coconut and went into a gin mill.

I followed, and took a plant behind a cuspidor. I watched him drink six fast bourbon-and-waters in a row. I was ready to turn to the next page in my notebook—we average six drinks a page—when he took the glass away from his face for a split second, and I saw it wasn't Simmons. It was Charlie Gratz, another private eye.

"What's up?" I snapped at him. He said: "I was tailing Willie Jones. I had him in a rundown between Fourth and Betel-nut, but he got away." "Kicked the ball out of your hands, I suppose?" I sneered—and I meant it to hurt. But he wouldn't tell me any more. He was low—mighty low.

We left the joint together. There, walking down the street right in front of us, was Jim Konstanty. At least, it looked like him. We were on him like a couple of wildcats. I socked him in the pit of the stomach. Charlie kicked him in the knee. Then the guy socked, kicked, gouged and butted us, tied us up, and threw us into the meat wagon. He turned out to be Sergeant Delehanty, the light heavyweight champion of the riot squad.

As Mr. Carpenter says, if the players aren't watched, what will become of the game?

* * *

Case 2

You remember me. Jack Larkin, private eye. They had me tailing the Philadelphia Phillies some weeks back, to see where they went. I found out. They went into the second division.

Back at the office, the Old Man told me: "New orders just came in. You're the Phillies' manager. That puts you on the inside, where you can look around."

It surprised me. But I kept my face dead, lit a cigarette, and said: "That means I replace Big Fred Fitzsimmons." The Old Man knocked the cigarette out of my mouth. He hates my insides. I appeal to dames; he doesn't. He said: "Who're you voting for this year, Garfield? They fired Fitzsimmons. Then they fired Big Ed Sawyer. Then they fired Big Steve O'Neill. You're next. You'll work under the name of Terry Moore."

I said: "I get it. Nice casting. Moore could catch anything." The Old Man said: "You couldn't catch a spoon in a cup of coffee. But you're the only op I got available. Now get out of here. Grab a train West, and pick up your ball club."

I caught the team in Cincinnati, and we lost four straight. Then we hit St. Louis. You could cook your dinner on the sidewalk. There was a doubleheader Sunday. We won the first one, 11 to 10, according to the scoreboard, which I cased all the way. This Stanky was handling the other club. I could see he wasn't feeling good. Every now and then he shot a dirty look across at me. I ignored him. When you're a guy women go for, you get used to dirty looks from your own sex. Besides, if I had the kind of pitching this fellow has, I'd be sore, too.

In the second game, we were leading 8 to 1 in the fifth inning when they dusted Torgeson, my first baseman. He hollered like a moose. Then he started an argument with Yvars, the Cardinal catcher. It sounded like the kind of stuff I was after, so I beat it out there with my notebook and took a plant behind the umpire.

Yvars looked my man right in the kisser. He said: "You slugged me in June 1952. Now it is July 1954, and I am going to slug you." I could see the case had a lot of background.

The next thing I knew, Stanky came at me. He said: "Are you Moore, the guy that said I was temperamentally unsuited to manage a ball club?" Hell, I thought, here's more background. In my grift, you learn to think fast. I stalled him. I said: "Well, I'm not G. David Doubleday." Stanky said: "I think you're the guy that said I was temperamentally unsuited to manage a ball club." Then he knocked me down.

I didn't go for my gun. In a stranger's town, you have to play it easy. But I promised myself that the first time I met him in my own yard, I would look down his throat and tell him that I thought he was temperamentally unsuited to manage a ball club.

By the time they ran us off the field, it was nearly dark. I kept an eye on Stanky, over the way. I thought he might try a shot from the hip. Pretty soon, I got a feeling that he was up to something else: Delaying the game. It was hard to put your finger on; just a shadow of a hunch. He sent the bases out to be dry-cleaned. He recited the Gettysburg Address at the plate. He called in new pitchers. Then he waved at the distance and yelled: "Corcoran!"

Pinelli, the umpire, said: "Who?" Stanky said: "Corcoran. He's a pitcher in Rochester. He ought to be able to catch the next train."

Pinelli threw us all out of the park. He told me: "It's a forfeit. You win, 9 to 0." I gave him a wink, to show him the rib wasn't getting across. I knew the score. I'd seen them make a run in the second inning. I said to Pinelli: "Don't forget, kid, I'm Terry Moore. I know the score." Pinelli said: "If you're Terry Moore, I'm Chief Justice Warren."

Maybe he was, at that. The next thing I knew, I was back in Philadelphia, and Moore had the job. The Old Man put me on a stolen-dog call. A blonde had lost a chihuahua. He told me to remember which was which. Then he knocked the cigarette out of my mouth. But it didn't scare me. I had another, and he knew it.

TONY ON THE WATERFRONT

By Stanley Woodward

From The Newark Star-Ledger, December 28, 1954

LAST WEEK this department saw a motion picture with one of the members of the cast and was interested to learn the ins and outs of movie making from a professional. The picture was "On The Waterfront," a production which the cognoscenti say is just beginning to win the awards it deserves.

In view of the fact that Marlon Brando was unavailable, we attended with one of his colleagues. The actor was Tony Galento, once known as "Two-Ton," who challenged Joe Louis for the heavyweight championship in 1939 and now keeps a tavern in Orange, N. J.

Tony is the only actor we have met who has the class to play a 110-minute movie without taking off his hat and coat. Our boy is cast as Louis O. (Truck) Giranda, vice-president of a racketeering longshoreman's union. He has many appearances and his principal job is to look sinister. He has several lines, however, and never fluffs a one.

Early in the picture the strongarms heave a stool pigeon off the roof of a tenement building in Hoboken (incidentally, the picture was made there). The union bosses stand below and, as the stoolie's dummy smashes in the street, Tony says:

"He's no canary. He can fly but he can't sing."

Later on, when John "Friendly," the big boss, is conducting a consultation on what must be done about another stoolie, Tony sits at his right, still wearing his hat and Chesterfield, and works over the racing form with a long white pencil. "Had one in the third at Suffolk," he explains. Later he intones: "Definitely," when the big boss decrees the stoolie shall be "interviewed" at 437 River Street.

There is a lot of slugging in the movie. Even when the mob has Brando down and is beating him goggly behind a pier shack, Tony keeps his hat and overcoat on and stays on the edges showing no such enthusiasm for mayhem as when he knocked Louis down with a left hook.

267

Tony had seen the movie five or six times before. He went to it once with Walter Winchell, once with Dorothy Kilgallen and a couple of times al fresco. We were strictly third run as far as the press was concerned, but we had the advantage of Tony's earlier spectatorial experience.

"That Brando!" he said. "Look at him. You wouldn't get me to run up those ladders and over those roofs. He must be nuts."

He did almost everything in the picture except get thrown in the harbor. Another guy took that.

"Did you see the dead guy who was hung up with a bale-hook in the alley . . . That was the guy himself, no dummy. Kazan (director) likes to do it real. He wanted to throw a real guy off the roof of the house but they finally decided not to.

"The movies get kind of rough—like playing football. Anybody is goofy to play that game."

When he came around to pick me up, Tony made the speech we taught him when he criticized Mickey Walker's painting for television in the Waldorf:

"Your perspective is distorted and the subordination of the motif of composition is vacuous."

It's nice to know he can make it now because he couldn't say "vacuous" until the fifth try on the original occasion.

Tony has all his buttons and much of the money he made in twenty years of boxing, wrestling and performing such feats as fighting bears and grappling under water with octopuses.

He has a busy tavern in Orange, but he hankers for another movie role. "I'da had more lines in 'Waterfront' if I hadn't kept skipping over to First Street for a beer. When Kazan couldn't find me, he gave the lines to another guy.

"I like the movies, but the next time I think I ought to play a lover."

BASEBALL PAGLIACCI

By Bill Roeder

From The New York World-Telegram and Sun, April 30, 1954

A TALL, SKINNY, melancholy trouper called Slivers was the first baseball clown. If you go back 40 to 50 years you may remember him. Slivers traveled chiefly with the circus (MacDonald's, Barnum and Bailey, Ringling Brothers) but sometimes he'd perform in a ball park. He worked alone, always in pantomime, and he was considered a great artist. One of his bits became a classic that clowns still use. The high foul ball that won't come down.

Slivers, whose real name was Frank Oakley, did several well-known skits including the duck hunter, the golfer and the bumbling carpenter. His trademark, though, was the baseball act for which he originated the costume as well as the business.

He dressed as a catcher, with a bird cage for a mask, a washboard for a chest protector and a couple of pillows for knee guards. Slivers wore shoes that looked as long as skis, and flapping from one hand was a glove the size of a bicycle wheel. He would walk on in this outfit and begin creating vivid effects with his gestures.

Slivers began by laying out the bases. Very intent, but wildly in error as to distance and direction, he would pace off a lopsided diamond and soon the spectators could picture the cockeyed game being played on it.

There would be Slivers himself fearfully crouched behind the plate; hovering over him a cold tyrant of an umpire; coming to bat a series of incredibly menacing hitters; off in the distance the infielders and outfielders retreating in unison as Slivers waved them back, back; and on the mound a pitcher so hapless that Slivers shuddered with every windup. Some times he would drop his glove, turn his head aside and put his fingers to his ears as he waited for the unfailing crack of the bat.

About halfway through the skit the high foul ball would be hit. Slivers, dramatically whipping off the bird cage, would look up, up, up and then he'd go weaving about the infield, holding the great glove out in front of him in both hands. Colliding with invisible teammates, he would stumble, fall and get up again without ever taking his eyes from the sky.

The ball seemed to go up out of sight. Slivers would begin searching the heavens with his binoculars, a pair of pop bottles strapped together. After a while he'd shrug, yawn and then he'd sit down and eat a sandwich.

The game would resume with the ball still unaccounted for. Minutes later, perhaps at the height of an argument with the umpire or while registering bewilderment as he counted off six, seven, eight runners crossing the plate on one home run, Slivers would absently glance upward and then he'd give it the double take. The ball was coming down at last.

Oh, how Slivers would go into action then. Officiously he'd wave everybody away, then stalk straight to the point where the ball would land. Planted for the catch, he smiled confidently as his eyes followed the downward flight until—oops! Right through his hands.

Poor Slivers. A sad, shy, sensitive creature, he led an unhappy life behind the laughs, and in time the world grew to be too much for him. One day in 1916, still at his prime, he turned on the gas in a rooming house on W. 71st St. One of his death notices took the form of an injured reprimand.

"We resent the intrusion of the man of cares, of trials and errors, of disappointments in our picture of the merry Andrew," said an editorial in the New York Sun. "We would know only his trappings, the artful caricature he presents for our inspection. The human being should be decently reticent, comfortably obscure. Slivers should have been immortal; it was not within the proper rights of Frank Oakley to slay him."

Slivers, it turned out, didn't die. Al Schacht is Slivers in a tailcoat and a top hat and baseball pants. The trimmings are different and the effects have been broadened, but neither Schacht nor any other successful baseball clown has strayed far from the basic old formula of a silent buffoon who gets the worst of things in a mixed-up ball game.

A team of Ringling clowns headed by Paul Jung revived the Slivers skit a few years ago. They do it with four performers—pitcher, catcher, umpire and a dwarf as the batter—but otherwise it follows the original pretty closely, right down to the bird cage, the washboard and the disappearing foul ball.

There have been few famous player-clowns. Germany Schaefer was the first. He used to think up gags like going to bat with an umbrella when it looked like rain. Later Schaefer teamed with Nick Altrock while the two were with the Senators. Then, also with Washington, it was Altrock and Schacht who entertained before and between games and at the World Series.

Schacht and Altrock haven't spoken in 25 years. "There was no one thing that came between us," Schacht says. "We just didn't get along from the start and it got worse. When we weren't speaking, I'd tell the clubhouse boy what props to bring out and that's how Altrock would know what was expected of him."

Eventually Schacht went on his own. He did so well that he's now in semi-retirement. He has a restaurant that does a million-dollar business and he goes on tour for only a month every summer, mostly in minor league towns. His fee scale runs from $100 for Class D parks to $500 for the major leagues, plus bonuses according to the attendance. The act still sells, too. Last time he played Seattle, Schacht pulled in $1800 for his half-hour stint.

MY OLD KENTUCKY DERBY HOME

By Hy Goldberg

From The Newark News, May 1, 1954

OLD FOLKS at home, or Derby Day in the living room: Well, it's almost an hour before post time, therefore ample opportunity to prepare. How many guests are there going to be? Six? Better figure on at least 10. Some of the neighbors might be overnight entries. Oops, the language of the race track has slipped in already.

Need lots of room for this operation, so the kitchen is put to use instead of the portable bar. Let's see now, where's that recipe we brought from Louisville several years ago. Ah, here it is. Surprised it didn't get lost in the shuffle.

(Sounds of tinkling ice mingle with the off-key humming of "My Old Kentucky Home.") Large, thin glasses, the book says. Dissolve one teaspoon of fine sugar in water. Add a dash of maraschino. Mm, never knew that before. One jigger of bourbon. Better make it one and a half, big glasses and drinks won't be strong enough. Four or five sprigs of mint, held to the side of the glass.

"Hey Lulu, how do you make the mint stick to the side of the glass?"

"Don't worry about it, just poke it into the glass."

Oh, the sun shines bright . . . Mmm . . . fill with fine ice. Yup, that will keep the mint in place . . . trim with fruits. A few slivers of pineapple and a slice of orange will do the trick. The front doorbell rang and a half dozen guests filed into the living room.

"Hiya, folks. Come right in, Colonel suh. This isn't the blue grass you're walking on, just a blue carpet, but we'll do the best we can to make up for any slight deficiencies or inconveniences, eh Lulu?

"Turn the knob and make sure the set is in focus, while I step out into the kitchen for a moment. You can warm up watching Pvt. Schine while we're waiting for Churchill Downs to come in, or doesn't he work on Saturday? Heh, heh."

The host's appearance in the room with a tray of frosted glasses was greeted with gasps of admiration. "Don't they look beautiful. Do you drink from those beakers or use them as center pieces for

272

the dining room table? Perhaps we're supposed to let 'em set and watch the leaves grow? What sort of a plant is it, a perennial or an annual?"

"Never mind, just taste one of these and you'll agree you never could get anything to match it in Louisville. All this and a horse race too, with no crowds to push you around, no outrageous charges for the libations, and no transportation to worry about. Ah, the horses are starting out of the paddock. That gives me time to go out and start a fresh batch."

Dissolve the sugar . . . a few leaves of mint . . . Mmm, it's running kind of low . . . jigger of bourbon, let's make it two . . . ice . . . Aah, won't bother with the fruit. That's just for decorative purposes anyway.

Two rounds of refreshments later, the horses on the screen were slowly approaching the starting gate, and mine host was out in the kitchen again. Lessee now. Sugar. Aw, won't bother with the sugar. No more mint. Throw some parsley in. They won't know the difference. Still a little ice left. Fruit? Bah!

"Waya mean Cor-relashun ishn't gonna win it? Besht horshe in the race, by far. Whoosh gonna beat 'im," murmured one of the guests.

"Lesh not bring relashuns into thish. We've been having a pleashant party up to now. I'm here to shee a hawss race, suh, and it's my first Kentucky Derby. Mint juleps and all! Boy!"

Sounds coming out of the mechanical box in the corner intruded occasionally on the conversation. "* * * Now Fisherman is moving into the stall . . . There goes Determine . . . The grooms are having a bit of difficulty with blaa . . . blaa . . . blaa. . . They're off!"

"Hey, the screen looks blurry," shouted the host above the din. "Will some one tinker with the gadgets while I go out for another drink. Who will have a straight shot of bourbon?"

THE MONK AND THE BALL GAME

By Peter Clarke

From The Waterbury Republican, December 8, 1954

THIS IS THE story of a Cistercian monk and a ball game.

The monk, Brother Anselm, was a baseball fan—and the game was the seventh of the 1952 World Series.

Every baseball fan in America knows that the Yankees beat the Dodgers, 4-2, that day to cop the World Championship—every baseball fan except Brother Anselm, that is.

But I'll start the story at the beginning.

That was the day Brother Anselm became a Cistercian—or a Trappist as they are more familiarly known. That was the day he left the world to devote himself entirely to the things of God . . . to get up every day at 2 a.m. from his hard bed and enter the dark recesses of the chapel where the monks chanted the night office— to eat frugal meals, such as a slice of bread and a cup of soy bean coffee for breakfast—to spend a good portion of each day in the fields at back-breaking labor. That and many other things.

And for Brother Anselm they were easy. He fell right in with the life and had only one difficulty. Baseball, or rather the lack of baseball and baseball news.

He had entered the monastery in 1947 at the beginning of the baseball season and for months wondered how the Yankees were making out. The Yankees were his team.

He tried hard to dismiss the thoughts from his mind, but it was hard. Specially on real good "baseball days" when the sun was bright and accompanied by a cool breeze.

However, time took care of this difficulty. After about four years if anyone had mentioned baseball to him, he would possibly have said, "Baseball, what's baseball?"

Some baseball fans I know couldn't understand that. How could anyone lose interest in baseball, they would figure. Once it gets in your blood, it's there to stay until your blood goes dry, they would say.

They don't realize that Brother Anselm got something else in his blood after a few years in the monastery. God!

274

He was busy almost every minute of the day working, studying, or praying. There is no recreation period in a Cistercian monastery, and no radio or newspaper.

He never had any trouble until October, 1952, when his mother and father visited him. Brother Anselm was permitted to spend three days with them. He was free from all monastery exercises except those which took place in chapel.

The first morning he and his parents whiled away the time talking about the Cistercian life, but in the afternoon his father drove his car over near where they were sitting and turned on the radio to listen to the World Series. He invited the monk to listen, but Brother Anselm said, "No, you go listen to it—I'll stay here and talk with mother."

When the game was over, he didn't even ask his father the score. However, his dad volunteered the information—"The Yanks won 2-0 and evened up the series two-all," he said. But Brother Anselm had no comment.

But next day while talking with his mother, he heard snatches of the fifth game coming from the car radio. The Dodgers were leading 4-0 when the Yankees came to bat in the fifth.

Brother Anselm heard something about Martin singling into center. Then he heard nothing for a time until there was a great roar—"It's going—going—gone," the high pitched voice of the announcer screamed. Brother Anselm hurried to the auto and sat down next to his father.

"What's up, Dad?"

"Mize just homered into the stands near the Yankee bullpen. It puts the Yanks ahead 5-4," his father told him.

Five years of monasticism rolled off Brother Anselm like hot oil pouring from a drum.

The Dodgers tied it up in the seventh when Cox beat out an infield grounder, advanced on Reese's sacrifice and scored on Snider's single to center. The Brooklyns won it in the 11th when Cox again scored on a double by Snider into right center.

The monastery wasn't the same place when Brother Anselm entered it that night. He was the only monk in the house who knew that the Dodgers were leading the Yankees 3-2 in the series. He felt like he was carrying an atom bomb under his cowl. Brother Anselm didn't sleep well.

And the next day he was on edge until the game got started. He heard the entire nine innings and was exultant when the Yankees tied the series at three-all. When the last Dodger was out, he slapped his father on the back and shouted, "Dad, we won—and we'll take them tomorrow again."

But the three-day visit was up that night and his parents left after dinner. Brother Anselm didn't sleep much that night and had insomnia for two weeks after, wondering who won the seventh game.

He still doesn't know for his parents haven't visited him since and he had no other way of learning. People who write him had no way of knowing he wanted to learn who won the seventh game. And Brother Anselm didn't ask—somehow or other it wouldn't be fitting for a Cistercian monk to write home and ask who won the seventh game of the World Series.

And then again, after a few months, he probably didn't care.

"SOME OF MY BEST FRIENDS ARE GHOSTS"
By Jerry Mitchell
From The New York Post, September 28, 1954

CASEY STENGEL sat in his hotel suite counting his money.

"Two million and four," he was saying, "two million and five, two million and six, two million and. . ."

Begging the Professor's pardon, but what did he think of the World Series ahead?

"It should be a great one for the ghostwriters," he said. "I asked my players what they planned to do after that last game Sunday. Hunt, fish or just loaf, an' you know what most of 'em said?

" 'Go home?' they said. 'With the World Series about to start? I'm stayin' to cover it for the papers. Maybe do some television work, too.'

"Take a tip from me an' get to the park early or you won't get a seat," the Professor went on. "The press box will be crawlin' with ballplayers an' their ghosts.

"You know I had a ghost once myself. A paper signed me up to write about a World Series while I was managin' the Dodgers.

" 'We'll want about 500 words right after every game,' the editor told me.

"But I never wrote for a paper, I told him. 'Go get Frankie Frisch. He went to Fordham an' wrote for the college paper. He even wrote the ads for his old man's linen company. He's your man.'

" 'No, we want you,' the fella said. 'An' don't worry. All you'll have to do is show up at every game an' talk to the reporter we send with you. He'll do all the work. He'll be your ghostwriter.'

"Well, I forget the name of this here fella who was to be my ghostwriter. He was a good friend of the editor's an' his main job was writin' the death notices on his paper. The editor probably thought he'd reward him with an outdoor job for a few days an' give him somethin' happy to write about.

"I get to my seat ready to go to work at the first game but there's no one in the seat next to me. The game starts an' my fella's still not there. Five innings go by an' still no ghost. Finally, in the seventh inning, he comes in. It seems he wasn't used to workin' outdoors so he'd stopped off at some joint to warm himself so he wouldn't get cold at the game. He had enough liquid heat in him by then to ward off triple pneumonia.

"I started puttin' all the notes I'd made together so he could get to work, but when I turned around he's sound asleep in his seat.

" 'Hey ghost,' I said. 'We'd better get goin'. Hey ghost!' But the fella didn't budge. Just kept snorin' away.

"I let him alone then, figurin' he might sleep it off an' be all right by the end of the game. But when it's all over he's still sound asleep an' I can't get a move outa' him.

"Tommy Holmes, one of my newspaper friends from Brooklyn, was sittin' near, so I went to him.

" 'I got a problem, Tommy,' I said. 'I'm supposed to do 500 words for this paper but my ghost can't make it. He passed out on me back there an' pretty soon his paper will want to know where's my story. I don't want to get the fella in dutch. Got any ideas?'

" 'Gee, Case,' said Tommy, 'I'd do it myself for you but I'm in the middle of my own story now an' can't stop. Why don't you see little Joe Soandso over there. He doesn't have to write his stuff until around midnight, so he's free.'

"So I went to this other fella an' made a deal with him to write the story for my ghost's paper an' to sign my ghost's name under it. I gave him 50 bucks for himself an' some ideas an' pretty soon he was typewritin' away. Wrote a good piece too. I got the paper that night an' it read all right.

"But the next day when I get to my seat the next one's empty again. No ghost. An' along about the sixth inning he arrives, an' in the same shape. Once again I gotta go to the other fella an' ask him to write the piece an' once again I shell out 50 bucks.

"Well, I'm in my hotel room around midnight when the phone rings an' who is on the other end but my ghost—wide awake an' sober. Also mad from the sound of his voice.

" 'This is Whatsishisname, your ghost, Case,' he says.

" 'Hello, ghost,' I said, 'What's on your mind?'

" 'Who's that you got writin' the pieces the last two days while I've been sufferin' from those faintin' spells?' he wants to know.

" 'Why, little Joe Soandso,' I said. 'Why?'

" 'Well, he's no good,' my ghost says. 'The stuff's awful. You'd better get someone else tomorrow or we'll both be in trouble.'

"Now, how do you like those apples? I pay a ghost to write stories for my own ghost who's supposed to write for me an' get bawled out because he don't like the writin'. That's the last time I ever had any dealin' with a newspaper ghost."

And what happened at the next game, Professor?

"I don't know," he said. "I went home to California. I was beginnin' to feel too haunted."

THE FOURTH ESCAPE

By Blackie Sherrod

From The Fort Worth Press, October 29, 1954

Copyright, 1954, Fort Worth Press
Reprinted by permission of copyright owner

BACK THERE in the dear dead days, just after we finished reform school cum lawdy, we were faced with a tough career decision.

Two professions beckoned—bank robbing and sports writing. Frantic friends recommended the former, pointing out the security, safety and respectability advantages.

But somehow we leaned toward the typewriter and its surroundings. In bank robbing, you are sometimes thrown with strange companions. Some of them wear skirts and can't even be trusted.

But the Fourth Escape, there it's different. Men are men and hairy-chested fellowship exists in high health.

And several times a month, you can draw away from the frills and lace, lug your typewriter to the top of the stadium and have a peaceful afternoon. The gathering of the clan. Camaraderie overfloweth. You slap the backs, tell the salty jokes, maybe split a vial of the vintage stuff, spit on the floor, scratch where it itches and be masculine as the dickens. A sweet reclusion from the powder puff and spilled perfume.

So, maybe you will join us today with bowed head and tearful eyeball.

The sanctity of the press box has been ravished.

You may have noticed last week that the United Press used a WOMAN sportswriter to cover the SMU-Kansas game. Giggling with success, the UP this week sends the same citizen to Baltimore to cover the biggest game in the country, Notre Dame and Navy. The biggest game in the nation and a gal typewriting the report in the treasured old press box.

The last fort has fallen. Shot down in flames.

Not an unchivalrous bone in our body. Nary a thing against this person. Faye Loyd she is, a charming citizen of pleasing proportions, a chic young woman who turns phrase or ankle with equal trimness.

She wrote sports in college, knows a punt from a pitchout, and works like a man. But she bulges in the wrong places. Or right places.

But what of the schools who absolutely bar women from the press box? What of the cracks shouted to and fro, some purplish in color and resplendent in waterfront humor? What of the loud appraisal of that blond in the green dress, sitting over there on the 30-yard line, just above the exit, here, take the binoculars? What of the 105-degree day in Lawrence, Kan., when we all shucked our pants and covered the game in underwear?

We spake not when they bobbed their hair to male length. They climbed into slacks and we looked silently into the distance. They invaded our poker games with such wildness as spit-in-the-ocean, doctor pepper, peep-and-turn, high-low split and one-eyed jacks. We suffered quietly.

Shove a skillet in their hands, and they'll play ping-pong with it. They fly airplanes, charge into bullrings and race downhill on bobsleds.

But press boxes, please no. Someone help, we are sinking into the gulf. Spare the last straw. Keep the last standard, tattered though it is, nailed to the mast.

Help, Grantland . . . **Westbrook** . . . help, Ring . . . Damon . . . . . . help . . . help . . .

MY OLD PALS

By Gordon Cobbledick

From The Cleveland Plain Dealer, September 15, 1954

WELL, SIR, it's a fine, heart-warming thing to know you have so many friends. Not just here-today-and-gone-tomorrow friends, but friends who've stuck to you through thick and thin and aren't too proud to admit it. Friends from the good old grade-school days. Friends from high school and college. Friends who remind you that they used to live only three or four streets away and boy, those were the happy, carefree years.

Friends who think it's a pity you haven't gotten together these last 40 years. Friends who wonder how about lunch one of these days. Friends who ask who was that girl you married and how is she and why don't you and her drop over some evening and meet the wife?

Good, loyal, old friends who want to know how many kids you've got and how're they doing? Friends who remember you were a helluva tackle and say, "Yeah, that's what I mean" when you tell 'em you were a halfback. Friends who always knew you'd make good.

I tell you there's nothing like the tried-and-true friends who think you write terrific stuff and some of it's good enough to be in a magazine and not just a newspaper. Makes you realize that all the sweating and straining hasn't been in vain.

Friends who wonder if you could get 'em a few world series tickets. Friends who just gotta have world series tickets. Friends who wouldn't think of asking except that they've got an uncle coming in from Nebraska and he wants to see the world series but he's got a gimpy leg and can't climb steps and would prefer boxes right behind the Indians' dugout.

Friends who admit they aren't such hot baseball fans, but they've got this business deal cooking and it would sure help if they could hand the sucker of the second part a brace of tickets for real good seats down front between home and first. After all, what are friends for if you can't use 'em once in a while ha-ha.

Friends who never met you but they had a brother-in-law who

heard you make a speech to the Kiwanis Club of Lower Whichburg back in '37 and he'd sure get a kick out of it if they could tell him you'd fixed 'em up with seats that Eisenhower himself couldn't of bought.

Friends who can tell from your picture in the paper that you're a kind-hearted man and if you would speak to Greenberg and maybe get 'em six good ones and if you can't get six make it four but they'd rather have six on account of these people that used to live next door are going to be visiting from Iowa the first week in October.

Friends who read your column every day before they even look at the first-page headlines and why don't you write something sometime about how stupid Greenberg is and if you could maybe latch onto a couple right behind the press box and not too high up it would certainly be peachy.

Friends who were real chummy with you at East High and when you tell 'em you didn't go to East High they think you're giving 'em the old brushoff but anyway they were chummy with some guy at East High and what's the difference, could you get 'em a few strips of world series tickets to distribute among the fellas at the office?

You're sorry, but you haven't any world series tickets and can't get any world series tickets. Still and all, it makes you feel good to know you have so many friends. Makes you think such popularity must be deserved.

In Memoriam

MY FRIEND GRANTLAND RICE

By Frank Graham

From Sport Magazine, November, 1954

WHAT KIND OF MAN was Grantland Rice? Well, to begin with, let's knock out some false notions about him.

When he died, there were things said of him in some of his obituaries that would have bewildered and embarrassed him. One was that he was the first sportswriter to write literate English. Another, that he was the first to be "accepted in the best social circles." And a third, that he never wrote a harsh word about anybody. There were others, but since these were the main points at variance with the truth, we'll take them one by one, and then go on from there.

Item One: Long before there was a Grantland Rice, there were sportswriters who wrote extremely well. Among Granny's earlier contemporaries, most of them older than he, were Hughie Keogh, whom he often quoted in later years; Joe Vila, Oscar Reichow, Charlie Dryden, another great favorite of his; Bozeman Bulger, W. O. McGeehan, Ring Lardner, Harry Cross, Ed Wray, George Herbert Daley, Sid Mercer, Bill Phelon, Ralph McMillan and Bill Keefe, whose bylines sold papers all over the country. These were the more famous. There were countless others, less known nationally, but gifted, too.

Item Two: These writers were not denizens of the boozing kens, unwashed, illiterate and uncouth. They knew and mingled with, at times, many kinds of men, as newspapermen must. But they bathed and shaved regularly, dressed as well as they could afford to, married nice women and reared children of whom they justly were proud. They went to church and were good neighbors. They were "accepted" wherever they went. They had friends in the high places in culture, in business, in government. Nothing ever could have

annoyed Granny more than to have known it was said of him that
he made sportswriters "respectable."

Item Three: As for the harsh words that he was supposed never
to have written about anybody, well, there were many. They were
widely spaced and therefore effective. It was his belief, to which he
clung all his life, that most persons in sports were inherently decent. But when the occasion arose, he could, and did, hammer the
daylights out of those who violated the code that he had set for all.
Many people, reading in the obituaries that Granny was all sweetness and light, even in the face of evil, must have squirmed again
in memory of the manner in which Granny had pilloried them.

Now then, this that was said of him was true: There never was
another just like him and there never will be again. You see, he was
Grantland Rice.

What set him apart from all the others with whom he walked
the world? It is not easy even for one who, like myself, was privi-
leged to know him for nearly 40 years and to travel unnumbered
thousands of miles with him through the last 20 years, to say.
What do you say . . . what would you say . . . if anyone asked you
to describe one of your closest friends? You would say, I am sure,
as I do of Granny, that he was one with whom you'd like to be,
always. That he was. . . .

Once Granny said, to the astonishment of some of his acquaint-
ances in an exclusive club, that perhaps the only true gentleman he
had ever known was Jack Dempsey.

"Dempsey?" one of them said. "Surely, you don't mean the
prize-fighter?"

"Yes," Granny said. "I do. I mean that he is a gentleman in the
finest and truest sense of the word. He is a *gentle man*. Kind, considerate, thoughtful of those around him. Trying to help everyone
who needs help, never hurting anyone's feelings."

When he told me of that, I agreed with him. To myself, I said:
"It is a perfect description of Jack Dempsey . . . and of Grantland
Rice."

What was it he had as a sportswriter that no other ever had?
A lyric style that made him the most widely syndicated columnist
in America—meaning in the world—and the most widely imitated.
And, back of the style, a warmth of feeling for the one in sports
who, winning or losing, fought against adversity, fought hard but
cleanly. His credo was expressed in many of his writings, prose
and poetry. In, for instance, "Ballade of the Gamefish," which, in-

spired by Col. John Trotwood Moore's line, "Only the gamefish swims upstream," began:

> "Where the puddle is shallow, the weakfish stay,
> "To drift along with the current's flow"

And ended:

> "Held with the current the Fates bestow,
> "The driftwood moves to a sluggish theme,
> "Nor heeds the call which the Far Isles throw,
> "Only the gamefish swims upstream."

Pardon me if I digress for a moment. In one of Granny's obituaries, written for a national weekly news magazine . . . not *Time*, I hasten to add . . . an obviously young man who obviously never had read Granny's collected poems, especially *Songs of the Stalwart*, published by D. Appleton and Company in 1917, referred to Granny's "verses" condescendingly.

When the young man comes of age, I should like him to read the foreword, by Irvin S. Cobb, which begins:

"Grantland Rice is a sweet and kindly human being who has a habit of saying things in a sweet and kindly way. Sometimes he says them in verse, which is still better."

And which ends:

"Some of these days, they are going to nominate a successor to the late James Whitcomb Riley as our most typical writer of homely, gentle American verse. I have my candidate already picked out. His name is Grantland Rice."

Then I should like the young man to read, among other verses in this book, "A Little Boy—and a Dream" . . . "At the Morning Gate" . . . "Ghosts of the Alamo" . . . "The Story of the Rose," and others that, as the titles indicate, have nothing to do with sports.

The moment of angry digression is over. Now to the sportswriter and the man.

There was a night in the Detroit Athletic Club in 1937, when Granny and I were there for a golf tournament on our way to Chicago for the Jim Braddock-Joe Louis fight for the heavyweight championship. In the living room of the suite I shared with Granny were the late Charlie Hughes, director of the club in that time, Francis Ouimet, Bobby Jones, and, of course, Granny. It occurred to me—and I made so bold as to speak of it—that I was seated in the presence of the three men who had done the most for golf in this country: Ouimet, who as a youth had beaten the great Englishmen, Vardon and Ray, in the 1913 U.S. Open and so had made other kids in this land aware that golf was not strictly an old man's game; Jones, who had excited the whole world by his Grand Slam in 1930; and Granny, who on the old and long-vanished New York *Evening Mail* had been the first "name" sportswriter to feature golf in his writings.

Granny did as much for football as he did for golf. Many other famous writers had written of football before he even played it at Vanderbilt University, but there would come a day when, as I well know, because I was roaming the country covering the big games, they would say, "The most important game every Saturday is the one that Grantland Rice covers."

Although I heard it everywhere, I doubt that Granny ever heard it. If he did, I'm sure he wouldn't have believed it. One of his greatest charms was that he never gave consideration to his own importance.

Well, one day just a few years ago, we were riding in a cab through Central Park on our way to a ball game at the Polo Grounds, and as we talked, the name of a mutual friend bobbed up in our conversation.

"I don't see much of him any more," Granny said. "I'm sorry, too, because I am very fond of him. I read about him, though. I guess he's become a celebrity. He's always with celebrities. Do you like being with celebrities?"

"No," I said.

"Neither do I," he said. "Come to think of it, I wouldn't know a celebrity if I saw one. Would you?"

The temptation was strong within me to tell him that every morning, when he shaved, he was seeing a celebrity in his mirror, but I resisted it.

There was the 1944 World Series between the Cardinals and the Browns. Long after I'd forgotten who won it I'll remember it because of Granny, for two reasons. One was an incident that illustrates what I've just been telling you about the man and the fact that he never realized he was a person of importance. The other was his appreciation of the services of one who might be described as his bodyguard.

All the games were played, of course, at Sportsmans Park. The Cardinals, home club in the first two games, issued white press badges. The Browns' badges were blue. When we arrived at the park for the third game, Granny said:

"I've got the wrong badge! What shall I do? Can I buy a ticket?"

"No," I said. "Hold still. Follow me and I'll get you in."

At the press gate, opening off the street, as the gate-tender was punching my badge, I said:

"This is Grantland Rice, right behind me. He has the wrong badge for today. Will you let him in?"

"Grantland Rice!" the man said.

He reached across my shoulder to clutch Granny's hand. "Mr. Rice!" he said. "This is the greatest thrill of my life, meeting you! Gosh! Wait 'till I tell my wife I met Grantland Rice! Why, she won't believe me! Come in, Mr. Rice! Come in!"

So Granny was in the park. There was another gate, on the upper deck, through which we had to pass to gain access to the press box. There was the same explanation, the same glowing reception. You can guess what Granny said once we had cleared the second barrier, can't you?

"You certainly have influence with these men. If it hadn't been for you, I never could have gotten in."

"Sure," I said. "I'm very important around here. I hope you noticed the men on the gate acted as though they never heard of you."

The bodyguard was my friend . . . and forever after, Granny's friend, too . . . Mickey Genaro, a former prize-fighter with a busted nose, two cauliflower ears and a heart of gold. At the time, he was in the Navy and stationed at Great Lakes on his way to the Pacific and as my guest, was attending the Series. He joined us at the Hotel Chase and Granny, forming an instant liking for him, put him in charge of both of us. Granny had hired a car, with a chauffeur, to take us to and from the ball park. Mickey rode with the chauffeur the first day, and impressed upon him, just by looking at him, the necessity for being at a given point at a stated time, to take us back to the hotel.

Once back at the Chase, Granny inaugurated a routine that held for the duration of the Series: On a table in the living room of the suite were bottles, glasses and bowls of ice in the normal expectation that, even as he was writing his column, guests would arrive, as they did everywhere he went. Mickey was posted at the door, with instructions:

"Let everybody in. If I call a visitor by name, he can stay as long as he wishes, even if he is interrupting my writing. And keep him supplied with drinks. If I just say 'Well! Well!' give him two drinks and then get rid of him as quickly, but as pleasantly, as you can."

The "Hello Joe's" got everything from Mickey but the red carpet and, being really friends of Granny's, left shortly, not wishing to impede him in his work. The crashers got two drinks, a gentle hint that Mr. Rice was working and a polite brush. A perfectly devised system, it worked perfectly. When the Series were over, Granny said, fervently:

"Mickey, I wish I could have you with me always."

"So do I, Mr. Rice," Mickey said. "And no kiddin'."

When the story was told to Miss Mecca, Granny's secretary, she said: "When you see Mickey again, tell him I wish the same thing —and that I'm not kidding, either. I try as hard as I can to protect Mr. Rice from people who impose upon him, but he outwits me. Maybe I should get a broken nose and two cauliflower ears and join the Navy, so that I could scare them, too."

All his life, Granny worked hard. In his early years around New York, he sought, and found, his relaxation in golf, which he played extraordinarily well. As the years closed about him, he relaxed at the race track, and while there are so many, in so many places, who miss him, it is likely they miss him most at the tracks, for there, in his declining years, they saw him so often. Owners, trainers, jockeys, turf writers and "regulars" on the tracks from Belmont Park to Santa Anita and Hollywood Park, by way of Jamaica, Aqueduct, Saratoga, Hialeah and Sunshine Park, were his friends.

He went to baseball games, football games and golf tournaments to work. He covered all the important races, such as the Kentucky Derby, the Preakness and the Belmont, naturally, but for sheer enjoyment, there were the afternoons at the handiest track—Sunshine Park being his favorite—the company of his friends and the everlasting hopeful assault on the mutuels.

Granny was a moderately enthusiastic bettor, meaning that he played the Daily Double and every race on the card, frequently backing as many as three or four horses in a race—but never, as they say around the tracks, going overboard.

"I have discovered," he once said, in a mood of gentle irony, "that there is a certain element of risk involved in betting on the horses."

To his friend George Widener, one of America's greatest breeders and president of Belmont Park, he said: "I don't care anything about a horse's breeding, George. All I ask for is six inches of his nose on the wire in front of the others in the race."

And George said: "You know, Grant, that's all I ask of the horses I breed."

Granny knew all the top horses but to him the platers were numbers.

"A horse named Number Seven," he would say, for instance.

He would go to the track armed with scratch sheets, buy all the tipsters' cards and, like the veriest chump, seek advice from even the raggedy bums who touched him for a dollar or two. He seldom sat down for more than a few minutes at a time, but prowled the clubhouse or the lawn, meeting his friends, taking their tips and playing them.

One day, on his way back to the clubhouse at Jamaica after a visit with his friend, Sunny Jim Fitzsimmons, dean of American trainers, he was scanning his program and his sheets and cards, looking for a winner in the next race. Though he was not lacking information—of sorts, anyway—he wanted reassurance by word of mouth.

"Do you know any of the owners in this race?" he asked.

"Here's one now," I said, intercepting a man hurrying through the paddock crowd. "Granny, this is Ike Pearlstein. He owns Miquelon."

"How do you do?" Granny said. "What about Miquelon?"

"Miquelon, Mr. Rice," Ike said with great feeling, "is a dirty no good————!"

"Thank you, Mr. Pearlstein," Granny said. Then turning to me: "Well, we've got the low down on Miquelon. See any other owners you know?"

He had a simple design for living. He rose early every morning, ate a hearty breakfast, then went back to bed, not to sleep but to read his papers and magazines. At noon he was up and off for the track, the ball park or wherever his fancy led him. When he was at home in New York, he would go to his midtown office at least a couple of days a week. Breakfast was the only meal that interested him. His luncheon seldom varied.

"I was looking for him in the dining room at Belmont," Frank Stevens, head of the catering firm, said, "and I knew how to find him. I heard he'd just arrived, and when a waiter came out of the kitchen with a tray on which there was a Martini, a glass of tomato juice, a chicken sandwich and a dill pickle, I followed him and he led me directly to Granny."

His choice at dinner, more likely than not, would be chicken, which he probably ate a couple of hundred times a year.

He cared little for the theatre, the movies or television, and the only thing on the radio that interested him was the news. His favorite after dark diversion when he was on the road was to sit and talk with his friends. His interests were wide and his opinions firm, although he never was hard-headed. He was pessimistic about the future, thought all old men, himself included, were fools and that, if the world was to be saved at all, the young men would have to do the saving.

Of one thing I'm sure: Granny will watch with interest while they go about it.

For The Record

CHAMPIONS OF 1954

ARCHERY
United States Champions

Target
Men—Robert J. Rhode, Minneapolis.
Women—Laurette Young, Detroit.

Flight
Footbow—Peter Martinek, Los
Angeles.
Unlimited Class—Peter Martinek.
Women's Unlimited Class—Margaret
Breneman, Columbus, Ohio.

AUTO RACING
A. A. A.—Jimmy Bryan, Phoenix,
Ariz.
Indianapolis Winner—Bill Vukovich,
Fresno, Calif.
Pan-American Road Race—Umberto
Maglioli, Italy.

BADMINTON
National Champions
Men's Singles—Eddy Choong,
Malaya.
Women's Singles—Judy Devlin, Bal-
timore.
Men's Doubles—Ong Poh Lim and
Ooi Teik Hock, Malaya.
Women's Doubles—Judy Devlin and
Sue Devlin, Baltimore.
Mixed Doubles—Joseph and Lois
Alston, Detroit.

BASEBALL
World—New York Giants.
National League—New York Giants.
American League—Cleveland Indians.
All-Star Game—American League.
Leading Batsman, N. L.—Willie Mays,
N. Y.
Leading Batsman, A. L.—Bobby
Avila, Cleve.
Little World Series—Louisville (A.
A.).
International League—Toronto (regu-
lar season); Syracuse (play-offs).
American Association—Indianapolis
(regular season); Louisville (play-
offs).
Pacific Coast League—San Diego
(regular season); Oakland (play-
offs).
Dixie Series—Atlanta (S. A.).
Texas League—Shreveport (regular
season); Houston (play-offs).
Southern Association—Atlanta (regu-
lar season and play-offs).
Eastern League—Wilkes-Barre
(regular season); Albany (play-
offs).

Colleges
N. C. A. A.—Missouri.

BASKETBALL
World—United States (Peoria, Ill.,
Caterpillars).
National Collegiate—La Salle.
National Invitation—Holy Cross.
Eastern Intercollegiate League—Cor-
nell.
Western Conference—Indiana.
Pacific Coast Conference—Southern
California.

292

Southeastern Conference—Kentucky.

Southern Conference—George Washington.

Atlantic Coast Conference—Duke.

Missouri Valley—Oklahoma A. and M.

Big Seven—Kansas and Colorado.

Southwest Conference—Rice and Texas.

Border Conference—Texas Tech.

Skyline Conference—Colorado A. and M.

Rocky Mountain Conference—Idaho State.

National Association (N. A. I. A.)— St. Benedict's.

A. A. U.—Peoria Caterpillars.

Women's A. A. U.—Wayland College (Texas).

N.B.A.—Minneapolis Lakers.

BILLIARDS

World Champions

Three-Cushion—Ray Kilgore, San Francisco.

Pocket—Willie Mosconi, Philadelphia.

BOBSLEDDING

World Champions

Two-Man—Italy (Guglielmo Sheibmeier and Andrea Zambelli).

Four-Man—Switzerland.

North American Champions

Two-Man—Stan Benham, Lake Placid, and Jim Bickford, Saranac Lake.

National A. A. U. Champions

Two-Man—Stan Benham and Jim Bickford.

Four-Man—Sno Birds of Lake Placid Club.

BOWLING

American Bowling Congress Champions

All Events—Brad Lewis, Ashland, Ohio.

Singles—Tony Sparando, Rego Park, Queens.

Doubles—Don McClaren, St. Louis, and Billy Welu, Houston.

Five-Man Team—Tri-Par Radio, Chicago.

Woman's International Congress Champions

All Events—Anne Johnson, Berwick, Pa.

Singles—Helen Martin, Peoria, Ill.

Doubles—Fran Stenett and Rose Caccioch, Rockford, Ill.

Team—Marhoefer Weiner, Chicago.

National Match-Game Champions

Men—Don Carter, Detroit.

Women—Marion Ladewig, Grand Rapids.

BOXING

World Champions

Flyweight—Pascual Perez, Argentina.

Bantamweight—Robert Cohen, France.

Featherweight—Sandy Saddler, New York.

Lightweight—Jimmy Carter, New York.

Welterweight—Johnny Saxton, New York.

Middleweight—Carl Olson, San Francisco.

Light Heavyweight—Archie Moore, Miami.

Heavyweight—Rocky Marciano, Brockton, Mass.

National A. A. U. Champions

112-Pound—Charles Branch, Philadelphia.

119-Pound—Billy Ramos, New Bedford, Mass.
125-Pound—Stan Fitzgerald, Buffalo.
132-Pound—Garnet Hart, Philadelphia.
139-Pound—Robert Shell, New York.
147-Pound—Joseph Bethea, Seattle.
156-Pound—John Houston, Oakland, Calif.
165-Pound—Donald McCray, Boston.
178-Pound—Warren Lester, Baltimore.
Heavyweight—Reuben Vargas, San Francisco.

National Collegiate Champions

119-Pound—Garry Garber, Maryland.
125-Pound—Seijo Naya, Hawaii.
132-Pound—Vince Palumbo, Maryland.
139-Pound—John Granger, Syracuse.
147-Pound—Herb Odom, Michigan State.
156-Pound—Bobby Meath, Wisconsin.
165-Pound—Gordon Gladson, Washington State.
178-Pound—Adam Kois, Penn State.
Heavyweight—Mike McMurtry, Idaho State.
Team—Wisconsin.

CANOEING

U. S. Paddling Champions

One-Man Single Blade—Frank Havens, Vienna, Va.
One-Man Double Blade—P. Beachum, Potomac B. C., Washington, D. C.
Tandem Single Blade—F. Krick and J. Haas, Philadelphia C. C.
Tandem Double Blades—A. Potter and J. Van Dyke, Potomac B. C.
Four-Man Single Blade—Philadelphia C. C.
Four-Man Double Blade—Yonkers (N. Y.) C. C.
Team—Potomac B. C.

U. S. Sailing Champions

Decked—Adolph Morse, Phoenix C. C., Lindenhurst, L. I.
Open Cruising—Stephen Lysak, Yonkers C. C.

CASTING

National Association Champions

All-Around—Jon Tarantino, San Francisco.
All-Distance—Jon Tarantino.
All-Accuracy—Marion Garber, Toledo.
Distance Baits—Richard R. Ward, Washington.
Distance Flies—Jon Tarantino.
Accuracy Baits—Warren Rector, Okla. City.
Accuracy Flies—Donald Meyer, Burbank, Calif.

CHESS

World Champions

Men—Mikhail Botvinnik, Russia.
Women—Mrs. Elizabeth Bykova, Russia.
Junior—Oscar Panno, Argentina.

United States Champions

Men—Arthur B. Bisguier, New York.
Women—Mona May Karff, New York.
Men's Open—Larry Evans, New York.
Women's Open—Mrs. Gisela K. Gresser, N. Y.
Speed—James T. Sherwin, New York.
Junior—Ross E. Siemms, Toronto.
Intercollegiate—Albert Weissman, N. Y. U.

COURT TENNIS

North American Singles—Alastair B. Martin, Glen Head, L. I.
National Singles—Alastair B. Martin.

National Doubles—Frank Shields,
New York, and Alastair B. Martin.
Tuxedo Gold Racquet—Alastair B.
Martin.
North American Pro—Jack Johnson,
New York.

CROSS-COUNTRY

National A. A. U.—Gordon McKenzie, New York.
National A. A. U. Team—New York
A. C.
National Collegiate—Allen Frame,
Kansas.
National Collegiate Team—Oklahoma
A. and M.
I. C. 4-A—George Terry, Boston University.
I. C. 4-A Team—Manhattan.
Heptagonal—John J. Rosenbaum,
Cornell.
Heptagonal Team—Cornell.

CURLING

Gordon International Medal—United
States.
Midwest Champion—Portage, Wis.
Northwest Champion—Duluth, Minn.
Women's U. S. Champion—Wauwatosa (Wis.) Granites.

CYCLING

Tour of France—Louison Bobet,
France.
U. S. Amateur Champions
Senior Open—Jack Disney, Altadena,
Calif.
Junior Open—Bob Zumwalt, San
Diego, Calif.
Girls' Open—Nancy Nieman, Detroit.

DOG SHOWS

Westminster—Mrs. Carl E. Morgan's
cocker spaniel, Ch. Carmor's Rise
and Shine.
Westchester—Dr. and Mrs. W.
Stewart Carter's Scottish terrier,
Ch. Edgerstoune Troubadour,
Buechel, Ky.

FENCING
United States Champions
Foil—Joseph Levis, Boston.
Epee—Sewell Shurtz, U. S. Navy.
Saber—George Worth, New York.
Women's Foil—Mrs. Maxine Mitchell,
Hollywood, Calif.

Team
Foil—Salle Santelli, New York.
Epee—Fencers Club, New York.
Saber—Salle Santelli.
Women's Foil—Fencers Club.

Collegiate
Foil—Robert Goldman, Pennsylvania.
Epee—Henry Kolowrat, Princeton.
Saber—Steve Sobel, Columbia.
Three-Weapon Team—Columbia and
N. Y. U.

Intercollegiate Association
Foil—Phil Mocquard, Cornell.
Epee—Richard Pew, Cornell.
Saber—Steve Sobel, Columbia.
Three-Weapon Team—Columbia.
Foil Team—Columbia and Cornell
(tie).
Epee Team—Columbia.
Saber Team—Columbia.

FOOTBALL
National—Ohio State (Associated
Press poll); U. C. L. A. (United
Press poll).
Eastern (Lambert Trophy)—Navy.
Ivy League—Cornell and Yale.
Western Conference—Ohio State.
Pacific Coast Conference—U. C. L. A.
Southeastern Conference—Mississippi.
Atlantic Coast Conference—Duke.
Southern Conference—West Virginia.
Southwest Conference—Arkansas.
Big Seven Conference—Oklahoma.

Skyline Conference—Denver.
Missouri Valley Conference—Wichita.
Rocky Mountain Conference—Montana State.
Border Conference—Texas Tech.
Midwest Conference—Carleton.
Yankee Conference—New Hampshire.
Canadian Intercollegiate—Toronto.
Canadian Professional (Grey Cup)—Edmonton Eskimos.

National Football League

Eastern Conference—Cleveland Browns.
Western Conference—Detroit Lions.
Play-off Winner—Cleveland Browns.

GOLF

Canada Cup—Australia.
Hopkins Trophy—United States.
Americas Cup—United States.
National Open—Ed Furgol, Clayton, Mo.
National Amateur—Arnold Palmer, Cleveland.
National P. G. A.—Melvin Harbert, Detroit.
British Open—Peter Thomson, Australia.
British Amateur—Doug Bachli, Australia.
Augusta Masters—Sam Snead, White Sulphur Springs, Ga.
World Pro (Tam O'Shanter)—Bob Toski, Livingston, N. J.
World Amateur (Tam O'Shanter)—Frank Stranahan, Toledo.
All-American Open—Jerry Barber, La Canada, Calif.
All-American Amateur—Arnold Palmer.
Canadian Open—Bob Fletcher, Saskatoon, Sask.
Canadian Amateur—Harvie Ward, San Francisco.
Eastern Open—Bob Toski.

Western Open—Lloyd Mangrum, Niles, Ill.
North and South Amateur—Billy Joe Patton, Morganton, N. C.
Trans-Mississippi—Joe Conrad, San Antonio.
U. S. Seniors—J. Ellis Knowles, Rye, N. Y.
U. S. Collegiate—Hillman Robbins, Memphis State.
U. S. Collegiate Team—Southern Methodist.

Women

Curtis Cup—United States.
U. S. Amateur—Barbara Romack, Sacramento, Calif.
U. S. Open—Mrs. M. D. Zaharias, Niles, Ill.
British Open—Frances Stephens, England.
All-American Open—Patty Berg, St. Andrews, Ill.
World Pro (Tam O'Shanter)—Patty Berg.
World Amateur (Tam O'Shanter)—Mary Wright, San Diego.
Western Open—Betty Jameson, San Antonio.
Western Amateur—Claire Doran, Cleveland.
Canadian Amateur Open—Marlene Stewart, Fonthill, Ont.
North and South—Joyce Ziske, Waterford, Wis.
Southern Amateur—Polly Riley, Fort Worth.
Trans-Miss.—Vonnie Colby, Hollywood, Fla.
United States Seniors'—Mrs. J. Walker Hoopes, Wilmington, Del.
Titleholders'—Patty Berg.
Eastern Amateur—Mrs. Mae Murray Jones, Rutland, Vt.
U. S. Junior—Margaret Smith, Mexico.

U. S. Intercollegiate—Nancy Reed, George Peabody, Nashville, Tenn.

GYMNASTICS

National A. A. U. Champions

All-Around—Charles Simms, Los Angeles Turners.

Free Exercise—Don Faber, U. C. L. A.

Horizontal Bar—Jean Cronstedt, Penn State.

Tumbling—Richard Browning, Champaign, Ill.

Long Horse—Charles Simms.

Trampoline—Robert Elliot, Maverick Boys Club, Texas.

Side Horse—Robert Diamond, U. C. L. A.

Parallel Bars—Jean Cronstedt.

Still Rings—Leonard Harris, Los Angeles City College.

Rope Climb—Don Perry, U. C. L. A.

Swinging Rings—Mark Gilden, Los Angeles.

Team—Los Angeles Turners.

Women

All-Around—Ruth Grulkowski, Lincoln Turners, Chicago.

Uneven Parallel Bars—Louise Wright, Roxborough Turners, and Ruth Grulkowski.

Free Exercise—Ernestine Russell, Windsor Gymnastic Club, Canada.

Balance Beam—Ruth Grulkowski.

Side Horse—Louise Wright.

Team Drill—American Sokol, Eastern District (N. J.).

Swinging Rings—Louise Wright.

Tumbling—Barbara Galleher, Dallas A. C.

National Collegiate Champions

All-Around—Jean Cronstedt, Penn State.

Flying Rings—Manuel Procopio, Penn State.

Free Exercise—Jean Cronstedt.

Horizontal Bar—Jean Cronstedt.

Parallel Bars—Jean Cronstedt.

Rope Climb—Don Perry, U. C. L. A.

Side Horse—Bob Lawrence, Penn State.

Trampoline—James Norman, Iowa.

Tumbling—Richard Browning, Illinois.

Team—Penn State.

HANDBALL

National A. A. U. Champions
Four-Wall

Singles—Bill Lauro, Brooklyn Central.

Doubles—John Abate and Joe Ingrassia, New York A. C.

One-Wall

Singles—Rubrecht Obert, New York.

Doubles—Ted Russell and Adrian Lightsy, Hebrew Education Center, Astoria, Queens.

U. S. Association Champions
Four-Wall

Singles—Vic Hershkowitz, Brooklyn.

Doubles—Sam Haber and Ken Schneider, Chicago.

HARNESS RACING

Mile Tracks

2-Year-Old Pacer—American Way.

2-Year-Old Trotter—Scott Frost.

3-Year-Old Pacer—Parker Byrd.

3-Year-Old Trotter—Stenographer.

Aged Pacer—Red Sails.

Aged Trotter—Kimberly Kid.

Half-Mile Tracks

2-Year-Old Pacer—Quick Chief.

2-Year-Old Trotter—Scott Frost.

3-Year-Old Pacer—Phantom Lady.

3-Year-Old Trotter—Stenographer.
Aged Pacer—Newport Chief.
Aged Trotter—Faber Hanover.

Other Champions

Leading Money-Winner—Katie Key.
Leading Driver—Billy Haughton.

HOCKEY

Stanley Cup—Detroit.
National League—Detroit.
American League—Buffalo (regular
season); Cleveland (play-offs).
Western League—Vancouver (regular
season); Calgary (play-offs).
International League—Cincinnati
(regular season and play-offs).
World Amateur—Russia.
A. H. A. of U. S. (senior open)—
Great Falls, Mont.
Allan Cup—Penticton V's.
Memorial Cup—St. Catherines (Ont.)
Tepees.

Intercollegiate

National Collegiate—R. P. I.
Pentagonal League—Harvard.
Canadian—Laval.

HORSE RACING

T. R. A. Champions

American Champion—Native Dancer.
Handicap Division—Native Dancer.
Handicap Filly or Mare—Lavender
Hill.
3-Year-Old Colt—High Gun.
3-Year-Old Filly—Parlo.
2-Year-Old Colt—Nashua.
2-Year-Old Filly—High Voltage.
Steeplechaser—King Commander.

Other Champions

Money-Winning Owner—King Ranch.
Money-Winning Horse—Determine.
Trainer (winners saddled)—Robert
H. McDaniel.

Jockey (winners ridden)—Willie
Shoemaker.

HORSE SHOWS

National Horse Show Champions (At Madison Square Garden)

International Individual Jumping—
Fritz Thiedmann, West Germany,
riding b. g. Meteor.
International Perpetual Challenge
Trophy (team jumping)—Mexican
Army.
Open Jumper—Morton W. Smith's ch.
g. Clay Pigeon, Cobham, Va.
Conformation Hunter—Waverly
Farm's b. g. The Cad, Warrenton,
Va.
Working Hunter—Mrs. Peggy
Augustus' bl. g. Defense, Cobham,
Va.
Green Hunter—Ren R. Perry's gr. g.
Bigeno, Shaker Heights, Ohio.
N. H. S. Equitation—Roberta Smith,
Upper Montclair, N. J.
A. S. P. C. A. Maclay Trophy—Ron-
nie Martini, Bronxville, N. Y.
A. H. S. A. Medal, Saddle Seat—
Martin Rosensweig, New York.
A. H. S. A. Medal, Hunter Seat—
Margaret McGinn, Norristown, Pa.
Three-Gaited Grand Championship
Stake—Dodge Stables' ch. m.
Meadow Princess, Lexington, Ky.
Five-Gaited Grand Championship
Stake—Dodge Stables' ch. g. Socko,
Lexington, Ky.

P. H. A. Season Trophy (Jumping)

Mr. and Mrs. A. H. Merkel Sr.'s gr.
g. Grey Dawn, Brookville, L. I.

HORSESHOE PITCHING

World Champions

Men—Guy Zimmerman, Danville,
Calif.

Women—Katie Gregson, Crestline, Calif.

A. A. U. Champions

Singles—Floyd Toole, Little Rock, Ark.

Doubles—C. Murphy and W. Thomas, Salem, N. C.

ICE SKATING

Figure

World Champions

Men—Hayes Alan Jenkins, United States.

Women—Gundi Busch, Germany.

Pairs—Frances Dafoe and Norris Bowden, Canada.

Dance—Jean Westwood and Lawrence Demmy, England.

United States Champions

Men—Hayes Alan Jenkins, Colorado Springs.

Women—Tenley Albright, Newton Center, Mass.

Pairs—Carole Ann Ormaca and Robin Grainer, Fresno, Calif.

Speed

North American Champions

Men's Outdoor—Art Longsjo, Leominster, Mass.

Women's Outdoor—Mrs. Barbara M. DeSchepper, Detroit.

Men's Indoor—Art Longsjo.

Women's Indoor—Mrs. Barbara M. DeSchepper.

United States Champions

Outdoor—Ken Bartholomew, Minneapolis.

Women's Outdoor—Pat Gibson, Madison, Wis.

Men's Indoor—Bob Olson, Glendale, Calif.

Women's Indoor—Mrs. Barbara M. DeSchepper.

LACROSSE

U. S. Open—Mt. Washington Club, Baltimore.

U. S. Intercollegiate—Navy.

North-South Game—North.

LAWN BOWLING

National Champions

Singles—Richard W. Folkins, Los Angeles.

Doubles—Hugh Folkins and Richard W. Folkins, Los Angeles.

Triples—Arroyo Seco L. B. C., Los Angeles (H. Folkins, R. W. Folkins and W. Gardiner).

MOTOR BOATING

National Inboard Champions

Gold Cup—Stanley S. Sayres' Slo-Mo-Shun V, driven by Lou Fageol.

President's Cup—Joseph L. Schoenith's Gale IV, driven by W. J. Cantrell.

Silver Cup—Horace E. Dodge's Dora My Sweetie, driven by Jack Bartley.

Detroit Memorial Cup—Schoenith's Gale V, driven by J. Lee Schoenith.

Imperial Gold Cup (New Martinsville)—Schoenith's Gale V, driven by J. Lee Schoenith.

Maple Leaf Cup—Schoenith's Gale V, driven by J. Lee Schoenith.

International Cup (Elizabeth City, N. C.)—Schoenith's Gale V, driven by J. Lee Schoenith.

Governor's Trophy (Madison, Ind.)—Schoneith's Gale IV, driven by W. J. Cantrell.

Hydroplanes

48 Cubic Inch—Gillette Smith, El Monte, Calif.

91 Cubic Inch—Sam Crooks, Madeira Beach, Fla.

135 Cubic Inch—J. C. Townsend, Port Arthur, Tex.

136 Cubic Inch—Wallace Rolland, Elkton, Md.

225 Cubic Inch—Dr. W. P. Lines, Highland Heights, Ky.

266 Cubic Inch—Ray Gassner, St. Petersburg.

Seven-Litre—Ray Fageol, Cayahoga Falls, Ohio.

Pacific One-Design—Marion Beaver, Parker, Ariz.

National Outboard Champions

Hydroplanes

M—Dr. R. D. Frawley, Dravosburg, Pa.

A—Orlando Torigiani, Bakersfield, Calif.

B—W. L. Tenney, Dayton, Ohio.

C—W. L. Tenney.

F—P. J. Owens, Bedford, Ind.

C Service Hydro—Oliver DePuis, Plains, Mont.

C Racing Runabout—W. L. Tenney.

C Service Runabout—William Rankin, Seattle.

F Racing Runabout—William Siemsen, Santa Rosa, Calif.

Cruiser Champions

A. P. B. A. National Trophy—Dr. Allen B. Du Mont, Cedar Grove, N. J.

Herbert L. Stone Trophy—Dr. Ellwood S. Schultz, Los Angeles.

POLO

Outdoor Champions

National Open—Meadow Brook-Triple C.

Waterbury Trophy—Meadow Brook-Triple C.

National 20-Goal—San Antonio P. C.

National 12-Goal—Farmington, Conn.

National Intra-Circuit—Fairfield, Conn.

Indoor Champions

National Senior—Squadron A, New York.

National 12-Goal—Long Island.

Metropolitan League—Squadron A.

National Intercollegiate—New Mexico M. I.

Sherman Memorial Handicap—Huntington, L. I.

RACQUETS

National Singles—Geoffrey Atkins, Chicago.

National Doubles—William Wood-Prince, Chicago, and Geoffrey Atkins.

Tuxedo Gold Racquet—Geoffrey Atkins.

ROWING

United States Champions

Single Sculls—John B. Kelly Jr., Vesper B. C., Philadelphia.

Assn. Single Sculls—Pat Costello, Detroit, B. C.

Quarter-Mile Single Sculls—George Loveless, New York A. C.

Double Sculls—Detroit B. C.

Quadruple Sculls—Detroit B. C.

Paired-Oared Shell With Coxswain—Fairmount R. A., Philadelphia.

Paired-Oared Shell Without Coxswain—Rutgers R. C.

Four-Oared Shell With Coxswain—Vesper B. C.

Four-Oared Shell Without Coxswain—West Side R. C., Buffalo.

Eight-Oared Shell—Vesper B. C.

Intermediate Eight-Oared Shell—Old Dominion B. C., Alexandria, Va.

150-Pound Single Sculls—James Barker, Undine B. C., Philadelphia.

Team (Barnes Trophy)—Vesper B. C.

Intercollegiate

I. R. A. Varsity—Navy (disqualified).

Eastern Association—Navy (disqualified).

Harvard-Yale—Yale.

Adams Cup—Navy.

Blackwell Cup—Pennsylvania.

Carnegie Cup—Cornell.

Childs Cup—Pennsylvania.

Compton Cup—Harvard.

Dad Vail Trophy—Dartmouth.

I. R. A. Junior Varsity—Cornell.

I. R. A. Freshmen—Cornell.

Eastern Association Lightweight—M. I. T.

Goldthwait Cup—Princeton.

Oxford-Cambridge—Oxford.

British Henley

Diamond Sculls—Peter Vlasic, Yugoslavia.

Grand Challenge Cup—Krylia Sovetov, Russia.

Thames Challenge Cup—M. I. T., United States.

SHOOTING

Rifle and Pistol

United States Champions

Pistol—Harry Reeves, Detroit.

Small-Bore Rifle—Alonzo Woods, Elbridge, N. Y.

High-Power Rifle (match)—Lieut. Clifford Tyrone, San Diego, Calif.

High-Power Rifle (service)—Chief Warrant Officer C. R. Carpenter, Encinitas, Calif.

Women's Pistol—Lucille Chambliss, Winter Haven, Fla.

Women's Small-Bore Rifle—Mrs. Eleanor Bell, Santa Ana, Calif.

Women's High-Power Rifle—Helen Orme-Johnson, El Paso, Tex.

Trap

Grand American Handicap—Nick Egan, Flushing, Queens.

Women's Grand American Handicap—Dianne Williamson, Compton, Calif.

North American Clay Target—Julius Petty, Stuttgart, Ark.

Women's North American Clay Target—Mrs. Helen Watkins, Wasco, Ore.

Champion of Champions—Arnold Riegger, Seattle.

Women's Champion of Champions—Iva Pembridge, Phillipsburg, Kan.

Skeet

All-Gauge—Howard Confer, Detroit.

Women's All-Gauge—Mrs. Carola Mandel, Chicago.

Industry All-Gauge—Fred Missildine, Sea Island, Ga.

High-Over-All—Col. Salvadore P. Roig, Puerto Rico.

Champion of Champions—Col. Salvadore P. Roig.

SKIING

United States Champions

Jumping—Roy Sherwood, Salisbury, Conn.

Downhill (open-closed)—Dick Bueck, Sun Valley, Idaho.

Slalom (open-closed)—Chiharu Igaya, Hanover, N. H.

18-Kilometer Cross-Country—Tauno Pulkkinen, New York.

30-Kilometer Cross-Country—Tauno Pulkkinen.

Alpine Combined—Chiharu Igaya.

Giant Slalom—Dean Perkins, Sun Valley, Idaho.

Women's Downhill (open)—Nancy Banks, Seattle.

Women's Downhill (closed)—Nancy Banks.

Women's Slalom (open-closed)—Jill Kinmont, Bishop, Calif.

Women's Alpine Combined (open-closed)—Nancy Banks.

Women's Alpine Combined—Nancy Banks.

Women's Giant Slalom—Jerryann Devlin, Sun Valley, Idaho.

SOCCER

World Cup—Germany (at Zurich).
National Challenge Cup—New York Americans.
National Amateur Cup—Beadling S. C., Western Pennsylvania.
National Junior Cup—Hansa Juniors, Chicago.
American Soccer League—New York Americans.

SOFTBALL

Amateur Association

Men—Clearwater (Fla.) Bombers.
Women—Leach Motors Rockets, Fresno, Calif.

SQUASH RACQUETS

Lapham Trophy—United States.

National Champions

Open—Henri Salaun, Boston.
Singles—G. Diehl Mateer Jr., Philadelphia.
Women's Singles—Lois Dilks, Upper Darby, Pa.
Doubles—Richard Squires, New York, and G. Diehl Mateer Jr.
Women's Doubles—Mrs. John Newlin and Mrs. Donald Manley-Power, Philadelphia.
Professional—John Warzycki, Cleveland.
Intercollegiate—Roger Campbell, Princeton.

SQUASH TENNIS

National Singles—H. Robert Reeve, Bayside Tennis and Squash Club.

SWIMMING

Men's National Senior Outdoor Champions

100-Meter Free-Style—Dick Cleveland, Hawaii.

200-Meter Free-Style—Ford Konno, Honolulu.
400-Meter Free-Style—Wm. Woolsey, Honolulu.
1,500-Meter Free-Style—Ford Konno.
100-Meter Backstroke—Albert Wiggins, Pittsburgh.
200-Meter Backstroke—Albert Wiggins.
100-Meter Butterfly—Dick Fadgen, N. C. State.
200-Meter Breast-Stroke—Dick Fadgen.
400-Meter Medley—Burwell Jones, Ann Arbor.
400-Meter Medley Relay—North Carolina State.
800-Meter Relay—New Haven S. C. "A" team.
Three-Meter Dive—Joaquin Capilla, Mexican Swimming Federation, Mexico City.
Ten-Meter Dive—Joaquin Capilla.
Team—North Carolina State.
Long-Distance—Frank Brunell, Philadelphia.
Long-Distance Team—Huntington (Ind.) Y. M. C. A.

Men's National Senior Indoor Champions

100-Yard Free-Style—Dick Cleveland.
200-Yard Free-Style—Ford Konno.
440-Yard Free-Style—Ford Konno.
1,500-Meter Free-Style—Ford Konno.
100-Yard Backstroke—Yoshi Oyakawa, Hawaii.
150-Yard Backstroke—Yoshi Oyakawa.
100-Yard Butterfly—Dave Hawkins, Harvard.
200-Yard Breast-Stroke—Dick Fadgen, Woonsocket (R. I.) Y. M. C. A.
400-Yard Individual Medley—Jack Wardrop, Ann Arbor.
400-Yard Free-Style Relay—New Haven S. C. "A" team.

400-Yard Medley Relay—New York A. C.

One-Meter Dive—Dick Browning, Pensacola, N. A. S.

Three-Meter Dive—Dick Browning.

Team—New Haven S. C.

Women's National Outdoor Champions

100-Meter Free-Style—Jody Alderson, Community Builders Club, Chicago.

400-Meter Free-Style—Carolyn Green, Fort Lauderdale (Fla.) S. C.

800-Meter Free-Style—Carolyn Green.

1,500-Meter Free-Style—Carolyn Green.

100-Meter Back-Stroke—Shelley Mann, Walter Reed S. C., Washington.

200-Meter Back-Stroke—Barbara Stark, Crystal Plunge Club, San Francisco.

100-Meter Butterfly—Shelley Mann.

200-Meter Breast-Stroke—Mary Jane Seers, Walter Reed S. C.

400-Meter Medley—Marie Gillett, W. Reed S. C.

400-Meter Medley Relay—Walter Reed S. C.

800-Meter Relay—Fort Lauderdale S. C. "A."

One-Meter Dive—Mrs. Patricia K. McCormick, Los Angeles A. C.

Three-Meter Dive—Mrs. Patricia K. McCormick.

Ten-Meter Dive—Mrs. Patricia K. McCormick.

Team—Walter Reed S. C.

Long Distance—Helen Hughes, Lafayette, S. C.

Long-Distance Team—Women's City Club, Detroit.

National Collegiate Champions

50-Yard Free-Style—Dick Cleveland, Ohio State.

100-Yard Free-Style—Dick Cleveland.

220-Yard Free-Style—Jack Wardrop, Michigan.

440-Yard Free-Style—Ford Konno, Ohio State.

1,500-Meter Free-Style—Ford Konno.

100-Yard Backstroke—Yoshi Oyakawa, Ohio State.

200-Yard Backstroke—Yoshi Oyakawa.

100-Yard Breast-Stroke—Dave Hawkins, Harvard.

200-Yard Breast-Stroke—Dave Hawkins.

150-Yard Medley—Burwell Jones, Michigan.

300-Yard Medley Relay—Ohio State.

400-Yard Free-Style Relay—Michigan.

One-Meter Dive—Fletcher Gilders, Ohio State.

Three-Meter Dive—Morley Shapiro, Ohio State.

Team—Ohio State.

TABLE TENNIS

United States Champions

Men's Singles—Richard Miles, New York.

Women's Singles—Mildred Shaihan, Chicago.

Men's Doubles—Tibor Hazi, Washington, and Bernard Bukiet, Chicago.

Women's Doubles—Mrs. Leah Thall Neuberger, New York, and Mildred Shaihan.

Mixed Doubles—Sally Prouty, Chicago, and Sol Schiff, New York.

TENNIS

Wightman Cup (Women)—United States.

Wimbledon Champions

Men's Singles—Jaroslav Drobny, Egypt.

Women's Singles—Maureen Connolly, San Diego, Calif.

Men's Doubles—Rex Hartwig and Mervyn Rose, Australia.
Women's Doubles—Louise Brough, Beverly Hills, Calif., and Mrs. Margaret Osborne du Pont, Wilmington, Del.
Mixed Doubles—Victor Seixas, Philadelphia, and Doris Hart, Coral Gables, Fla.

United States Outdoor Champions
Men's Singles—Victor Seixas.
Women's Singles—Doris Hart.
Men's Doubles—Tony Trabert, Cincinnati, and Victor Seixas.
Women's Doubles—Shirley Fry, Akron, Ohio, and Doris Hart.
Mixed Doubles—Victor Seixas and Doris Hart.
Junior Singles—Jerry Moss, Modesta, Calif.
Boys' Singles—Alan Silverman, Brooklyn.
Girls' Singles—Rosa-Maria Reyes, Mexico City.

CLAY COURTS
Singles—Bernard Bartzen, San Angelo, Tex.
Women's Singles—Maureen Connolly.
Men's Doubles—Tony Trabert and Victor Seixas.
Women's Doubles—Maureen Connolly and Doris Hart.

COLLEGIATE
Singles—Hamilton Richardson, Tulane.
Doubles—Robert Perry and Ron Livingston, U. C. L. A.
Team—U. C. L. A.

United States Indoor Champions
Men's Singles—Kurt Nielsen, Denmark.
Women's Singles—Mrs. Dorothy Levine, Chicago.

Men's Doubles—William Talbert, New York, and Tony Trabert.
Women's Doubles—Mrs. Barbara Ward, Moorestown, N. J., and Mrs. Dorothy Levine.
Mixed Doubles—Lois Felix, Meriden, Conn., and Winslow Blanchard 2d., Boston.

TRACK AND FIELD
Men's National Senior Outdoor Champions
100-Yard Dash—Arthur Bragg, Baltimore.
220-Yard Dash—Arthur Bragg.
440-Yard Run—Jim Lea, Los Angeles A. C.
880-Yard Run—Mal Whitfield, Los Angeles A. C.
Mile Run—Fred Dwyer, New York A. C.
Three-Mile Run—Horace Ashenfelter, New York A. C.
Six-Mile Run—Curtis Stone, New York A. C.
120 Hurdles—Jack Davis, Los Angeles A. C.
220 Low Hurdles—Jack Davis.
440 Hurdles—Josh Culbreath, Morgan State.
Two-Mile Steeplechase—Bill Ashenfelter, New York A. C.
Two-Mile Walk—Henry Laskau, 92d St. Y. M. H. A., New York.
Broad Jump—John Bennett, Marquette.
High Jump—Ernie Shelton, Los Angeles A. C.
Discus—Fortune Gordien, Los Angeles A. C.
56-Pound Weight—Bob Backus, New York A. C.
Hammer—Bob Backus.
Hop, Step and Jump—Claudio Cabrejas, Cuba.
Javelin—Franklin Held, Olympic Club, San Francisco.

Pole Vault—Robert Richards, Los An-
geles A. C.
Shot-Put—Parry O'Brien, Los
Angeles A. C.
Team—Los Angeles A. C.
Decathlon—Robert Richards.
Pentathlon—Brayton Norton,
Occidental Coll.
All-Around—Merwin Carter,
Baltimore.
Marathon—Ted Corbitt, N. Y. Pioneer
Club.
440-Yard Relay—Chicago C. Y. O.
One Mile Relay—New York Pioneer
Club.
One and ⅞ miles Medley Relay—New
York Pioneer Club.
10-Kilometer Walk—Henry Laskau.
15-Kilometer Walk—Henry Laskau.
20-Kilometer Walk—Henry Laskau.
30-Kilometer Walk—Leo Sjogren,
Finnish-American A. C., New York.
35-Kilometer Walk—Leo Sjogren.
40-Kilometer Walk—John M. Deni,
Pittsburgh.
50-Kilometer Walk—Leo Sjogren.
20-Kilometer Run—John A. Kelley, un-
attached.
25-Kilometer Run—Nick Costes, Boston Univ.

Men's National Senior Indoor Champions

60-Yard Hurdles—Jack Davis.
60-Yard Dash—John Haines, Pennsylvania.
600-Yard Run—Reginald Pearman,
New York Pioneer Club.
1,000-Yard Run—Mal Whitfield, Los
Angeles.
One-Mile Run—Josy Barthel, Luxem-
bourg.
Three-Mile Run—Horace Ashenfelter.
One-Mile Relay—Morgan State.
Sprint Medley Relay—New York Pioneer Club.

Two-Mile Relay—Fordham.
One-Mile Walk—Henry Laskau.
35-Pound Weight—Bob Backus.
Broad Jump—Neville Price, Oklahoma
U.
High Jump—Herman Wyatt, Santa
Clara Y. C.
Pole Vault—Jerry Welbourn, Colum-
bus, Ohio.
Shot-Put—Parry O'Brien.
Team—New York A. C.

National Collegiate Champions

100-Yard Dash—William Williams, Il-
linois.
220-Yard Dash—Charles Thomas,
Texas.
440-Yard Run—Jim Lea, Southern
California.
880-Yard Run—Arnold Sowell, Pitts-
burgh.
Mile Run—Bill Dellinger, Oregon.
Two-Mile Run—Kikuo Moriya,
Wheaton.
120-Yard Hurdles—Willard Thomson,
Illinois.
220-Yard Hurdles—Joe Corley, Illi-
nois.
Broad Jump—John Bennett,
Marquette.
High Jump—Ernie Shelton, Southern
California.
Discus—Jim Dillon, Auburn.
Javelin—Leo Long, Stanford.
Pole Vault—Larry Anderson,
California, and Earl Poucher,
Florida (tie).
Shot-Put—Tom Jones, Miami (Ohio).
Team—Southern California.

Intercollegiate A. A. A. Outdoor Champions

100-Yard Dash—Art Pollard, Penn
State.
220-Yard Dash—Henry Thresher,
Yale.
440-Yard Run—Lou Jones, Manhattan.

880-Yard Run—Arnold Sowell, Pittsburgh.

Mile Run—Richard Ollen, Northeastern.

Two-Mile Run—Robert Hollen, Penn State.

120-Yard Hurdles—Joel Shankle, Duke.

220-Yard Hurdles—Lester Goble, Alfred.

Mile Relay—Manhattan.

Broad Jump—John Bennett, Marquette.

High Jump—Frank Gaffney, Manhattan, and John Bennett (tie).

Discus—Stewart Thomson, Yale.

Hammer—Martin Engel, N. Y. U.

Javelin—Al Cantelio, La Salle.

Pole Vault—James Gulick, Temple; Bruce Hescock, Boston University; Daniel Lorch, Penn State, and Robert Owen, Pennsylvania (tie).

Shot-Put—Roosevelt Grier, Penn State.

Team—Penn State.

Intercollegiate A. A. A. A. Indoor Champions

60-Yard Dash—John Haines.

600-Yard Run—Lou Jones.

1,000-Yard Run—Tom Courtney, Fordham.

Mile Run—Richard Ollen, Northeastern.

Two-Mile Run—Edward Shea, Northeastern.

60-Yard High Hurdles—Warren Lattof, M. I. T.

Mile Relay—Princeton.

Two-Mile Relay—Syracuse.

Broad Jump—Bernard Bruce, Boston U.

High Jump—Frank Gaffney, Manhattan; William Antoine, M. I. T., and Wilfred Lee, Pennsylvania (tie).

Pole Vault—Bruce Hescock, Boston University.

Shot-Put—Albert Thompson, Columbia.

35-Pound Weight—Martin Engel, N. Y. U.

Team—Yale.

VOLLEYBALL

U. S. Volleyball Association

Open—Stockton (Calif.) Y. M. C. A.

Y. M. C. A.—Stockton, Calif.

Intercollegiate—U. C. L. A.

Armed Forces—Hamilton (Calif.) Air Base

Women—Houston (Tex.) Houstonettes.

WATER POLO

A. A. U. Champions

Outdoor—New York A. C.

Indoor—Illinois A. C., Chicago.

WEIGHT LIFTING

World Champions

Bantamweight—Bakir Farchudinov, Russia.

Featherweight—Rafel Tchimichkian, Russia.

Lightweight—Dimitri Ivanov, Russia.

Middleweight—Pete George, Akron, Ohio.

Light Heavyweight—Tommy Kono, Oakland, Calif.

Middle Heavyweight—Arkadin Vorobyev, Russia.

Heavyweight—Norbert Schemansky, Detroit.

Team—Russia.

National A. A. U. Champions

123-Pound—Charles Vinci, Cleveland.

132-Pound—Yas Kuzahara, York, Pa.

148-Pound—Joseph Pitman, York, Pa.

165-Pound—Bert Elliott, Puente, Calif.

181-Pound—Tommy Kono, Oakland, Calif.

198-Pound—David Sheppard, York, Pa.

Heavyweight—Norbert Schemansky, Detroit.

WRESTLING

National A. A. U. Champions

Free-Style

114.5-Pound—Richard Delgado, San Diego.

125.5-Pound—Jack Biabaugh, Tulsa Y. M. C. A.

136.5-Pound—Shozi Sasahara, Japan.

147.5-Pound—Tommy Evans, Tulsa Y. M. C. A.

160.5-Pound—Jay Hold, San Francisco R. C.

174.5-Pound—Dan Hodge, Tulsa Y. M. C. A.

191-Pound—Dale Thomas, Michigan State.

Heavyweight—William Kerslake, Case A. C., Cleveland.

Team—Tulsa Y. M. C. A.

National Collegiate Champions

115-Pound—Hugh Peery, Pittsburgh.

123-Pound—Richard Govig, Iowa.

130-Pound—Norvard Nalan, Michigan.

137-Pound—Myron Roderick, Okla. A. and M.

147-Pound—Tommy Evans, Oklahoma.

157-Pound—Bob Hoke, Michigan State.

167-Pound—Joe Solomon, Pittsburgh.

177-Pound—Ned Blass, Oklahoma A. and M.

191-Pound—Peter Blair, Navy.

Heavyweight—Gene Nicks, Oklahoma A. and M.

Team—Oklahoma A. and M.

YACHTING

National Champions

Mallory Trophy (men's North American)—Eugene Walet 3d, New Orleans.

Adams Trophy (women's national)—Mrs. James M. Mertz, American Y. C., Rye, N. Y.

Sears Cup (junior national)—Harry Jemmett, Kingston (Ont.) Y. C.

National Intercollegiate Dinghy (Morss Trophy)—Horacio Garcia and Alain de Berc, M. I. T.

One-Design Classes

World Star—Carlos de Cardenas, Havana.

National Snipe—Tom Frost, Newport Harbor, Calif.

Western Hemisphere Snipe—Harris Whittemore, Lake Quassapaug, Conn.

Lightning—Tom Allen, Buffalo, N. Y.

Comet—Howard Lippincott, Riverton, N. J.

Penguin—Runyon Colie, Mantoloking, N. J.

Raven—Donald Matthews, Oyster Bay, L. I.

110—Stephen Chadwick, Seattle.

210—Gregg Bemis, Cohasset, Mass.

L-16—Donald McClave, Greenwich, Conn.

Atlantic—Theodore Reyling, Sea Cliff, L. I.

Distance Racing

Newport-to-Bermuda—D. D. Strohmeier's yawl, Malay, Scarsdale, N. Y., and South Dartmouth, Mass.

Port Huron-Mackinac—Wendell W. Anderson's yawl, Escapade, Detroit.

Chicago-Mackinac—Edgar B. Tolman's cutter, Taltohna, Chicago.

(In Alphabetical Order)

JESSE ABRAMSON is no stranger to the readers of "Best Sports Stories". He has appeared in every volume of this anthology since '44. In '49 and '53 he captured the prizes for news coverage. As a sports reporter for the New York Herald Tribune, he has labored in their vineyards for over thirty years and he has been acclaimed as one of the country's finest sports writers.

FURMAN BISHER was born in Denton, North Carolina. He is now 36 years of age, married and has one son. He won the Georgia State sports writing award two out of the three years he entered. He came from the Charlotte (N.C.) News to the Atlanta Constitution in 1950.

HARRY T. BORBA was born in 1899 in Sebastopol, California and graduated from Stanford University in 1923. He spent some time on country journals to learn the writing business and went on to the San Francisco Bulletin, which folded in '27. He later worked on the Oakland Tribune and then joined the San Francisco News as its "first" football editor. In 1933 he was hired by the San Francisco Examiner and he has been there ever since.

SI BURICK, the "Si" is for Simon, has been the sports editor of the Dayton News since November, 1928. He attended the University of Dayton as a pre-med, got a job on the paper in that town and since 1930 has covered every important event, including the Derby and all the Big Ten and Notre Dame football games. He likes his job and does not regret his passing up the medical career. "The Doc's have the money; I have the fun!"

BEN BYRD is a thirty-year old writer who joined the Knoxville Journal while an undergraduate of the University of Tennessee. Except for a three-year Navy hitch, including participation in the Normandy invasion, his entire life has been passed in the South. He covers all the major sports at his university and the Southeastern Conference.

FRANK CASHEN is 28 years old and has been working for the Baltimore News-Post and Sunday American for the past 13 years, having started as a copy boy. After graduating from Loyola College at eighteen he joined the sports department and for the past ten years has covered football and basketball. Cashen is married and has two sons, Gregory, age 4, and Terry, age 3.

PETER F. CLARKE is a reporter on the Waterbury (Conn.) Republican. He also has worked at the United Press Philadelphia Bureau, The Trenton, (N.J.) Trentonian and the Chester (Pa.) Times. He is a native New Yorker, 35 years of age and is married. During World War II he saw service as a merchant seaman and Army officer. His story is based on an experience at the Cistercian Monastery of the Holy Ghost, Conyers, Ga., where he was a monk for four years.

GORDON COBBLEDICK was born in Cleveland and educated at Case Tech. In 1923, he joined the Cleveland Plain Dealer as a city-side cub. He has been there ever since, except for a few months on the now-defunct Cleveland Times. He has been a reporter, copy reader, sports writer, war correspondent, editorial writer, general columnist, sports columnist and since 1946, sports editor. He served in U. S. Marines in World War I. He lives on a 55-acre farm outside of Cleveland, has two sons and four grandchildren.

ED DANFORTH won the '54 "Best Sports Stories" award with his news coverage report on the Derby. He is a graduate of the University of Kentucky and has worked as a writer for many Southern papers before joining the Atlanta Journal where he has been sports editor since 1940. He has written for all types of media, served a hitch on a destroyer, is married and has two daughters.

ALLISON DANZIG was born in Waco, Texas and is a Cornell graduate, class of '21. He played football under Gil Dobie as a regular back, weight 127 pounds. He has been working for the New York Times since he left school except for a year's stint with the Brooklyn Eagle. He has authored many books including "Sports Golden Age", "Greatest Sports Stories of the Century" and a number of books on tennis. He won the "Best Sports Stories" prize for news reporting in 1950.

DON DONAGHEY was hired in 1915, while still a student in high school, to write for the Philadelphia Evening Telegraph. In 1916 he went to the Bulletin and with the exception of a 1944 hiatus when he accompanied his typewriter to the Pacific, he has been there ever since.

DAVID EIZENBERG has been writing sports nearly all his life. Born in Manhattan, he taught at New York University, has done public relations and authored a book on golf with Ernest Jones, the famous golf teacher. He was with the New York Evening Journal until 1930, later joined up with Journal-American sports staff and is still there. His great many readers look to him mainly for their golf, pro football and basketball news.

TIL FERDENZI earned six varsity letters in football and baseball at Boston College. Prior to his enlistment in the Marines in '42 he taught French and English in a Massachusetts High School and upon his discharge joined the New York Journal-American where he is writing football and tennis mainly. This is his first appearance in "Best Sports Stories."

LEO FISCHER is one of the oldest writers, from point of service, of the Middle West. In 1923 he joined the old Chicago American and became its sports editor after it changed its name to the Herald American. He has won a host of readers all over this country with his fine analysis of the sporting scene.

STANLEY FRANK is a free lance writer whose work always impresses with the amount of effort and lucidity of style that is found in his writing. He originally got his start with the New York Post and began to free lance shortly after the second World War. He has appeared in every major magazine in this country with articles on many different subjects other than sports.

JOHN GILLOOLY was born in 1908 in Boston. His father was sports editor of the Boston American until his death in 1924. John went to work for the Record-American and Sunday Advertiser upon his graduation from high school in '25 and has been with that paper ever since. He covered the Braves until they moved to Milwaukee. He was married at the age of 45, when his legs gave out.

HY GOLDBERG started in the newspaper business in 1926. He worked on two Newark papers before he joined the Newark News staff in 1931. He covered general sports, mostly baseball (International League) until 1940 and has been doing a column "Sports in the News" since then. He has covered virtually every major sports event in the country during the last 15 years plus the 1948 Olympics in London. He is also the editor of the Dell Magazines

"Dell Baseball Annual" and "Baseball Stars". He was born in Newark in 1908, is married and has two children.

FRANK GRAHAM was born in 1893 and worked for the New York Telephone Company from 1909 to 1915. He joined the Evening Sun in '15 and in '43 he went over to the magazine "Look" to become its sports editor. He left that periodical a year later to write two books and then went to the New York Journal-American. He has four children, lives in New Rochelle and was one of the early judges of "Best Sports Stories".

CURLEY GRIEVE is 52 years of age and has been sports editor of the San Francisco Examiner for the past twenty-five years. He has covered many major events from the Tunney-Dempsey fights to World Series, Kentucky Derby to Olympic Games. Grieve also writes a column "Sports Parade". He graduated from the University of Utah in '24 and started his newspaper career with the Salt Lake Tribune where he became sports editor at the Rocky Mountain News of Denver in 1946. He moved to the Examiner in 1931 and is married and has one child, Vernon David, Jr.

WILL GRIMSLEY is a native of Nashville, Tennessee who worked on the Nashville Tennessean before joining the AP in Memphis in 1943. He came to New York with the same organization in '48 where his specialties include golf, tennis, football and amateur sports. He helped in the coverage of the Olympic Games at Helsinki and has made two trips to Australia to cover the Davis Cup Challenge Round.

MILT GROSS has been writing sports for the New York Post for twenty years and for the last five has had his own column "Speaking Out". He has contributed many articles to national magazines including Saturday Evening Post, Colliers, Sports Illustrated, Argosy, etc. In 1948 he published a book, "Yankee Doodles", which dealt with the New York Yankees. He was graduated from Fordham University in '33 and received his M.A. from Columbia a year later.

W. C. HEINZ has garnered four prizes from the volumes of "Best Sports Stories". He won outright in '48, '50 and '54. He shared the award in '52. Now a free lance writer, Heinz was a member of the staff of the late New York Sun, for which he wrote a column. He is a graduate of Middlebury College and served as a war correspondent.

BOONTON HERNDON is a free-lance writer who has contributed to nearly all national magazines and who has also written some sports fiction. A newspaper man for seven years (with the New Orleans Item) he left the newspaper business to serve with the Army, winning five battle stars in the European theater, and then returned to writing. He is also the author of two books. Married, father of two and a half children (at this writing), a graduate of the University of Missouri.

HERMAN HICKMAN is a fabulous 326-pounder (most of it gristle) who has played football with Tennessee, coached at Army and Yale, played professionally with the Brooklyn football team and indulged in over 300 wrestling bouts. He is an orator, a philosopher and a gentleman who eats more than moderately well—as a matter of fact "he can eat anything that won't eat him". His book "The Herman Hickman Reader" published by Simon and Shuster in 1953 found a wide reading public.

BOB HUNTER left Southwestern Law School when he was offered a job as sports writer with the Los Angeles Examiner in 1933. He covers baseball, college football and basketball. He also has his own column "Bobbin Around" and authored the Loraine Day TV series which had such an enthusiastic reception on the West Coast.

OLIVER E. KUECHLE has been writing sports for almost thirty years. He was graduated from Marquette University and is at present associated with the Milwaukee Journal. In 1944 he handled the Journal's New York Bureau.

JOHN LARDNER has the "touch" in his writing. Not only does he have a provocative style, but his humor and fluency grace the pages of Newsweek, where readers look forward each week to his wonderful satire and comment. His father, the great Ring, certainly passed on more than a little of his talent to his son John. He is the author of "It Beats Working," a book that was very well received.

EDWARD LINN is a free lance writer who has been doing sports and fiction for the Saturday Evening Post, Collier's, True and other national magazines since he was discharged from the Army. Boston born, he is a graduate of Boston University, but now lives in Brooklyn with his wife and one son.

WHITNEY MARTIN is represented for the fouth time in "Best Sports Stories," and was a winner in the news-feature competition in 1952. He was born in Chicago in 1896 and is a graduate of Coe College. For the past 16 years he has been writing a sports column out of the New York office of the Associated Press.

GRANT MATTHEWS is being published by Best Sports Stories for the first time. He is a dyed-in-the-wool Westerner, having been born in Seattle some 43 years ago. He attended Washington State University and has been with the San Francisco Chronicle since 1939, writing Fish and Game news. He is married and has a 15-year-old son.

TEX MAULE is a Texan who by a strange twist of fate was born in Florida. He attended the University of Texas, worked with the Flying Codona Trapeze act, investigated for the War Department, became a flight purser and finally wound up with the Austin American-Statesman and later the Dallas News. He is 30 years old.

TOM MEANY was born in Brooklyn and still lives there. He began his writing career with the Brooklyn Eagle, covering high school sports. From 1923 to 1928 he covered the Dodgers for the Brooklyn Times and later on for the World-Telegram, The Morning Telegraph and the now defunct, PM. He has been a contributing editor for Colliers since 1950 and has written for CBS-TV. He has written seven books under his own name and ghost-authored two more. His latest is "The Incredible Giants".

JERRY MITCHELL has been with the New York Post for over twenty years. Before that he was with the now-defunct Graphic, the old New York American and the Daily Mirror, all in New York. A native of Plattsburgh, New York, he is married and has one son, Michael Patrick. He has served as the president of the New York Baseball Writers Association.

ARCH MURRAY is Princeton's contribution to sports writing. He has been with the New York Post for the last twenty years, covering football and baseball. Before that he worked for a short while for the Boston American. Married and lives in Manhattan. This is Tiger Arch's first appearance in Best Sports Stories.

JERRY NASON won the news reportage for "Best Sports Stories" in '45. He began his career with the Boston Globe about 25 years ago as a cartoonist, switched over to sports in '32 and in '41 took over as sports editor of a morning-evening-Sunday setup plus writing a sports column. He is 45 years of age and his writing has merited inclusion in every edition but one of the "Best Sports Stories" series.

JIM OBERT makes his debut in "Best Sports Stories". He joined the Peoria Star sports staff while he was a junior at Bradley University and graduated in 1950. In World War II he served 26 months in the infantry. At present he is the golf and bowling editor of the Star and has had some stories published on these subjects. He has assumed the promotion of the Star's annual Brother's Bowling Tournament, the largest of its kind in the world, drawing 1,937 pairs of blood brothers from five states. He is married and has two boys.

DON OLLIS is a free lance magazine photographer. After a stint as a Navy photographer, he graduated from Art Center School in Los Angeles then "settled down" with his wife and two small sons to free lance in Santa Barbara, California. During the last year he travelled some 50,000 miles covering sports, scientific, family life and movie star subjects for various magazines. His work has appeared in nearly all of the nation's leading publications.

PAUL O'NEIL was born in Seattle, Washington. He worked on the Star, the Times and the Post-Intelligencer in that community. At the same time he continued as a free lance writer for magazines until Time Inc. asked him to take over its Seattle Bureau in '44. Last June he joined the staff of Sports Illustrated in New York City. He received his education at the University of Washington, ran the hurdles there and now lives in Rye, New York with his wife and two children.

LOUIS P. O'NEILL has been working in the Metropolitan area for over thirty years. He is the sports editor of the Long Island Star-Journal and has made many fans with his humorous comments and appraisals of the horse racing scene. His selections appear in many other papers throughout the country.

JOE REICHLER is a St. John's graduate who joined the Associated Press in 1943 and has been with them ever since. He specializes in baseball but also does football and basketball. He is the author of "The Ted Williams Story", a three-installment series that ran in the Saturday Evening Post. He has also written series on Stan Musial, Leo Durocher, Robin Roberts and many other well known baseball personalities. He has covered every important baseball event since 1944.

JOHN RENDEL, a member of the New York Times sports staff for almost thirty years, became a dog specialist for the paper ten years ago. He has since written a book on dogs and one on horses and has won many prizes, one of which was the Kilbon Award of 1955. He also specializes in yacht races and horse shows.

ARTHUR RICHMAN is the younger of the two Richman boys and started his career with the New York Mirror as a copy boy at the age of 16. He was attending Brooklyn College at the time and he has been with that paper ever since. At present he is a staff writer, single and lives in the Bronx.

MILTON RICHMAN is 33 years of age and is a former professional baseball player who put in brief stints with minor league teams. He went to work for the United Press in 1944 after two and a half years with the military service. Like his brother, Arthur, he is single, lives in the Bronx and specializes in human interest baseball yarns.

BILL RIVES has been the sports editor of the Dallas News since 1949. He won the E. P. Dutton news feature award in 1951 on his first submission to the Best Sports Stories series. Before he joined the News, Rives was with the Associated Press in Dallas, Houston and New York. During World War II, he was a lieutenant-colonel in the U. S. Strategic Air Forces in Europe. This is his fourth appearance in this series. He is a native Texan, a graduate of St. Mary's University, San Antonio, Texas and is 43 years old.

EDITH ROBERTS, novelist and publicist, is a graduate of the University of Chicago. She has written seven novels, including That Hagen Girl, which was filmed by Warner Brothers. Mrs. Roberts served several years on the editorial staff of Coronet and is at present publicity director of the Chicago Heart Association. The title of her article, Football's Finest Hour, appearing in Coronet and Reader's Digest, was adopted as an official name for the East-West Shrine game.

BILL ROEDER has been with the New York World-Telegram (later and Sun) since 1943. Early in his career he covered high school sports, then baseball (mostly Brooklyn Dodgers) and basketball and occasionally football. He worked briefly for the Aurora

(Ill.) Beacon News and United Press (Chicago) before starting his job in New York. He was born in Brooklyn, attended the University of Vermont, is married and has two children.

HAROLD ROSENTHAL has been represented by stories in a half-dozen editions of Best Sports Stories. He is a member of the New York Herald Tribune's sports staff and has covered major-league baseball for the past decade. He lives in New York and writes scientific articles as a change of pace from the daily balls-and-strikes routine.

STAN SAPLIN became a sportswriter for the New York Journal-American three years ago, after an extensive career in publicity which included pro football (Newark Bears), harness racing (Roosevelt Raceway), ice hockey (New York Rangers) and the 1952 New York City Olympic Committee. At the Journal-American he specializes in track and field, hockey and sports promotions for the Hearst Free Milk Fund. He was in the Navy in World War II and is the alumni editor of New York University. Native New Yorker, married and father of two girls.

BLACKIE SHERROD is a native Texan, 35, who left a newspaper job in 1946 to make his way to West Coast, after discharge from the Navy. He stopped off in Fort Worth to gather a stake, taking a writing job with a radio station. Nine years later, he is still at Fort Worth, no closer to the West Coast than occasional jaunts out to cover football games for the Fort Worth Press. He is its sports editor and for the past five years he has his own daily column. Second entry in "Best Sports Stories."

WALTER W. (Red) SMITH has appeared in every volume of the Best Sports Stories series and has been a prize winner once. He gravitated from St. Louis to Philadelphia to New York, where he now works for the New York Herald Tribune. He is also the author of two books of his columns, is a prolific magazine writer and lecturer. Married, has a son and daughter and lives in Stamford, Conn.

WALTER STEWART was born in Memphis, Tenn. and graduated from the University of Illinois. He also attended Columbia University for another year. He worked for the Memphis Press-Scimitar, 1932-34, World-Telegram, 1935-37, and at the Journal-American in 1937. He then became sports editor of the Commercial Appeal in 1938 and has been there ever since, except for a stint in the Guadalcanal and China-Burma-India area. He came out a full colonel.

STANLEY WOODWARD has won the prize this series offers on two occasions and is generally recognized as one of the finest sportswriters in the country. He has written a very fine book called "The Sports Page". At present he is sports editor of the Newark Star-Ledger. He has also been the sports editor of the Miami Daily News and the New York Herald Tribune.

DICK YOUNG, a writer for the New York Daily News, has emerged as one of the fine sports reporters of Greater New York. Since 1941 his columns have tickled the risibilities of pro and con Dodger fans. He is still on the sunny side of thirty-five, married and a graduate of New York University.

Thirty of the Year's Best Pictures

PHOTOGRAPHERS

PAUL VATHIS, *The Associated Press*
FRANK LYERLA, *Detroit Times*
ERNEST SISTO, *The New York Times*
ERNEST ANHEUSER, *Milwaukee Sentinel*
CHARLIE HOFF, *New York Daily News*
FRANK STANFIELD, *Milwaukee Sentinel*
BARNEY STEIN, *New York Post*
BILL DYVINIAK, *St. Louis Post Dispatch*
GENE HERRICK, *The Associated Press*
GENE LESNEY, *United Press Associations*
CARMEN REPORTO, *The Chicago Sun-Times*
TED KELL, *New York Herald Tribune*
ART ROGERS, *Los Angeles Times*
NIELS LAURETZEN, *Milwaukee Journal*
MAURICE MAUREL, *United Press Associations*
EARL SEUBERT, *Minneapolis Star and Tribune*
JOHN C. LENT, *The Associated Press*
MATHEW ZIMMERMAN, *The Associated Press*
TONY CORDERO, *Des Moines Register*
MARTY LEDERHANDLER, *The Associated Press*
WILLIAM SEAMAN, *Minneapolis Star and Tribune*
BOB CAMPBELL, *San Francisco Chronicle*
HALL FILAN, *The Associated Press*
BOB DOTY, *Dayton Journal-Herald*
EDWARD KITCH, *The Associated Press*
A. B. RICKERBY, *United Press Associations*
ED JERRY, *United Press Associations*
DAVE DAVIS, *United Press Associations*
LLOYD T. FLOWERS, *Columbus Citizen*
JACK FRANK, *New York Herald Tribune*

PHOTOGRAPH WINNERS

PAUL VATHIS, who snapped the co-winning prize picture is of Greek extraction and was born in Mauch Chunk, Pa. in 1925. He graduated from high school there, joined the Marine Air Corps and served 18 months overseas. Shortly after his discharge in 1946 he joined the AP in Philadelphia and became an AP wirephoto operator. Later he was transferred to the AP bureaus at Pittsburgh and Harrisburg where he has been since 1950. He is married and the father of two children.

FRANK W. LYERLA, who shared first prize in the photo competition was born in Irving, Illinois in 1900. He has been with the Detroit Times since 1930 and has been the chief photographer since 1942. His specialty is sports and he covers all Big Ten football, the Detroit Lions and the Detroit Tiger home games. He is married, lives on a 120-acre farm in Fenton, Michigan and boasts of three grandchildren.

TTLE LEAGUER By Paul Vathis, *The Associated Press*

When Clarence Brumm, the catcher of the Colton, California, team blew this big bubble preparatory to playing the Schenectady Little Leaguers the photographer captured a scene that the judges could not resist making a co-winner in this year's photo contest.

© 1954. *The Associated Press*

COME CLEAN BOYS

By Frank Lyerla,

Detroit Times

This damp shot of two high school teams battling under almost impossible conditions contained all the elements necessary to convince the judges that this picture should rank among the very highest sport shots of the year. Consequently it has been awarded a share of the first prize money.

IANT AT WORK By Ernest Sisto, *The New York Times*

Hank Thompson of the New York Giants making a spectacular stop on a one-point stance
in the second World Series game with the Cleveland Indians.
© 1954.. *The New York Times*

EADS UP By Ernest Anheuser, *Milwaukee Sentinel*

This striking pose was created when Bobby Morgan of the Phils popped high into the air.
The hopeful catcher is Del Crandall of the Braves and the man in blue is Frank Secory.
© 1954. *Milwaukee Sentinel*

WILLIE MAY—
WILLIE DOES

By Charlie Hoff,

New York Daily News

A piece of banditry committed by the Giant outfielder at the Polo Grounds. The person robbed was a Dodger by the name of Duke Snider.

© 1954. *New York Daily News*

OUT? By Frank Stanfield,

Milwaukee Sentinel

The umpire waved Billy Bruton of the Braves out, but was he? Jackie Robinson, Dodger third baseman, is attempting to make the play and Ted Gorman, the umpire, is calling the play as he sees it.

© 1954. *Milwaukee Sentinel*

HE RHUBARB PATCH By Barney Stein, *New York Post*

Clem Labine beans Joe Adcock of the Milwaukee team and Ebbets Field takes on a very familiar look, that of a battleground. © 1954. *New York Post*

)UMP IN THE AIR By Bill Dyviniak, *St. Louis Post-Dispatch*

Babe Pinelli is practicing self preservation as Alex Grammas of the Cards scores in the first inning against the New York Giants. The catcher is Wes Westrum.
© 1954. *St. Louis Post Dispatch*

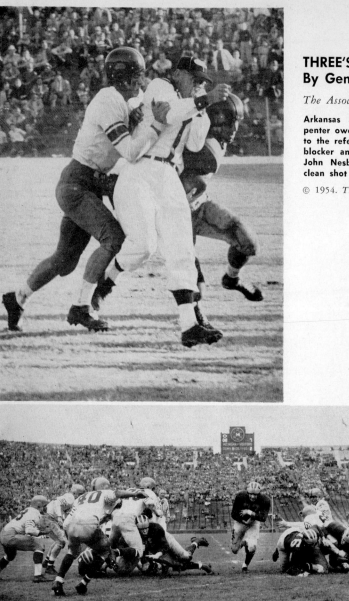

CLEAR TRACK FOR THE WOLVERINE By Gene Lesney,

United Press Associations

A hole "big enough to drive a truck through" is opened for Michigan's Lou Baldacci
he romps for yardage to score Michigan's TD against Minnesota in the battle for
Brown Jug. © 1954. *United Press Associations*

PIGSKIN PIGGY BACK By Carmen Reporto,
The Chicago Sun-Times

Loren Singer of Senn High, Chicago, tried for this pass and found himself on the shoulder of a Harrison High player.
© 1954. *The Chicago Sun-Times*

LOOSE BALL By Ted Kell, *New York Herald Tribune*

The ball is up for grabs in the Princeton-Harvard football game and this fumble resulted in Harvard touchdown. The Cantabs won, too. © 1954. *New York Herald Tribune*

BRUIN STEAMROLLER By Art Rogers, *Los Angeles Times*

The tremendous power ahead of the ball carrier shows why U C L A was the No. 1 te
in the United States for '54 © 1954. *Los Angeles Times*

INTERFERENCE! By Niels Lauretzen, *Milwaukee Journal*

An excellent shot of a flagrant violation. © 1954. *The Milwaukee Journal*

SPRINGTIME
FOR PADDY

By Maurice Maurel,

United Press Associations

Exuberant Paddy DeMarco executed this victorious leap upon hearing himself announced the world's lightweight champion at Madison Square Garden, where he beat the heavily favored Jimmy Carter for the crown.

© 1954. *United Press Associations*

ET OFF MY BACK

y Earl Seubert,

inneapolis Star and Tribune

high flying Golden Glover out to be restrained by the feree. The fight took place in inneapolis.

1954.
inneapolis Star and Tribune

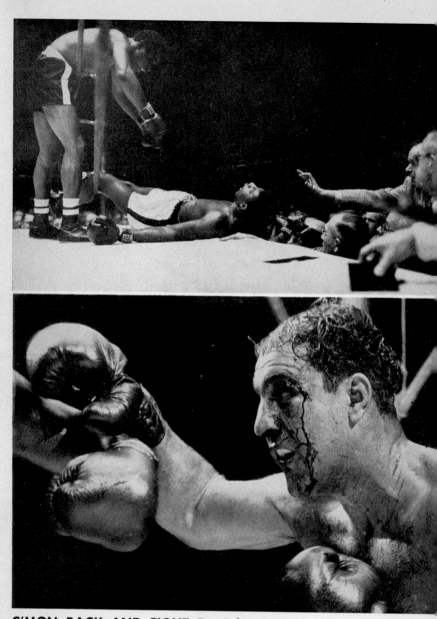

C'MON BACK AND FIGHT By John C. Lent, *The Associated Press*

This scene occurred at Madison Square Garden when Floyd Patterson knocked Jim
Slade out of the ring in the third round. Patterson won a unanimous decision.
© 1954. *The Associated Press*

GORY CHAMPION By Mathew Zimmerman, *The Associated Press*

In the 14th round Rocky Marciano presented this bloody picture as Ezzard Charles,
challenger, opened up a cut over the left eye. But Rocky scored a unanimous decision
over Charles anyway. © 1954. *The Associated Press*

INDEPENDENCE
UNASHAMED

By Tony Cordero,

Des Moines Register

Scene in the dressing room shortly after Roosevelt High beat Independence High for the Iowa state basketball championship.

1954. *Des Moines Register*

DERRIERE DRIBBLER

By Marty Lederhandler,

The Associated Press

Bill Uhl, the Dayton University's seven-foot center crashed to the floor in Madison Square Garden and gave the photographer this unusual picture as Dayton defeated St. John's, 70 to 56.

1954. *The Associated Press*

FLYING HIGH
By William Seaman

Minneapolis Star and Trib

Graceful action in a basket
game between two high sch
in Minneapolis, Minnesota.

© 1954.
Minneapolis Star and Tribune

HIDDEN FEET
By Bob Campbell,

San Francisco Chronicle

Monty Upshaw leaped into the
sand and came out with a new
high school record for broad
jump. Action took place in
Berkeley, California.

© 1954. *San Francisco Chronicle*

FALL TO A FINISH

By Hall Filan,

The Associated Press

Dramatic finish registered at the Invitational Track Meet at Compton, California. Jim Lea, Southern Cal's quarter-mile champion, breaks the tape a winner over J. W. Washburn, of Oklahoma A. and M.

© 1954. *The Associated Press*

ONE SHOE OFF

By Bob Doty,

Dayton Journal-Herald

Going off the high jump bar half shod in Dayton high school meet.

© 1954. *Dayton Journal-Herald*

BODY ENGLISH
By Edward Kitch,
The Associated Press

Mrs. Stanley Emmerson of Dayton, Ohio, attempts to steer her golf ball into the cup during Women's Western Open at Waukegan, Illinois.

© 1954. *The Associated Press*

THE GAMBLE THAT WON
By A. B. Rickerby,
United Press Associations

The spectators and the golfer, Ed Furgol, are caught in wrapt pose by big stroke of the National Open Tournament—out of the rough on the eighteenth hole at Baltusrol. The shot was a beauty and led to Furgol's victory in the National Open.

© 1954. *United Press Associations*

KICKING CAPER

By Ed Jerry,

United Press Associations

Rear guard action that took place when a player of Castle Shannon team made the mistake of interjecting himself between the ball and Lloyd Monson of the New York Americans. The Americans shut out their Pittsburgh rivals, 3-0.

© 1954. *United Press Associations*

"JOHNNY CAME TOO LATELY"

By Dave Davis,

United Press Associations

New York Rangers goalie, Johnny Bower, watches Bruin puck fly past him for a goal in a game at Madison Square Garden.

© 1954. *United Press Associations*

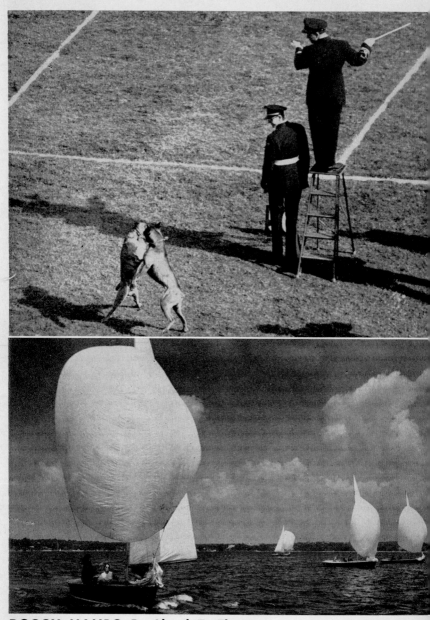

DOGGY MAMBO By Lloyd T. Flowers, *Columbus Citizen*

Ohio State University's band director, Jack Evans, on the ladder couldn't believe his e
when he caught this canine choreography behind his back. He thought he was lead
the university band in a victory march. © 1954. *The Columbus Citizen*

SHEETS TO WINDWARD By Jack Frank, *New York Herald Tribune*

This panoramic shot of boats heading for run with full spinnakers in the Syce Cup Se
was taken on Long Island Sound. © 1954. *New York Herald Tribune*